# It's NOT an Option

**Learning How To Trade Options Is No Longer An Option, IT'S A NECCESSITY!**

*by Jon & Pete Najarian*

**It's NOT An Option**

Learning How To Trade Options Is No Longer An Option,
IT'S A NECCESSITY!



Questions, simply reach out to our team.

Najarian Education

351 W. Washington St.
Kearney, MO 64060
1-800-330-4352
Support@NajarianEducation.com

Cover Design by Command G Design
Internal Design by Jeffective Design & Illustration
Published by Paradigm Direct, LLC
Printed in the United States of America

First Edition

Paperback ISBN: 979-8-9878784-5-3

 All the information provided in this book pertaining to investing, options, stocks, and securities is educational information and not investment advice. Specific securities are mentioned for informational purposes only. Nothing in this book, including references to specific securities, constitutes a recommendation, solicitation or an invitation to buy, sell or hold a security, buy or sell options, or engage in a particular trading strategy. Any examples shared in this book, including hypotheticals, are not guarantees of a return on investments. Najarian Education is not a registered investment adviser or a broker dealer. Individuals should seek advice from a registered professional securities representative before deciding to invest in any trading strategies outlined in this book. None of the material within this publication shall be construed as any kind of investment advice. Neither Najarian Education nor Jon and Pete Najarian are engaged in rendering legal, accounting, or other professional services. Information within this publication may contain "forward looking statements" within the meaning of Section 27A of the Securities Act of 1933 and Section 21B of the Securities Exchange Act of 1934. Any statements that express or involve discussions with respect to predictions, goals, expectations, beliefs, plans, projections, objectives, assumptions or future events or performance are not statements of historical fact and may be "forward looking statements." Forward looking statements are based on assumptions, expectations involving various risks and uncertainties, estimates, and projections at the time the statements are made that involve a number of risks and uncertainties which could cause actual results or events to differ materially from those presently anticipated. The reader of this book should not place undue reliance on forward looking statements contained in this book. All investments involve risk, and the past performance of a security, industry, sector, market, financial product, trading strategy, or individual's trading does not guarantee future results or returns. Investors are fully responsible for any investment decisions they make. Such decisions should be based solely on an evaluation of the investor's financial circumstances, investment objectives, risk tolerance and liquidity needs. Charles Payne is a professional trader and his results are not typical of the average individual. Background, education, and experience, of individuals will affect their overall experience. Readers' results may vary. THE BOOK USES SEVERAL HYPOTHETICALS TO ILLUSTRATE INVESTMENT TECHNIQUES AND STRATEGIES. HYPOTHETICAL PERFORMANCE RESULTS HAVE MANY INHERENT LIMITATIONS, SOME OF WHICH ARE DESCRIBED BELOW. NO REPRESENTATION IS BEING MADE THAT ANY ACCOUNT WILL OR IS LIKELY TO ACHIEVE PROFITS OR LOSSES SIMILAR TO THOSE SHOWN. IN FACT, THERE ARE FREQUENTLY SHARP DIFFERENCES BETWEEN HYPOTHETICAL PERFORMANCE RESULTS AND THE ACTUAL RESULTS SUBSEQUENTLY ACHIEVED BY ANY PARTICULAR TRADING PROGRAM. ONE OF THE LIMITATIONS OF HYPOTHETICAL PERFORMANCE RESULTS IS THAT THEY ARE GENERALLY PREPARED WITH THE BENEFIT OF HINDSIGHT. IN ADDITION, HYPOTHETICAL TRADING DOES NOT INVOLVE FINANCIAL RISK, AND NO HYPOTHETICAL TRADING RECORD CAN COMPLETELY ACCOUNT FOR THE IMPACT OF FINANCIAL RISK IN ACTUAL TRADING. FOR EXAMPLE, THE ABILITY TO WITHSTAND LOSSES OR TO ADHERE TO A PARTICULAR TRADING PROGRAM IN SPITE OF TRADING LOSSES ARE MATERIAL POINTS WHICH CAN ALSO ADVERSELY AFFECT ACTUAL TRADING RESULTS. THERE ARE NUMEROUS OTHER FACTORS RELATED TO THE MARKETS IN GENERAL OR TO THE IMPLEMENTATION OF ANY SPECIFIC TRADING PROGRAM, WHICH CANNOT BE FULLY ACCOUNTED FOR IN THE PREPARATION OF HYPOTHETICAL PERFORMANCE. Najarian Education or Jon and Pete Najarian are not liable for any damages, either directly or indirectly, arising from the use and/or misuse of the book. Neither Najarian Education nor Jon and Pete Najarian are make any guarantees that the strategies outlined in this book will be profitable for the individual investor, and they are not liable for any potential trading losses related to these strategies. Even though every precaution has been taken in the preparation of this publication, the publisher and author do not assume any liability for errors and/or omissions. This book is published "as is," without warranty or guarantee of any kind, either express or implied. You, as the reader, agree to release and hold harmless Najarian Education and Jon and Pete Najarian, their members, employees, agents, representatives, affiliates, subsidiaries, successors and assigns (collectively "Agents") from and against any and all claims, liabilities, losses, causes of actions, costs, lost profits, lost opportunities, indirect, special, incidental, consequential, punitive, or any expense and other damages whatsoever (including, without limitation, court costs and attorney's fees) ("Losses") asserted against, resulting from, imposed upon or incurred by any of the Agents as a result of, or arising out of your use of this book.

## *Dedications*

We dedicate this book to our mother and father, Mignette Anderson Najarian and Dr. John S. Najarian, who stressed the importance of faith, education, and discipline. Their unconditional love allowed us to make mistakes, choose our paths, and celebrate our successes. Their memories continue to shape our future.

*-Jon & Pete Najarian*

I dedicate this book to my wife Brigid McGrath for her love, advice, patience, strength, and support, as well as my beautiful daughters Tristen and Finola Najarian. I'm so very proud of all three of you. I want to also dedicate this book—our fourth book together—to my brother Pete who is the yin to my yang. He calms me when I need to relax and energizes me on those rare times when I struggle.

*-Jon Najarian*

I dedicate this book to my amazing wife Lisa Najarian, who is and always has been my rock. She is supportive and creative and helps to drive me to be better every day. And for that I am extremely fortunate. Additionally, my daughter Alexis, my grandson Kayo, and my son Kole for always providing me a smile when things are rough and giving me the energy to continue stepping forward. My brother Jon never stops moving forward and has taught me to never be satisfied with ok, but to always shoot for greatness.

*-Pete Najarian*

*Acknowledgements*

We've been blessed to have found a vocation that is both interesting, satisfying and fun. We've not met anyone that does not enjoy using the skills we discuss in the pages of this book to enrich themselves. Just like winning feels great, so does making money using the strategies we teach. This allows us to support those who are less fortunate as well as inspiring our family members and friends to become financially literate.

We've likewise been fortunate to work with fantastic traders on the floors of the exchanges, as well as our editors, and educators at MarketRebellion.com. This book could not have come together without the skill and insights of our head of education, Bill Johnson. If you have the opportunity to attend one of Bill's webinars about understanding option strategies, do yourself a favor and make that a priority on your trading journey!

We'd like to thank our many friends in the media and investing. This is by no means a complete list, but please know we've been inspired by and learned from these wonderful souls: Grant Cardone, Barry Josephson, Anthony Zuiker, Tony Dungy, Tom Osborne, Lou Holtz, Bob Nardelli, Adam Carolla, Leon Cooperman, Kevin O'Leary, Peter Kellogg, Maria Bartoromo, Charles Payne, Larry Kudlow, Liz Claman, Jim Cramer, Brian Sullivan, Bryn Talkington, Kelly Evans, and Ross Levinsohn.

*Scan the QR code to access the digital version of this book*

# CONTENTS

*Introduction*
*The Market Rebellion* .......... 1

*Chapter One:*
*How Much Would You Pay to Walk Away?* .......... 11

*Chapter Two:*
*When the Tide Goes Out, All Ships Sink* .......... 43

*Chapter Three:*
*Manage Your Risk, Not Your Profits* .......... 67

*Chapter Four:*
*It's Easier Said Than Done* .......... 101

*Chapter Five:*
*It's DDA or the Highway* .......... 131

*Chapter Six:*
*Blurring the Lines–Hedging vs. Speculating* .......... 157

*Chapter Seven:*
*There's Nothing Unusual About UOA* .......... 169

*Chapter Eight:*
*Ignoring Technicals is NOT an Option* .......... 187

*Postface:*
*The Archer & the Arrow* .......... 217

*Appendix:*
*A Starter Guide to Essential Options Strategies* .......... 221

# Introduction:

## The Market Rebellion

Some think of ocean-front mansions, luxurious yachts, and private jets. Others imagine endless greed, blatant corruption—and extended jail sentences. No matter what your view may be, Wall Street is no longer just a stadium for the daily clash between bulls and bears. New battles are brewing—market rebellions—that are changing the views and challenging the street.

Wall Street wisdom says to generate wealth, you must invest your money into stocks, which isn't too surprising. After all, it is a stock market. Toyota dealers want you to buy Toyotas, and Tesla dealers want you to buy Teslas. Stockbrokers want you to buy stocks. It's all they offer, so if you want to invest, they take your money, and you take the risks.

Getting thrown into the Wall Street coliseum to battle bulls and bears is not the kind of thing you want to keep simple. These beasts have a reputation for putting up good fights with lots of spirited pre-game trash talk. Occasionally, however, the bears back it up, go on an all-out blitz attack, and shred shares into sawdust. Remember the Enron Invasion, the Battle of Lehman Brothers, and the Extermination of Silicon Valley Bank? These and other famous battles left shareholders with nothing—and Wall Street with everything. No matter how many Psycho shower scenes we endure, Wall Street never adapts and continues to send investors to battle with just one weapon—shares of stock. Gas stations give you three. Baskin-Robbins gives you 31. Wall Street? Just one.

Don't expect things to change. It's part of a long-standing tradition, passed on through centuries, long before the Wall Street coliseum as we know it. In 1309, the Van der Beurse family of Bruges, Belgium, created an over-the-counter exchange where buyers and sellers could meet, and it's one of the earliest known formations of a stock market. It's from their name the word "bourse" was created—French for stock market. It was a difficult and slow way to match buyers and sellers, but when they did meet, not surprisingly, there was only one thing to buy—shares of stock.

The idea spread to the Netherlands, where they aimed to make sweeping improvements by creating an actual stock exchange where investors could quickly and easily meet to buy—you guessed it—only shares of stock. The earliest recordings of a physical stock exchange were in Amsterdam in 1611 when the *Dutch East India Company* decided to raise money by selling shares to investors, which led to the creation of the Amsterdam Stock Exchange. It was the first publicly traded company, and for many years, the only stock listed. Not only did the exchange limit investors to just shares of stock, but also to just one company. Those were the days when stock picking was easy.

New companies eventually followed suit. More stocks were listed, but investors were still stuck trading the same stuff—shares of stock. The names changed—not the risks. With more shares available to sell, the exchange flourished, but investors wouldn't be so lucky. The lure of easy money caused a market bubble to form in 1720, and like all bubbles, it burst. This turned that large selection of stocks into shredded sawdust. On a positive note, it was the earliest recorded win for the bears. Despite the crash, investors got a taste of money, and were hooked on buying stocks, so the game wasn't over. Brawls between bulls and bears would just get transferred to a different coliseum. Fast forward to 1792.

That's when 24 stockbrokers signed the Buttonwood Agreement to create the New York Stock Exchange. The agreement had two simple rules: Brokers were to deal only with each other, and commissions were fixed at 0.25% to eliminate the incentive to undercut each other. The idea was to increase investor confidence and the financial stability that was missing in Amsterdam. Investors would have more confidence—just not more choices. The long history that led to the New York Stock Exchange has been passionately fixated on only trading shares of stock. Yes, it's simple, but simple is rarely profitable. If you want simple, don't invest. But if you want to put money to work, invest in your future, and take only the risks necessary to meet your goals, you need more than what Wall Street is offering. You don't need more stocks. You need flexibility and more ways to manage the risks.

## The Idea of Stock Options is Born

Traders began wondering if there was a way to alter the hidden risks of buying stocks. Could a market be created where an investor could transfer unwanted risk to someone else willing to hold that risk for a fee? Both investors would be better off, so the overall stock market would benefit too. It was the early musings of an insurance market for stocks, and the idea of stock options was born. It's a modern sounding concept, but the idea of options has been around for a long time, long before the Chicago Board Options Exchange (CBOE)—and even long before television.

In 1896, Leonard R. Higgins, a trader at the London Stock Exchange, published a book called The Put-And-Call where he explains two types of daily options. So, if you think the recent creation of zero days to expiration, or 0DTE options, is something new, you're off by about 125 years. Back then, they were called *Call O'more to-morrow* and *Put O'more to-morrow*. If "0DTE" options seems like a peculiar term, just be glad these didn't catch on. Higgins also reveals a strategy called the "double option," where traders buy a call and a put with the same strike and expiration. The idea was to profit whether prices rise or fall. In his words, the double option was used for stocks such as railroads where "fluctuations are generally violent and uncertain." Today's traders would call the double option a "straddle," and it's still a popular strategy. So, before the turn of the 20th century, the idea of options and straddles existed. Why didn't they take off back then?

Well, kooky names aside, the real problem was determining an option's value. Think of an option like a black box with an unknown amount of cash inside, anything from pennies to thousands of dollars. How much would you be willing to pay for it? Probably not much. At the same time, sellers didn't know what to charge, so bid-ask spreads became unacceptably wide. The idea of an options market at least sprouted wings but could only fly slightly better than an ostrich. That would change when two academics published a pathbreaking paper that would give options flight. Fast forward to 1973.

## The Start of a Market Rebellion

In 1973, Fischer Black and Myron Scholes showed how to quickly calculate an option's fair value by using the Black-Scholes Option Pricing Model. Some experts say the prize-winning formula is the biggest breakthrough in modern financial history, and Myron Scholes won the Nobel Prize in 1997 for his work. (Unfortunately, Fischer Black died in 1995, so was ineligible for the prize.) Awards or not, it was the missing link that allowed the Chicago Board Options Exchange (CBOE) to successfully list exchange-traded options in 1973. The biggest prize of all, however, is that for the first time in history, investors now—finally—had choices other than shares of stock to battle bulls and bears. They could now manage risks. Trading without managing risk is not only dangerous—it's financially reckless. The world has changed—and so have the risks.

## The Intricate Web of Unknown Risks

If you buy shares, you're no longer just holding the risks of the shares. You're caught in a complex spider web of international, political, interest rate, exchange rate, commodity, liquidity, counterparty, and inflation risks. Every company, no matter how small, is intricately tied to the world, and in the future, probably the Moon and Mars

> **Risk is what's left over when you think you've thought of everything.**
>
> **– Carl Richards**

No matter how many risks you can think of, it's the ones you didn't consider that matter. After all, if a risk can be identified and measured, it's not much of a risk, as it can be hedged or avoided. In the words of Carl Richards, *"Risk is what's left over when you think you've thought of everything."* Well, how extensive are global risks, and are they really a threat to U.S. shareholders?

The world is now a complex network of financial connections, too tricky, knotty, and obscure for anyone to follow. Thirty years ago, few people could find Cyprus on a map. In 2012, however, the tiny island country nestled in the Mediterranean Sea, representing just 0.2% of the Eurozone's GDP, nearly collapsed the entire Eurozone's banking system and threatened the future of the euro. That could have created a rippling effect into the U.S. economy, crippling many American firms. Which ones? It's impossible to say. Even if you could come up with a reasonably good list, they're not the only risks. It's the ones you never thought of that count.

Global connections are too hard to track, and they can lead to puzzling outcomes. For example, the 1979 Iranian Hostage Crisis caused the U.S. dental budgets to shrink. The connections aren't easy to see, but they make sense once you realize that, in a global economy, everything is connected to everything else. Investors feared the crisis would spark a war in the Middle East, which caused financial market disruptions, which caused a flight to safety, which caused gold and silver prices to skyrocket.

Silver, at the time, was also the most expensive component of X-ray film, so increased gold and silver prices meant higher dental costs—and lower dental budgets. Who would have guessed?

In 2008, the California housing collapse caused some British towns to reduce the budgets of their police forces and other social services. What's the connection? Many British towns banked in Iceland to earn higher interest rates. The Icelandic banks offered higher rates because they took greater risks by investing in sub-prime CDOs (collateralized debt obligations). When the California housing market collapsed, the CDOs became unsellable—and the Icelandic banks failed. These British towns lost money and had to cut back on public services. Did you see these connections? Don't feel bad. Nobody else did either, which is why dental budgets caved in and British towns lost money. With today's globalized markets and information moving at the speed of light, there's too much room for too many things to go wrong—things you'd never dream of.

## The E-risk Danger

An alarming example of hidden risk occurred in July 2023, when the United Kingdom's Ministry of Defense inadvertently sent *millions* of emails with classified information on hypersonic missile research to an African nation closely tied to Russia. The UK was trying to send emails to the Pentagon, which uses the domain extension ".mil" but they were sent to the extension ".ml"—the domain for the West African nation of Mali. What if the information caused Russia to retaliate, which caused global fears, oil prices to spike, interest rates to plummet, unemployment to rise, and traders to panic, which caused your shares to disintegrate into sub-atomic particles? In the past, it would take something like missing uranium from Libya to cause market disruptions. Today, it can be a missing letter "i" on an email. Don't think a typo risk is a farfetched idea—it happened before.

Historians showed that Japan planned to declare war shortly before the bombing of Pearl Harbor, but a series of errors by typists and translators prevented the Japanese embassy from giving Washington the declaration in time. In *The Rising Sun*, John Toland said it was "a war that need not have been fought was about to be fought because of mutual misunderstanding, language difficulties, and mistranslations." In today's globalized economy, it's not just the stock market risks you can think of that matter. It's the ones you don't see, never thought of, and never happened before that matter—like a missing letter "i" from an email address. Stories like this show why it's unimpressive when you hear a market "expert" on television make a bold prediction like, "Tesla's shares will rise because the demand for electric cars is growing, and gas prices are rising." Out of the millions of factors and conditions that could cause Tesla's shares to rise or fall, that's it—just two? What about LFP cells made in China, or the parts made in the Netherlands, Germany, and Canada? The gigafactory in Mexico? Autopilot liability claims? Shipping costs or supply chain disruptions? What about interest rates, currency fluctuations, and competition? And because Tesla accepts Dogecoin, there's cryptocurrency risk. Of course, there's always the "Musk risk." And yet, despite millions of unknowns, investors will rush out to buy shares and hold 100% of all unknown risks, just because one person was able to give two examples of painfully obvious things that might increase Tesla's price. Today's risks are too intricately connected for a single person to understand. To succeed in today's markets, it's more than managing risk. It's managing risk you can't even see or imagine.

## The New Market Rebellion

When options began trading in 1973, they were alternative assets that shook up the traditional way of thinking—a market rebellion. The volume was only 911 contracts. In 2020, it exploded to an average of over 10 million contracts per day and over 2.5 billion for the year. The explosive growth isn't a surprise to Pete or me. Early in our careers, we knew options would play a key role for our success as professional market makers. Options allowed us to profit from the biggest bull market runs in history—1990 to 2000, and 2009 to 2019. We also had to survive the biggest market catastrophes, including Black Monday (October 19, 1987), Asian Contagion (1997), Dot-com bubble (2000), Financial Crisis of 2007-2008, and the 2020 market crash during COVID-19.

We've traded through countless bull and bear markets, sideways markets, high and low interest rates, explosive and stable volatility, and every curveball the market has thrown. After decades of experience, we've learned what works, what doesn't, and why. We also discovered options were a doorway into the market's mind, a way to see what everybody else thinks, so we created *Heat Seeker™* to profit from unusual option activity—a way to *follow the smart money.*

*Scan the QR code to get access to the digital version of our book* ***"Follow the Smart Money"***

Rebellions always begin with a need for change, a challenge between old and new. We're on a mission—a market rebellion—to show investors and traders they do have other choices than to hold all the unknown risks that come with shares. Whether you're looking for safer ways to trade shares of stock, interesting income-generating strategies, or wishing to speculate with unusual option activity, we want to share some of the tips and tricks for selecting the right options strategies. You'll learn how to manage the risks of global markets by hedging, rolling, and morphing—techniques that aren't possible with shares of stock. These are the strategies we used to survive as market markers, and we're sharing them with you.

It's often said there are three sides to every story: Yours, mine, and the truth. Wall Street has had hundreds of years to convince you to only buy shares. Now, it's time to rebel. We're going to reveal our side of the story, which is how options expand your choices, manage and reduce risk, and create higher probabilities for reaching goals. If you're going to battle bulls and bears, you need more than shares of stock. You need ways to manage the risks. Once you understand the benefits of options, you'll discover ways to reduce—or eliminate—the risks you don't want. You'll find ways to get paid for risks you're willing to accept. You'll know the choices that are right for you, and that's where you'll find the truth. That'll be your story. One thing is for certain: It's no longer sensible to just hold shares that are surrounded by the unpredictable forces and hidden risks of a global market.

It's not safe. It's not sensible. It's not an option.

# Chapter One:

## How Much Would You Pay to Walk Away?

Each weekday at 9:30am, a brass bell rings nine times throughout the trading floors of the New York Stock Exchange (NYSE) to mark the opening of the battle between the bulls and bears. And today, probably the bots too. Are today's prices worth more or less than yesterday? That's the tough question the market is tasked with answering each day. Big money is on the line, so traders wait with high hopes—and alarming anxiety—for the 4:00pm decision. But when Pete and I were on the floor of the Chicago Board Options Exchange (CBOE), there was a different battle brewing—the clash between stocks and options. Should you trade the shares—or the options? New York traders chose shares. That's not surprising. They're a stock exchange, remember? But the Chicago traders chose options. Now, we understand the rivalry between the Giants and Bears, but why such a difference of opinions between stock and options? And what mentally stable person would pick stock—or the Giants?

Anyway, it's a raging debate that continues today. However, after years of market making, we realized there's a better way to settle the score. The answer doesn't lie between New York and Chicago. The answer is found in a question: *Is there a price you'd be willing to pay to guarantee limited losses?*

It's a simple question that clearly tells the options story—and ends all debates. If you buy shares of stock at $100, the future price may be much lower—that's the risk. What's it worth to guarantee a maximum loss of $5, $10, $20, or any number you choose—including zero? If you answer, "I'd be willing to pay $5 to limit losses down to $90 for the next three months," then you understand the idea behind options. That's all there is to it. All the fancy-sounding strategies just allow you to divide risk into different pieces. What if you're willing to risk more than $5 but not as much as $10? A "short iron condor" or "vertical spread" may allow you to risk $7.50. If you want to limit risk while pursuing profits, options are your only answer. On the other hand, if you say, "I'm willing to watch my shares get pulverized like a pinata if I can squeeze out a few extra dollars of profit" then, by all means, stick with shares of stock, and you can stop reading now. Options will do you no good.

As we go through the book, you'll see that's all options do. They just give different choices about risks and rewards. When it comes to reducing risk, would you rather have more choices or fewer? As Henry Ford famously said about the Model T, "Any customer can have a car painted any color he wants, so long as it's black." So, the New York traders would say, "You can have any shade of stock risk you want, so long as it's

100%." The Chicago traders would answer, "You can have any shade of risk you'd like, from 0% to 100%—or well above." Once you learn options, a whole new menu appears. One side of the menu is the acceptance of risk, but the other is the avoidance of risk. Once you learn options, you can still buy shares of stock, but you can reduce the risks. However, you can also choose to increase the risk—and get paid to do so. Options traders are stock traders with a distinct difference: They have choices. It's the most powerful idea behind options, and the one everyone misses. When you're trading inside a globalized web of intricate risks, we think you'll agree that having only one choice—stock—is just not an option. We decided to write this book to show why options are now an essential part of trading and investing. We know you have many questions, and sometimes, the best answers are given by questions. So, let's open the menu and begin by answering some very tough questions.

## Are Options Risky?

There's no such thing as a bad question—except this one. It's usually the first question we get, but it's the wrong question. Everything is risky. Knives are risky. Ropes are risky. Fire, water, and air are risky. Withdrawing money from an ATM is risky. After the recent regional bank collapse of 2023, *depositing* money into a bank can be risky. If you've ever seen videos of trading floors during market meltdowns, just standing at your post minding your own business can be risky. Everything involves risk. It's risky to be alive.

Back to the question—are options risky? Once you understand options, you'll see it was the abuse—not the use—that created risk. If you decide to juggle machetes while riding a unicycle on a tightrope over a flowing river of lava, it's not fair to say machetes are risky if you end up immortalized at the ocean floor. So why does everyone think options are so risky? Well, they're derivatives, and everyone knows derivatives are the psychotic serial killers of the financial world. Because everyone knows it, nobody questions it. How can they not be?

They're responsible for the biggest financial firestorms in history. It was futures, options, swaps, and other derivatives that blew up Enron, Barings Bank, Bear Stearns, Lehman Brothers, Worldcom, Conseco, and Silicon Valley Bank. Oh, and let's not forget the mortgage-backed securities (MBS), credit default swaps (CDS), and collateralized debt obligations (CDO) for being responsible for the 2007-2008 housing crash. How can options not be risky?

Well, with derivatives, there's one long position for every short position. One side wins, and the other side loses. Long-Term Capital Management's (LTCM) debacle was caused by using over-levered positions—250:1—with a shockingly short-sighted computer model. Every computer programmer knows GIGO—garbage in, garbage out—and LTCM's model was fed a diet of radioactive hazardous waste. LTCM would probably have met the same fate if it had been trading baseball cards on eBay.

Nick Leeson destroyed Barings Bank by trading in derivatives. That's the side everyone hears. But it was one billion dollars in *unhedged* and *unauthorized speculative* trades. That's a gambling problem, not a derivatives problem. If you lose your family fortune by betting on roulette, it's hardly fair to blame the chips for being risky. And yet, that's what people are claiming who say derivatives caused the bank's collapse.

Enron had a host of problems, but most sources point to the complex financial statements as being the downfall. Like LTCM, it used complex business models but also combined them with unethical accounting practices to misrepresent earnings and modify the balance sheet to show favorable performance. Arthur Andersen, then one of the Big Five accounting firms, was found guilty of illegally destroying documents relevant to the SEC investigation, which voided its license to audit public companies. According to a 2003 Connecticut Law Review article, *Risk Management and Corporate Governance: The Case of Enron*, author Robert Rosen said even though Enron extensively relied on derivatives for its business, the company's finance committee and board did not have enough experience with derivatives to understand what they were being told. The Senate subcommittee argued that had there been a detailed understanding of how the derivatives were organized, the board would have prevented their use.

So, let's see if we have this straight: An inexperienced board would have prevented the use of something it didn't understand if it only had better explanations? That's like denying they have dementia, because if they did, they'd remember. The purpose of the finance committee and board is to do the explaining—not the excusing. Before its bankruptcy in 2001, Enron employed 21,000 people and earned $101 billion in 2000. *Fortune* magazine named Enron "America's Most Innovative Company" for six consecutive years. The board understood that just fine and took full credit for it. So, if you want to point fingers, let's start with the people who selected the finance committee and board. Or blame the people for accepting positions for which they were clearly unqualified. What about Arthur Anderson for violating its rigorous Code of Professional Conduct? Nope, blame the derivatives. Everyone knows derivatives are responsible, so they're always the scapegoat. And yet, if you dig deeper, you'll find the derivatives did exactly what they were put in place to do. They were the only thing in the entire miserable chain of events that didn't fail.

In 2001, Warren Buffet famously said, "Derivatives are weapons of mass destruction." If options were heading for trial and Buffett was on the witness list, let's just say the attorneys would be settling out of court. What other endorsement do you need to avoid options? Well, hold on a second. He's also one of the biggest sellers of naked put options, which are considered among the riskiest of options strategies. In 2008, Berkshire Hathaway was a party to 251 derivatives contracts totaling $37.1 billion. So, there's obviously more to the "derivatives are risky" story. Sure, options can be used in risky ways, but so can any other asset. Treasury bills are considered the safest investment in the world, but if you short them with $250 million in borrowed funds, it's now an insanely risky position, but that doesn't mean T-bills are risky. So, what's the best way to think of options?

The best way to understand options is that they are tools for adjusting risk. Just like a hot water faucet, you can turn risk up, you can turn it down—but you can also shut it off. That's right, you can completely shut all risk off with options. You can combine options in ways to behave exactly like a Treasury bill—no risk at all. You can't take dynamite, mix it with more dynamite, and end up with less risk. Why? Because dynamite is inherently unstable. It's risky no matter how you divide it. That's how most people see options. They think there's just something inherently unstable and risky about them. If that were true, how can options be combined in ways that create less risk, or even no risk at all? Now that's a good question. To answer, you must understand a bit more about options, so that means more questions. And we promise not to consult ex-members of the Enron finance committee or board.

## What is an Option?

*Scan the QR code*
*to watch our video*
***"Introduction to Options"***

All option strategies boil down to just two types of options—calls and puts. If you buy an option, you have some type of *right.* If you sell an option, you have some type of *obligation.* At the most basic level, options are a market for rights and obligations. Those rights and obligations depend on what you're buying or selling.

Call options give the buyer the right, not the obligation, to buy shares of stock, at a fixed price, over a given time. Call options get their name because you have the right to "call shares" away from another trader. In other words, it's your *right to choose* to be the buyer. Put options, on the other hand, give the buyer the right, not the obligation, to sell shares of stock, and the fixed price, over a given time. Put options get their name because you can "put shares back" to another trader. That is, you have the *right to choose* to be the seller. Notice that both definitions are the same, but one gives you the right to buy shares while the other gives you the right to sell shares. So, if trading shares of stock is relatively safe, how can having the right to decide to buy or sell suddenly make them risky? Options are derivatives, because their price is based on, or derived from the price of a stock or index, which is called the *underlying*. It's the thing that "underlies" the option's value. If you buy a Microsoft call option, Microsoft is the underlying. Changes in Microsoft's share price will change the value of the calls and puts. So, options are just calls and puts. Option buyers, whether calls or puts, have rights.

## Can I Sell an Option?

For every buyer, there must be a seller. So yes, you can sell an option. Selling an option is also called *writing* the option. While there may be margin requirements for selling options, the mechanics are just as easy as they are for buying options. Click on the asking price to be the buyer. Click on the bid to be the seller. So, which should you choose? That depends on what you're trying to do. If you sell an option, you have some type of *obligation*. Option buyers have rights, but sellers have obligations. What are the seller's obligations?

Since option sellers are on the opposite side of the trade, they have the opposite set of conditions. Call sellers have the *obligation to sell* shares of stock while put sellers have the *obligation to buy* shares of stock:

| | CALL | PUT |
|---|---|---|
| **LONG (Buyer)** | Right to Buy | Right to Sell |
| **SHORT (Seller)** | Obligation to Sell | Obligation to Buy |

Notice that everything is opposite between the buyer and seller. The call buyer has a right while the call seller has an obligation. If the call buyer has the right to buy, the call seller must have the obligation to sell. If the put buyer has the *right to sell* shares, the put seller must have the *obligation to buy* shares. Sometimes, new traders think that rights are good and obligations are bad, so you should only buy options. Who wants an obligation?

Think about what you've been doing with shares of stock. If you place a limit order to buy shares, that's an obligation to buy. If you place a limit order to sell shares, that's an obligation to sell. If you place a stop order, that's an obligation to buy or sell. If you short shares of stock and it pays a dividend, you have an obligation to deliver the dividend. So, long before the options market existed, stock traders had obligations. However, if you buy an option, the big difference is that you have the right to buy or the right to sell. It's that single word "right" that makes all the difference. It's the "right" that gives you the right to walk away from the deal if the stock doesn't perform as you expected. You'll never get that deal by trading shares of stock. If you buy a $100 call and the stock falls to $90, you can just say, "Nah, I think I'll pass. I don't want the shares now that I know the price is $90." Try calling your broker and saying you'd like to get your money back for the shares you bought six months ago because they're down $10. Well, there's obviously a value in having that right. How much would you be willing to pay for the right to walk away? That's not a stock question. It's an option question. Options are a market for rights versus obligations, and it's your "option" to choose. Long options (buyers) have rights. Short options (sellers) have obligations.

## Are Call Options Complicated?

They sound that way, but believe it or not, you've used options in other ways. You just didn't know it. For instance, imagine you're at Walmart just before the holidays and find the new Apple iPad was on sale for $500—but sold out. The manager expects to get a new shipment at the beginning of the year, but you're afraid the price will rise. So, for your inconvenience, he gives you a rain check to buy the same iPad for $500 during the next two months.

The rain check gives you control over the iPad. You don't own it, but you have the option to do so for $500 *if you choose.* It's your right to "call it away" from Walmart at any time by paying the $500 fixed price. No matter how high iPad prices may rise over the next two months, your price is fixed at $500—guaranteed. But what if the price falls?

If the price falls, you'll just buy the iPad at the current price and forget about the rain check. If the price is now $450, throw away the rain check and pay the lower price. In trading terms, you let the rain check expire worthless. In other words, you chose to walk away from the deal. For the options market, this fixed $500 rain check price is called the *strike price* since that's where the deal was "struck." It's also called the *exercise price* because if you choose to buy the iPad, you'd "exercise" your right to pay $500. For any optionable stock, you'll find many different fixed prices. So, if you've used a rain check, you've used an option. The idea isn't complicated at all, right? But it gets better.

As soon as you're in possession of the rain check, it becomes an asset to you. You can make money if iPad prices rise but can't lose if they fall. How can a piece of paper giving you the right to buy something be an asset? Because it can gain value. Let's say next month there's a shortage of chips and the same model sells for $600. Even if you decide you don't want the iPad anymore, the rain check still has value to others. It's now worth the $100 difference. All you'd have to do is stand outside Walmart, or perhaps list on eBay, that you have this rain check giving the holder the right to pay $500. Someone should be willing to pay up to the $100 difference for that piece of paper. Who wouldn't want to save $100? The rain check provides that benefit, so it's financially worth $100. So, even if the price rises, you're not ever required to buy the iPad—just sell the rain check to someone else. Now, in this iPad example, you may not get $100, as that'll depend on the market and your negotiating skills. However, in the options market, this $100 difference will be there because of a process called arbitrage. Would the rain check buyer have to buy the iPad?

Not at all. The piece of paper gains a life of its own. It's a separate tradable asset. If you sell the rain check for $100 to another trader, in options lingo, you've *sold to close* the position. You've "closed" the position since you no longer own it. The person that buys it is *buying to open*, or to enter the position. Does that mean he's going to use it to buy the iPad? Not necessarily. He may be speculating that the price will rise further. If the iPad price rises to $650, he could sell the rain check to another person for the $150 difference thus making a 50% return on his money—and never buy the iPad. Had he not bought the rain check for $100, he could have speculated another way. He could buy the iPad for $600 and perhaps sell it on eBay for $650. It's the same $50 gain, but it's only an 8.3% return on his money—not 50%. By using the rain check, he gained leverage, as it only cost $100 rather than $600 to *control the ownership* of the iPad. This is exactly what investors do with call options. Even though call options allow investors to buy 100 shares of stock if they choose, most never do. Instead, they just buy and sell the call options. Just like the stock market, the options market is an organized exchange where investors can trade contracts back and forth among investors.

For example, let's say Jitters Coffee is trading for $100 per share, and you buy a three-month $100 call for $5. Each contract controls 100 shares, so that's really $500 total. If the stock is $100 or below at expiration, the contract expires worthless. But if the stock is higher, say $110, you can sell your call for the $10 difference. You paid $5, sold for $10, or 100% profit, even though the stock only rose 10%. The concept of call options isn't hard at all. If you've ever held a rain check, you had a call option. You just didn't know it.

## Are Put Options Complicated?

Once you understand call options, put options work the same way—just in the opposite direction. Put options give you the right, not the obligation, to *sell* 100 shares of stock, for a fixed price, over a given time. A simple analogy is a money-back guarantee. Most large retailers like Home Depot or Costco allow you to return an item within a certain time for a full refund. If you buy a vacuum cleaner from Home Depot and the store allows you to return it within 30 days for a full refund, it's as if the store has given you a free put option. You have the right, not the obligation, to "put it back" and receive the purchase price.

A better analogy is insurance. If you have a $52,000 car, you might buy an insurance policy that will pay $50,000 in the event it's totaled. So, if your car gets hit by a meteorite, you can call the insurance company and say, "Hey, I don't want my car anymore. Here, you take it. I'm putting it back over to you." That's "exercising" your right conveyed by the insurance contract. You deliver a car, and the insurance company delivers a $50,000 check to you. Now, admittedly, it never works this clean and neat with auto insurance. The company will, of course, argue that they're not paying $50,000 for a car that's as useless as a cup of decaf, so will try to get you to settle for something more reasonable, like $1,500. But that's not how it works in the options world. If you exercise your put option, you receive the strike price—no arguments at all.

For instance, say you own 100 shares of Jitters Coffee at $100 per share and buy a three-month $100 put for $5. If the stock is $100 or higher at expiration, the put expires worthless, and you lose the $500 paid. However, if the stock is below $100, you could sell your shares for the $100 strike—no matter how low the stock price may be. However, you have a second choice. If the stock's price is below the $100 strike, the put option gains value. If the stock is $90 at expiration, the $100 put is worth the $10 difference. You could keep your shares and just sell the put and collect the $10, or $1,000 total, difference. Just as with calls, you don't need to own shares to buy a put. Instead, you could buy a put to speculate that the underlying price will fall. If you didn't own shares of Jitters, you could still buy the $100 put to speculate that the price would fall over the next three months. If you paid $5, you could sell for $10, again doubling your money, even though the stock fell 10%. Put options are easy to understand if you just think of insurance. Meteorites not included.

## Can I Trade Options on All Stocks?

Not all stocks have listed options, but the ones that do are called *optionable* stocks. Most of the big names you're used to hearing and trading will be optionable. However, just because a stock isn't optionable now doesn't mean it won't be in the future. If there's big news or a sudden following, it may become optionable. By the same token, just because a stock is optionable today doesn't mean it can't lose that status in the future. For a variety of reasons, a stock may get delisted, and if that happens, no new options will be listed. However, the existing options will continue to trade until they expire.

## When Do Options Expire?

Options can currently be traded anywhere from one day to nearly three years. Standard options have nine months or less to expiration, but there's another category called LEAPS (Long-Term Equity Anticipation Securities) that can have nearly three-year expirations. The SPX (S&P 500 index) has Super LEAPS, which can go out as far as five years. In 2005, the CBOE introduced Weekly options, which were listed on Thursday and expired the following Friday. In 2016, Wednesday Weeklys were introduced, and later that year, Monday Weeklys were created. To complete the suite, in May 2022, the CBOE created Tuesday and Thursday Weeklys. Some of the larger indexes like S&P 500 (SPX), SPDR &P 500 ETF (SPY), Nasdaq 100 Index (NDX), and Nasdaq 100 Trust (QQQ) have Weeklys for every day of the week. Consequently, these indexes will always have options that expire each day, which are called 0DTE options, or zero days to expiration. Options are always listed according to their expiration date and strike. So, if you buy a Worldwide Widgets $100 call that expires on August 21, 2023, it'll be listed as Worldwide Widgets 21August $100 call. If there's no day listed, it's a standard option that expires on the third Friday of the expiration month. If you see Worldwide Widgets August $100 call, it expires on the third Friday of August.

## What's the Most I Can Lose?

For most financial assets, the most you can lose is the amount you paid, and that's true for options too. If you buy an option, the price you pay is called the *premium*, and it's the most you can lose. However, each option contract controls 100 shares of stock, so if an option's price is quoted as $3, it really means $300 plus commissions. If you buy shares of stock, the most you can lose is also the amount you paid—but it's a whole lot more to possibly lose. Just ask Enron shareholders. If you owned shares of Enron, you can't say, "Umm, now that I've read about the accounting scandal, I'd like to forget about the 1,000 shares I purchased last year." The shares are yours—and you're stuck. If you had a call option, however, you could forget about buying the shares by choosing to not exercise. That doesn't mean you couldn't lose money. It just means it offered protection from losing a whole lot more. Why? Because you had the right to walk away.

However, if you sell an option, you'll receive money. The buyer pays money while the seller receives it. As the seller, you have an obligation, so for some types of strategies, you could lose more than the amount received. For example, let's say you sell a $100 call by itself, which is called a naked, or *unhedged*, call. Perhaps you collected $3, or $300 total, cash up front from the sale. Later, however, the stock is $105 and the call buyer exercises. Because you don't own the shares, you must now go into the open market, pay $105 for the shares, but deliver them for the $100 strike, which is a $5 loss. But when you combine that with the $3 collected from the sale, it's a net $2 loss, or $200, total. What if you sold 10 naked calls? Now it's a $2,000 loss. What if the stock had risen to $110 rather than $105? You would pay $110 per share for 1,000 shares and deliver for $100 per share for a $10,000 loss, or a net $7,000 loss after accounting for the $3,000 collected from the sale. With naked calls, the losses only continue to grow since there's no theoretical limit on how high a stock's price can rise.

So, many of the nightmare stories you've heard about options are with naked short options. Selling options can still be a great strategy if used in the right ways. Throughout the book, we'll show you some safer ways to sell options as hedged positions.

## What's an Option's Moneyness?

Traders often describe options as in the money (ITM), at the money (ATM), or out of the money (OTM), which is sometimes called an option's *moneyness*. The best way to understand these terms is to think of the words "immediate benefit." If there's an immediate benefit conveyed in an option, it's in the money. For instance, if the stock is currently trading for $100, the $95 call is in the money. By owning the $95 call, you have the right to pay $95 for stock that's worth $100, and that's an immediate benefit. Put options work in the other direction. With the stock at $100, the $105 put gives you the right to sell shares at $105, which is an immediate benefit. Once you understand in-the-money options, out-of-the-money options are just the opposite.

If the stock is $100, the $105 call is out of the money, as it gives you the right to pay $105 for shares currently worth $100—hardly an immediate benefit. That's not to say it won't have value in the marketplace, as a trader may be willing to buy the call to speculate that the stock's price will rise above $105. So, out-of-the-money options can have value in the market—sometimes a lot. With the stock at $100, the $95 put would also be out of the money. If you owned shares, you could sell them at the current $100 market price. By owning this put, however, you have the right to sell for $95. That's not an immediate benefit, so it's an out-of-the-money put. If you like formulas, all call options with strike prices less than the current stock price are in-the-money options. All puts with strikes greater than the current stock price are also in the money. For any call that's in the money, the same strike put, also called the corresponding put, is out of the money. For all puts in the money, the corresponding calls are out of the money. So, if the $100 call is in the money, the $100 put is out of the money.

At-the-money options (ATM) are neither in the money nor out of the money. Their strikes equal the current stock price or are at least very close. With the stock at $100, the $100 call and put are at-the-money strikes. Because it's rare to find a strike that exactly matches the current stock price, the at-the-money strike is usually defined as the one that's closest to the current stock price, even if it's technically slightly in–or out of the money. On a technical note, the true at-the-money option must account for the cost of carry. If the stock is $100 and interest rates are 5%, the one-year $105 strike is the at-the-money strike even though most traders would still say the $100 strike is at the money. If you understand an option's moneyness, it makes discussing options and strategies much easier.

## What Are Intrinsic and Extrinsic Values?

For any option that's in the money, the amount of the immediate benefit is called the *intrinsic value*. If a stock is $100, the $95 call has a $5 immediate benefit, so it has $5 of intrinsic value. You could also say it's $5 in the money. Put options work in the opposite way. With the stock at $100, the $105 put is $5 in the money, so it has $5 of intrinsic value. If an option is in the money, it must trade for at least its intrinsic value at all times. However, prior to expiration, in-the-money options will trade for more than their intrinsic value, and this additional value is called the extrinsic value, or the time value. The extrinsic value is the amount traders are willing to pay since time remains on the option. For example, say the $95 call is trading for $6 with the stock at $100. There's $5 of intrinsic value, yet the option is trading for $6, so the additional dollar is extrinsic value. If the $110 put is trading for $12, it has $10 of intrinsic value and $2 of extrinsic value. At expiration, all extrinsic value falls to zero since there's no time remaining. However, any intrinsic value remains with the option. The extrinsic value is the option's true value. As you'll find out later in the book, the extrinsic value is the price you pay for the right to walk away.

## What's an Option Trading at Parity?

If an option has intrinsic value but no extrinsic value (or very little), it's trading at *parity*. So, if the stock is $100 and the $90 call is trading for $10, it has $10 of intrinsic value and no extrinsic value. The $90 call is trading at parity. Mathematically, the $90 call is behaving exactly like stock. Parity just means "equivalence," so a call option trading at parity is equivalent to stock. If the stock is $100, the $110 put trading for $10 would be trading at parity, which makes it equivalent to short shares of stock.

If I Exercise an Option, Will the Transaction Go Through?

If you buy an option, you're not really buying directly from another trader. Instead, you're buying from a clearing firm called the Options Clearing Corporation, or OCC. The OCC acts as the buyer to every seller and a seller to every buyer. It's a highly capitalized clearing firm, and since 1973 when options were first listed, not a single exercise has ever failed to go through. If you exercise an option, your broker submits a notice to the OCC. In turn, the OCC randomly notifies another brokerage firm with traders who are short that option. That broker, in turn, randomly selects a trader to give the notice, which is called an assignment. If you exercise a $100 call, you'll pay $100 strike multiplied by 100 shares per contract, or $10,000, and receive 100 shares. Another trader will get assigned and receive the $10,000 cash but lose the 100 shares. If you exercise a $100 put, the opposite occurs. You'll sell your shares and receive $10,000 cash. So, if you exercise an option, or get assigned, you're just buying and selling shares—just as you've always done. The OCC guarantees it.

## What is Volatility?

*Scan the QR code*
*to watch our video*
***"What is Volatility"***

Volatility is a term every options trader knows. It's the very thing that gives options value and the very essence of options trading. It's also the key input into an option pricing model discussed next. What's volatility? It's associated with things that are, well, volatile like volcanoes, dynamite, or the temper of Homer Simpson. If you look at a stock price chart, you'll see zigs and zags—fluctuations—in the price. As you've probably guessed, there's a calculation that can quantify the size of these fluctuations. If you took a college statistics class—and stayed awake—you'll remember a terrifying term called the standard deviation. Loosely speaking, volatility measures the standard deviation of stock price changes over a given time. Volatility is always reported as a percentage, say 20%, and the greater the number, the more fluctuations you can expect. Volatility is non-directional, which means a high-volatility stock isn't necessarily expected to rise or fall. Instead, regardless of direction, there'll be big zigs and zags over time, and that tends to make the stock drift further from its starting point. Below are three one-year charts of hundreds of hypothetical $100 stocks at 10%, 20%, and 40% volatilities, respectively. As volatility increases, you can see the spread in potential future prices becomes greater. Because there's more potential for the stock to rise or fall, call and put options become more valuable as volatility increases:

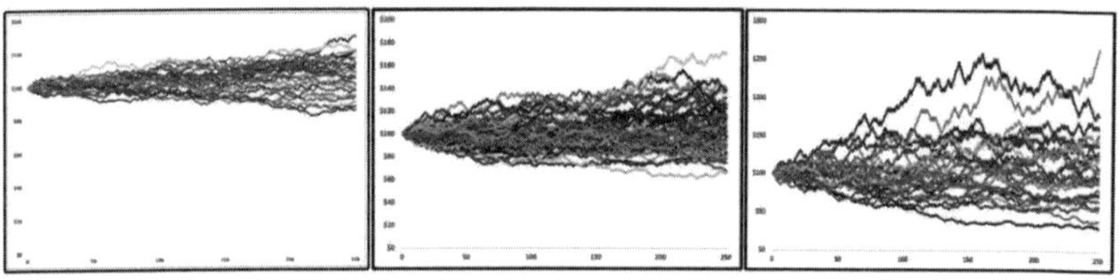

Volatility is a measure of risk. The more fluctuations in a stock's price, the less confidence you have in tomorrow's price, and that's the very definition of risk. Stock and bond prices fall in the face of risk, but option prices rise. This is another clue that options hedge risk—not create it—and that's because their value is in the ability to hedge unwanted risk. If you want to know how to trade options, you must have a good understanding of volatility.

## What's an Option Pricing Model?

Option pricing models are calculators designed to generate call and put *theoretical values*, also called *fair values*. The fair value is the price that doesn't favor the buyer or seller and is, theoretically, the price we'd expect to see in the market. If you always bought and sold options at fair value, you'd expect to break even in the long run, not counting commissions. Several option pricing models exist, and all give reasonably close answers, but the most famous is the Black-Scholes model. For the Black-Scholes model, you'll enter the current stock price, strike price, time to expiration, risk-free interest rate, volatility, and any dividends paid over the option's life, and out pops the fair value. Pricing models are an important source of information, as they allow you to gauge if the current market price seems reasonable under current market conditions.

## What Are the Greeks?

*Scan the QR code to watch our video* ***"Options Greeks"***

The Greeks are risk measures every options trader should know. They're mathematical outputs from a pricing model that show various sensitivities about your options. The five key Greeks are delta, gamma, theta, vega, and rho. Each is designed to show how sensitive your options are to various factors. One thing that makes options more difficult than stock is that multiple factors affect option prices, and that's what the Greeks are designed to track. Think of them as a GPS. Once you've driven with a GPS, you wonder how you ever backed out of your driveway without one. Greeks aren't hard to learn, but if you want to simplify options trading, they're a must. Most options trading platforms show these Greeks, but you must understand what they mean and how they change.

## What is Delta?

If you buy a call and the stock price rises one dollar, the call option's price will rise, but it usually won't be by the full dollar change in the stock. There are complex reasons for this, but you can easily estimate by how much your option's price will move by looking at *delta.*

Delta measures the rate of change of an option's price in relation to changes in the stock's price. Call options have positive delta, which means call option prices rise and fall in the same direction as the stock: Stock price up, call prices up. Stock price down, call prices down. But all option prices won't rise and fall to the same degree, and that's where delta comes in.

Think of delta as the percentage change in the option's price for a given change in the stock's price. For instance, if you own a $100 call trading for $3 with a delta of 0.50, it means the option will pick up 50% of the next dollar change in the stock's price. If the stock immediately rises one dollar, this option's price will only pick up 50% of that dollar move, or 50 cents, and increase to $3.50. If the stock rises 10 cents, the option picks up 50%, or five cents, and the call would trade for $3.05.

Deltas work in reverse too. If the stock price falls one dollar, the price would fall from $3 to $2.50. Regardless of the change in the stock's price, you'll end up with a new option price—and a new delta. For calls, deltas range from zero to 1.0. For puts, they're from 0 to -1.o. As you continue reading through the other Greeks, keep in mind that they're always listed for the long positions—options you buy. If you short an option, the Greeks are reversed. If you have a long $100 call with a delta of 0.70, the short $100 call has a delta of -0.70. If you want to know by how much your option's price will change for the next immediate one-dollar change in the stock, delta is your answer. Traders watch net deltas to gauge their profits or losses for the next dollar change in the stock.

## What is Gamma?

As the stock price changes, your option's delta changes. By how much? That's the question *gamma* answers. Gamma shows the rate of change in your option's delta and is sometimes called the "delta of the delta." Gamma is always positive for long options—options you buy—whether calls or puts. The math of gamma is easy: Add gamma to delta when the stock price rises and subtract it from delta if the stock price falls. Let's say your $100 call is trading for $3 with a delta of 0.50 and gamma of .05. If the stock price immediately rises one dollar, your option's delta rises to the old delta plus gamma, or 0.50 + .05, or 0.55. The option has moved a little bit in the money, so it's now a little more sensitive to changes in the stock's price, which is reflected by the new 0.55 delta. However, if the stock price fell one dollar, your call's delta would fall to 0.45. It's a little bit out of the money, so it has lost sensitivity to changes in the stock's price.

Gamma is like a gas pedal that accelerates deltas when prices are moving in your favor, but it also acts as a braking system, which reduces your deltas—and losses—as the stock price falls. If you have a $100 put with delta of -0.50 and gamma of .05 and the stock price rises, your put's delta changes the old delta plus gamma, or -0.50 + .05, which is -0.45. Your put option moved a little bit out of the money, so it lost some sensitivity to changes in the stock's price. On the other hand, had the stock price fallen one dollar, your delta would be -0.50 - .05, or -0.55. Gamma becomes zero when options are either far out of the money or deep in the money. Gamma is maximized for at-the-money options, but if you're right at expiration, gamma can skyrocket through the roof. Gamma is the reason you must be careful with options strategies. A trade that took weeks to build up a nice profit from a $10 move in the stock can be wiped out on a $3 move near expiration. Gamma is the reason.

## What is Theta?

Options have an expiration date, so option prices lose a little bit of value each day. However, it's only the extrinsic value that fades over time. The reason is simple: The extrinsic value is the amount you pay because time remains on the option. It's the price you pay for the right to walk away. Once the option has expired, the extrinsic value must be zero. So, with each passing day, some of the extrinsic value erodes—a process called time decay. How much will your option's price lose from the passage of one day's time? That's the question *theta* answers, and the Greek letter "T" was chosen to represent time. Theta is always negative for long options and positive for short options. If your $100 call is trading for $3 with a theta of -.05, it'll be worth $2.95 tomorrow, assuming all other factors are the same. At that time, you'll generate a new delta, gamma, and theta. Because at-the-money options carry the largest extrinsic values, their prices have the furthest to fall, so they decay at the fastest rate. As you move away from at-the-money strikes, theta gets progressively smaller. Theta is often viewed as the biggest risk of an option. Remember, however, that risk is always about uncertainty. Time moves in one direction at the same speed, so it's 100% certain. Therefore, theta should be viewed as a characteristic of an option—not a risk. Depending on your strategies, you may want to see the option decay and with others you won't. No matter what your view, there are other strategies that can mitigate—or accelerate time decay.

## What is Vega?

Option prices are also sensitive to a stock's volatility. *Vega* shows how sensitive your option's price is to changes in *volatility*. The Greek alphabet doesn't have a letter "V" so vega was chosen to sound like one. Vega shows the change in your option's price for a one-percentage point move, also called a one-tick change in volatility. For instance, if volatility is currently 20% and rises to 21%, or falls to 19%, that's a one-tick change. Vega is easy to use: Just add vega to your option's price if volatility rises but subtract it if volatility falls. Just like gamma, for any strike and expiration, call and put vegas will be equal.

Let's say the stock is trading at 20% volatility and your $100 call is trading for $3 with a vega of 0.10. If volatility immediately rises from 20% to 21%, your option's price is expected to rise to $3 + 0.10, or $3.10. If volatility falls to 19%, your option's price is expected to trade for $3 - 0.10, or $2.90. Those may not seem like big changes, but many times a stock's volatility may skyrocket, say from 20% to 80% from a single news announcement. That can be a huge boost to profits for long options—and your worst nightmare for short options. The reverse is true if volatility implodes. Vega is a Greek you want to watch, especially for large positions. Remember, options gain value in the face of uncertainty, which is why they hedge risk. But it also means they're sensitive to volatility changes. Vega shows by how much.

## What is Rho?

All financial instruments are sensitive to interest rates, as they're the price of money. The Greek letter *rho* was chosen to represent an option's sensitivity to "rate," specifically the risk-free interest rate. If rates rise, call prices rise while put prices fall. Rho, like vega, considers one percentage point, or one-tick changes. If the risk-free rate is 3% and immediately rises to 4% or drops to 2%, those are one-tick changes. Let's say you have an option trading for $3 with a rho of .04. If interest rates immediately rise from 3% to 4%, your option's price rises by rho to $3.04. If interest rates fell from 3% to 2%, your call would fall by rho to $2.96. Put options work in the opposite direction, and their prices will fall by rho if interest rates rise and rise by rho if interest rates fall. Most options aren't terribly sensitive to rho, so it's a Greek that's often ignored. Further, the Fed usually changes interest rates in ¼-point increments, so a rho of .04 is realistically more like .01. However, rho can be a significant risk if you're dealing with long-term options, high-priced stocks, or periods of rapidly rising or falling interest rates. It can also be the Greek to watch if you're trading currency options and short a currency that has runaway inflation. Call options are positively sensitive to interest rates, so they have positive rho. Put options are negatively sensitive, so they have negative rho. Remember, all option price expectations based on any Greek measurement always assume everything else remains the same. In the real world, when interest rates rise, stock prices usually fall, so you're more likely to see call prices fall and put prices rise—exactly the opposite of what rho predicts.

## What's a Profit and Loss Diagram?

*Scan the QR code*
*to watch our video*
***"Profit and Loss Diagrams"***

It's nearly impossible to teach options without learning risk graphs, also called risk curves, risk profiles, or profit and loss diagrams. Most students just call them headaches. But they're designed to make things easy, so don't avoid risk graphs because you hate math. Instead, think of them as your GPS monitor, showing where profits rise, fall, or may take sudden turns. If you can read your GPS, you can read a risk graph. The chart below is a risk graph for 100 shares of stock purchased at $100 per share:

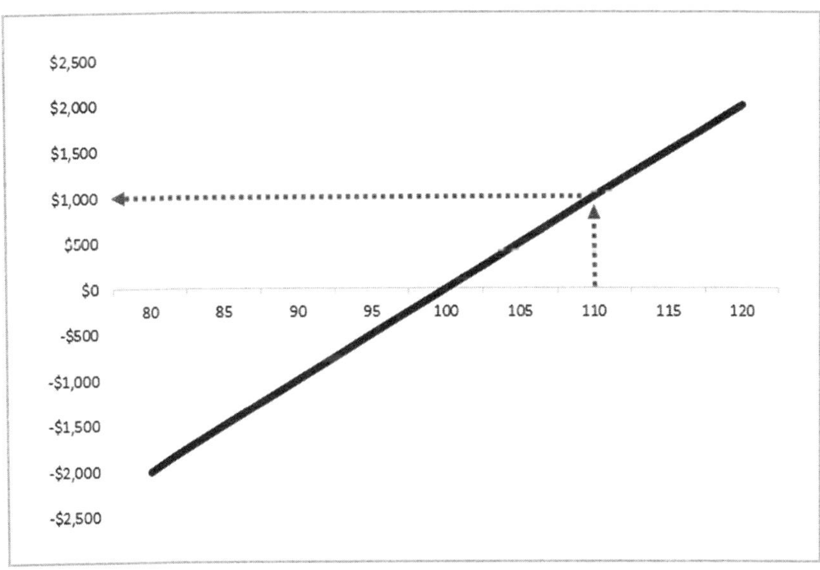

The horizontal axis shows various stock prices from $80 to $120, while the vertical axis shows the resulting profits or losses at each stock price. The horizontal line is $0, which means no gains or losses, so it's the breakeven level. If the risk graph sits above zero, there's a profit. If it's below zero, it represents a loss. For example, if you purchased 100 shares of stock for $100 per share and the price rose to $110, you'd have a $1,000 profit, and that's exactly what the chart shows at a stock price of $110 (dotted arrows). As a shareholder, you always earn—and lose—dollar for dollar with changes in the stock's price. The key insight about shares of stock is that your risk graph is always a straight line. Options, however, produce bent lines, so long calls and puts are sometimes called "hockey stick" graphs, for obvious reasons. Below is a risk graph for a $100 call purchased for five dollars:

For options, risk graphs may have two lines. The black line is the risk graph at expiration—the final seconds of the option's life.

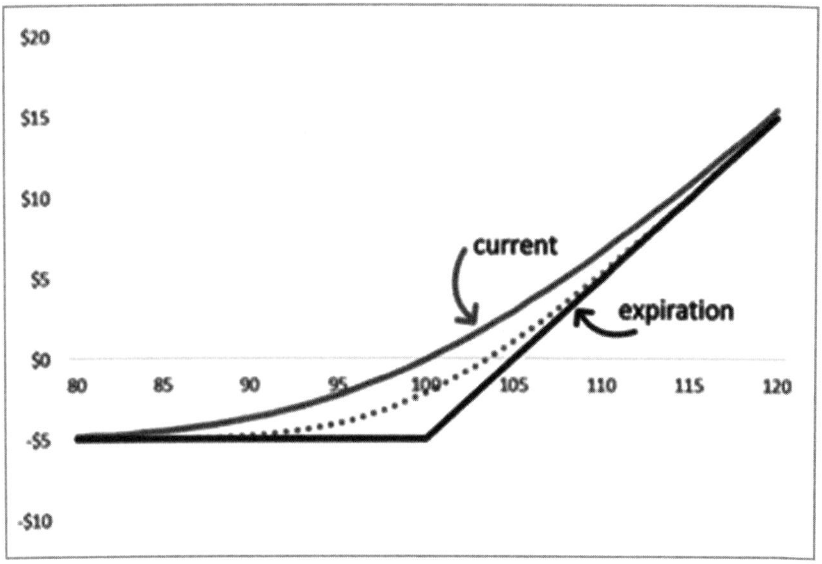

The gray line is the *current curve,* which shows what your profits or losses are expected to be right now based on a pricing model. As time goes by, the gray line moves toward the black line, as shown by the dotted line, eventually collapsing onto the black line at expiration. The current curve shows how much additional value over the intrinsic value resides in the option, which is the time value, or extrinsic value. The distance between the gray line and the black line is the option's extrinsic value, which must fall to zero at expiration, and that's why the gray line disappears. When expiration arrives, there's no more time value, so you're just left with the expiration curve, which shows your option will either be worthless (if the stock is below the strike), or it's worth the intrinsic value (if the stock is above the strike).

One of the key characteristics of an option's risk graph is that you'll always get a bend at the strike price. For long options, the strike price is the point at which you'd walk away, and that's what causes the bend. If the stock falls below $100 at expiration, would you want to exercise and pay $100 for the shares? Definitely not. Instead, you'd walk away and not exercise. If the stock is $100 or below, say $90, the call expires worthless, but who cares? You weren't going to use the option anyway. If you want the shares, just pay the current $90 market price. Because you wouldn't exercise for any stock price below the $100 strike, the expiration graph flattens out, and that's what creates the bend. You don't get that choice by holding shares. If you're holding shares and the stock falls to $90, you've taken that loss whether you want it or not. Some strategies use more than one option. If a strategy has two strikes, you'll get two bends. Each strike creates a bend, and bends are caused by either having a right (from a long option) or an obligation (from a short option).

## Options Are Zero-Sum Games

Do options destroy money as so many people believe? Well, there's another insight you can gain from risk graphs. Below is a comparison between a long $100 call (black line) and a short $100 call (gray line):

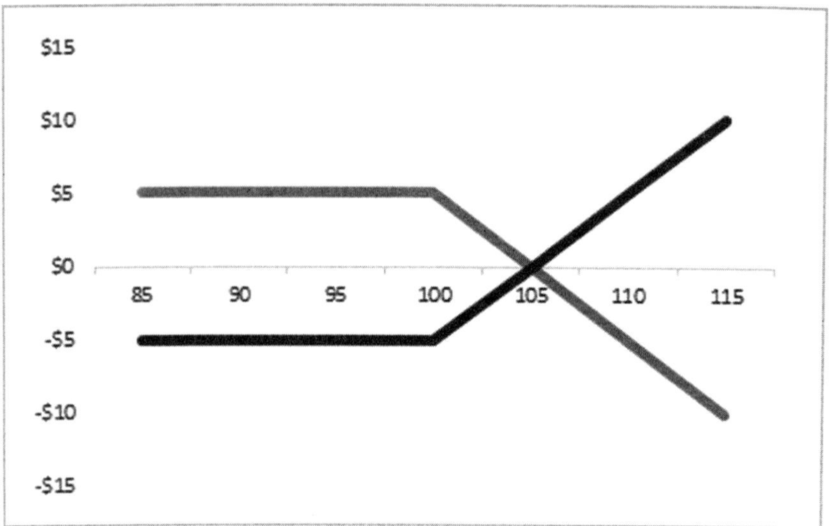


The black line represents the $100 call buyer while the gray line represents the risk graph for the call seller. The two profiles are mirror images of each other, which means the gains to the buyer are exactly the losses to the seller and vice versa. It's like betting on a coin flip—there's one winner and one loser. In the options market, the loser pays the winner, so options are a zero-sum game between the buyer and seller. Both curves cross at $105, which is called a *crossover point*. Whenever you compare two strategies, you'll always get at least one crossover point, which shows that one strategy isn't "better" than the other. Instead, one strategy will win in some areas of the chart while the other strategy will win in others. The options market doesn't create—or destroy—money. Instead, it allows traders the ability to transfer unwanted risk to another trader seeking to increase returns by accepting risk—a speculator.

If there's a risk you don't want, you can pay money to reduce or avoid it. On the other hand, if there's a risk you're willing to accept, you can get paid to accept the risk. Everyone can be made better off by using options. So, each day the NYSE rings the opening bell, you may have different opinions about that day's clash between bulls and bears, but we hope we've changed your opinion on the clash between stocks and options—and the Giants and Bears.

# Chapter Two:

## When the Tide Goes Out, All Ships Sink

Buy the rumor, sell the news. Never catch a falling knife. Cut your losses short, and let your profits run. Stocks take the stairs up and the elevator down. Oh, and don't forget, the market can stay irrational longer than you can stay solvent.

Whether you call them maxims, tenets, adages, or aphorisms, these words of wisdom are scattered over Wall Street like ticker tape after a Thanksgiving Day parade. They're lessons from the past to teach traders and investors the daily—but often forgotten—risks in the market. No matter which one you hear, the underlying message is about the destructive outcomes of mismanaged risk. Professional traders always ask what if things don't go as planned? That's what allows them to survive. Anyone can survive when things go better than expected. But will you survive if they don't?

And that means you must focus on managing risk. Retail investors, however, miss this point and focus on the windfall profits that might appear if a Ladybug lands on their computer screen just when Venus aligns with Mars. The more they can make, the better the deal, without any regard to thinking of the probabilities for profits or losses. As stock market expert and former hedge fund manager Jack Schwager observed, "Amateurs think about how much money they can make, while professionals think about how much money they could lose." Before you set out to make the big bucks, you must guard against big losses. What's the best way to do it?

> ***Amateurs think about how much money they can make, while professionals think about how much money they could lose.***
>
> ***– Jack Schwager***

Now that you understand the basics of options, Pete and I want to show you different types of risks in some of the following chapters and how options provide incredible solutions. So, let's start with the biggest risk that affects every type of trader or investor. Whether short-term, long-term, experienced or not, young or old—even with unshakable nerves of steel—this is the fear that gets every stock trader. And for those traders who think fear doesn't apply to them, we have our own Wall Street maxim: That's more bull than we can bear. So, what's the fear, and how do you manage it?

## A Rising Tide Lifts All Boats, But...

When Pete and I were market makers at the CBOE, we watched many traders burn out from a sudden, violent changing of the tides such as the Asian Contagion or Dot-com bubble. It happens when traders get overconfident and allow positions to grow to unacceptable levels. It's easy to let positions get too large when things are going great. Why manage risk when there doesn't seem to be any risk to manage?

John F. Kennedy said, "A rising tide lifts all boats." His message was that an improved economy benefits everyone, and economic policies should focus on broad efforts. Okay, good point, but that also means when the tide goes out, all ships sink. As a trader, that's the biggest risk you face. Losses are part of trading, so there's nothing wrong with taking an occasional hit. Just as basketball players expect missed shots, quarterbacks expect incomplete passes, and poker players expect losing hands, losing trades are part of trading. It's okay to be wrong. You just want to guard against being wrong for a long time. Jack Schwager has great advice for all traders: "Being wrong is acceptable, but staying wrong is totally unacceptable."

Of course, you probably think that'll never happen to you. Who's going to continue to hold as markets wilt away? Just sell your shares, right? Well, it's a psychological trap. Each day prices fall, you're more likely to see buyers step in, and the feeling of regret would be overwhelming if you sold at the low. So, you convince yourself tomorrow's the day prices will bounce, and you continue to hold—and lose money. That's why Wall Street warns, "Cut your losses short, and let your profits run." It's easier said than done, which is why it's a powerful pearl of wisdom. Now that you're caught in the trap and convinced selling is the wrong move—maybe you should buy? You continue to buy, but the market continues to drop.

Sometimes, panic selling causes a positive feedback loop where more selling creates more selling. Falling prices may trigger stop orders, which push prices lower, which causes more traders to sell, which causes speculators to short sell, which causes more people to panic, which causes prices to fall further, and the process just continues in a vicious cycle. Even though you thought you'd be rational and sell, you're now caught dumping more and more money into a rapidly falling market. Traders can just end up sitting there like a deer in headlights, and the only thing that moves is the losses. Eventually, prices get so low, traders can't take the pressure, and everyone sells on one massive selloff day, usually called capitulation. Everyone gives up and throws in the towel, and they sell at the low. When the tide goes out, all ships sink—and fast—and that can easily get you caught in the trap of holding on too long and selling near the low.

Every trader remembers the COVID-19 pandemic when we witnessed that very reaction. Below is a chart of the S&P 500 ETF (SPY), which shows the index hit a high of $338 on February 19, 2020, just prior to falling off a cliff. The low was March 23 at $223, a 34% drop in just five months:

Traders aren't wrong thinking prices will eventually bounce. They usually do. This is why you'll usually see "V" bottoms after market drops. That's when FOMO—fear of missing out—takes over. Eventually buyers will step in, and once the market turns, other traders think this is the big turning point and hop on for the ride too. Nobody wants to miss out on the potential wave of potential profits, especially if they need to make up losses, and that causes the opposite effect. We now get a positive feedback loop that creates a virtuous cycle of continued rising prices. The more prices rise, the more people jump in, and the more they continue to rise. Look at any stock chart, and most of the time, you'll see a "V" bottom after pullbacks—not a long sustained sideways motion at the bottom. That's the battle of bulls and bears, or more accurately, fear and greed.

The far-right side of the chart is August 18, about 10 months later, when the SPY closed at $338, the first day the index fully recovered. So, if you held all the way back to the highs during the 10-month period, the selloff didn't affect you one bit, but chances are, that's not what happened. While you're correct for expecting a bounce, it's a question of when. And when the tide is rapidly going out, it's probably going to be much later than you expected, which means it'll be well past your maximum pain threshold, and you'll sell near the lows. That's why Wall Street warns, "The market can stay irrational longer than you can stay solvent." That's the risk of the tide going out, and it's the biggest risk traders face because the math works against you. If you sell at a 25% loss, you need a 33% gain just to get back to even. If you sell at a 50% loss, you need 100% return just to get back to even. There goes your compounding—and your financial plan. All from one rapid shift in the tide.

From 1983 to 2007, the Dow Jones Industrial Average rose from 1,000 to 14,200 but took two years to lose half that amount from 2007 to 2009. Fear is a powerful motivator, and that's why professional traders call it "market risk." It's a sweeping risk that affects the overall market—not just an individual stock or sector. It's the risk of the tide going out and all ships sinking. No stock trader wants to get caught in that, but that's why it's a psychological trap. The more you're convinced it's going to turn, the longer you hold, until you just can't take the pressure anymore, and end up selling at the low. Good trading plans can get derailed when the tide goes out.

## Stock Gives You Lots of Choices—So Long as It's Delta One

The big risk with trading shares is that you get little flexibility—you either own shares or you don't. Your risk graph is a straight line, and that means you always gain or lose dollar for dollar with changes in the stock's price. And when the tide's going out, it's the worst risk profile to have. Think about that: It's the worst position to have, but the only choice you get. Holding 100 shares just multiplies those gains and losses by 100, so a one dollar rise or fall in the stock's price results in either a $100 gain or loss:

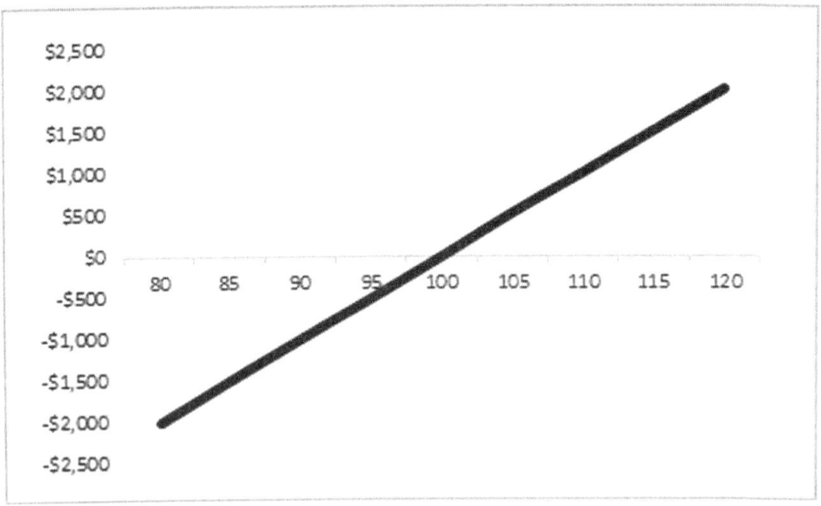

In options trading terms, stock is always delta one, which just means it rises and falls dollar for dollar with itself. As a stock trader, the only choice you have is to change the slope, which you can do by buying or selling shares. No matter how many shares you have, though, you'll always be delta one—dollar-for-dollar up, and dollar-for-dollar down. If you have 100 shares of stock but sell 50 shares, the line flattens a little bit. If you increase to 200 shares, the line gets steeper. If you sell all your shares, the line goes flat:

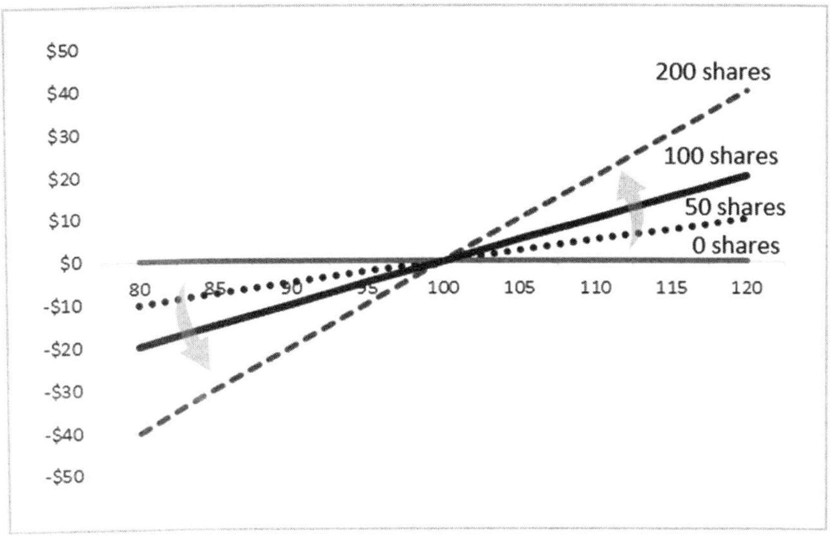


Except for selling all your shares and making the line flat, all choices require you to hold 100% of the downside risk. As a stock trader, that's the only control over risk that you have. In other words, not much. The Golden Rule of Financial Risk Management is simple: Avoid extreme outcomes. However, when your risk graph is a straight line, you're either making it all—or losing it all—and that's as extreme as it gets. Using shares of stock flies in the face of good financial risk management. Shares of stock simply don't allow you to do much with your risks and rewards. You can always double the potential rewards, but that means you must double the downside risk, and that's what makes stock so risky with today's global risks. How will options give you more flexibility in managing risk?

## Options Give You Options

Options allow you to bend your risk graphs, so you're not just dealing with straight lines. Instead, they look like a hockey stick, and that's because they limit risk to one side. Call options limit the downside risk while put options limit the upside risk. Remember, options give you the right to walk away, and that's why the line will flatten out at the strike. By changing the shape, you're changing risks and rewards. If you get rid of the risks you don't want, it's good risk management, and no other asset allows you to alter risks graphs like options. Remember, options give you options, and when you have more choices, you'll be better at managing risk. How can options help you when the tide goes out?

In too many ways to count, but let's start with some easy ones. Let's say you wanted to speculate on overall market conditions over the next three months. Rather than buying shares at $100, what if you bought a 90-day $100 call for $5. You're only paying 5% of the stock's cost, so that makes you more cash efficient. You can spread your money thinner, or even buy other hedges. When you free up money, you can do the same things more efficiently. But it gets better.

The chart below shows the risk graph for the $100 call (black line) with the long stock position (gray line) for comparison:

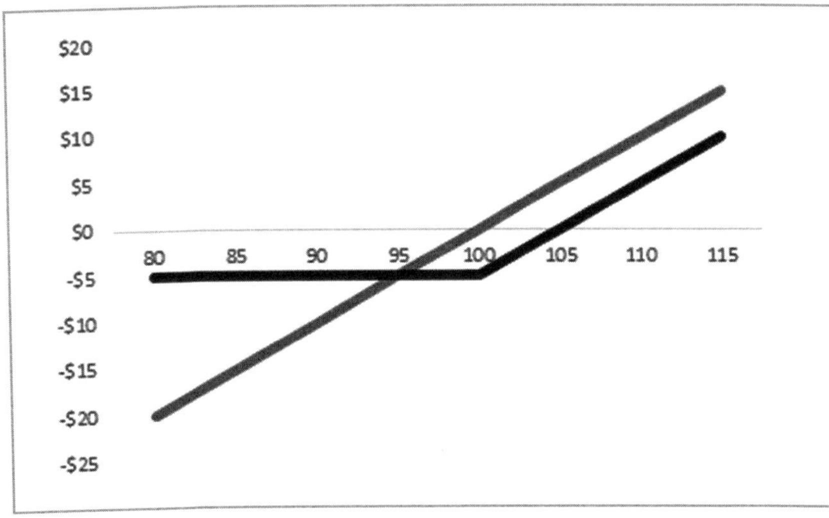


You're no longer dealing with straight lines, so you've altered risks and rewards. Remember, option risk graphs always bend at the strike price. For all stock prices above $100, you still have unlimited potential gains—just like the stock. However, for all stock prices below the $100 strike, things have changed. Now the most you can lose is the $5 price paid. That's the option coming to the rescue if the stock falls below the strike. The option hits bottom at $100, but the stock hits bottom at zero. However, because you paid a $5 premium, you need to make that up before showing a profit. How far?

You can find a call option's breakeven price by adding the option's premium to the strike price, or $100 strike + $5 premium = $105. With this call, you'd need the stock to rise 5% to $105 just to break even, which is where the risk graph crosses zero. So, is the call option better than shares of stock?

It's not better, it's just different. For all stock prices to the right of the $95 crossover point, the stock graph lies above the $100 call. So, the stock trader outperforms the call trader by the $5 premium if the stock rises. However, the call option outperforms the stock for all stock prices below $95. And if you're focused on risk management, this is the part that matters. Considering that some stocks may not move 5% in a year, this option is speculative. However, that's okay—if that's what you're speculating. You're still speculating in a safer, more efficient way. Options, however, don't have to be used speculatively. Options give you options, and you're free to change the risks and rewards to suit your needs. Remember, you can crank risk up—but you can also turn it down. How do you turn it down?

Just buy a lower strike call. The lower the strike, the more intrinsic value it has, and the less extrinsic value it has. If you're reducing the extrinsic value—the insurance—you're making the option behave a little bit more like shares of stock. For instance, if the $100 call is $5, the $95 may be $7.50. Now the breakeven is reduced from $105 to $95 + $7.50, or $102.50, so it's a little closer to the stock.

The chart below compares the $100 call for $5 (gray line) and the $95 call for $7.50 (black line):

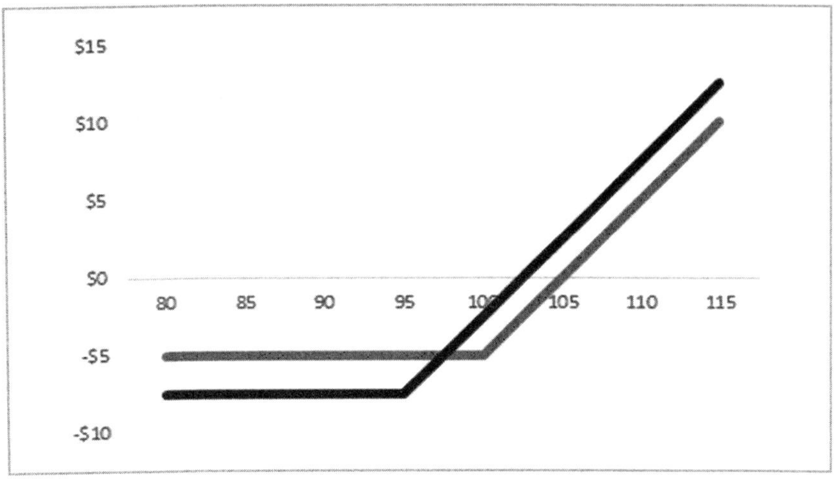


With the $95 call, you don't need the stock to move as high to break even, but you also may take a $7.50 loss instead of a $5 loss. Why can you lose more now? If you paid more for the option, why isn't there more insurance?

The $95 call is priced at $7.50, which has $5 of intrinsic value, but just $2.50 of extrinsic value—and that's the insurance. You paid $5 for the insurance policy with the $100s strike, but now you're paying $2.50. Even though you paid more in total for the $95 call, you paid less for the insurance. You've simply accepted a larger deductible, since you can now walk away at $95 instead of $100. With less insurance comes bigger losses, but that also means bigger gains. You've accepted a little more risk in exchange for more potential rewards. If you don't like the risk-reward profile of the $95 call, try the $90, the $85, and so on until you find one that suits you. There are no right or wrong answers, just lots of choices. That's the beauty of options. So why do they have such a risky reputation?

Most traders are terrified of losing money, so they're only willing to spend very small amounts and hope the stock makes the front page of the *Wall Street Journal* for making the biggest move in stock market history. If the $100 call is $5, the $120 call may be 20 cents. Yes, now the most you can lose is 20 cents—but it's virtually guaranteed. The breakeven price is $120.20, and there's very little chance for that to happen. But people buy them, lose money, and then scream it was the risky option's fault. Can you push the boundaries further and make the option behave even more like stock?

Rather than buying the at-the-money $100 call for $5, perhaps you could buy a deep in-the-money call, say the $80 call trading for $21. With the stock at $100, this call has $20 of intrinsic value, but only one dollar's worth of extrinsic value. Remember, the extrinsic value is the insurance value. It's the price you pay for the right to walk away. It's cheap because there's not much of a chance for the stock to fall below the $100 strike by expiration. Because it's a low chance of falling out of the money, the right to walk away doesn't have much value. This $80 call will have a high delta, maybe 95 or more, and that means this call is behaving far more like shares of stock. It's hardly an option at all. The breakeven point is $80 strike + $21, or $101, which means the stock only needs to rise one dollar by expiration to break even. If the stock falls all the way to $80 or lower, the call expires worthless, and you'd lose the $21 premium. However, had you bought the shares instead, you'd be down $20, so you're only worse off by the dollar's worth of extrinsic value. What's the advantage of buying the deep-in-the-money $80 call?

Even though you paid more than $5 as with the $100 call, you paid $21 to control 100 shares of stock, which is still a lot less than $100. That gives you about $100/$21, or

4.7x leverage. However, if the stock does fall below $100, you're out $21. The chart below compares the $80 call (black line) to shares of stock (gray line):

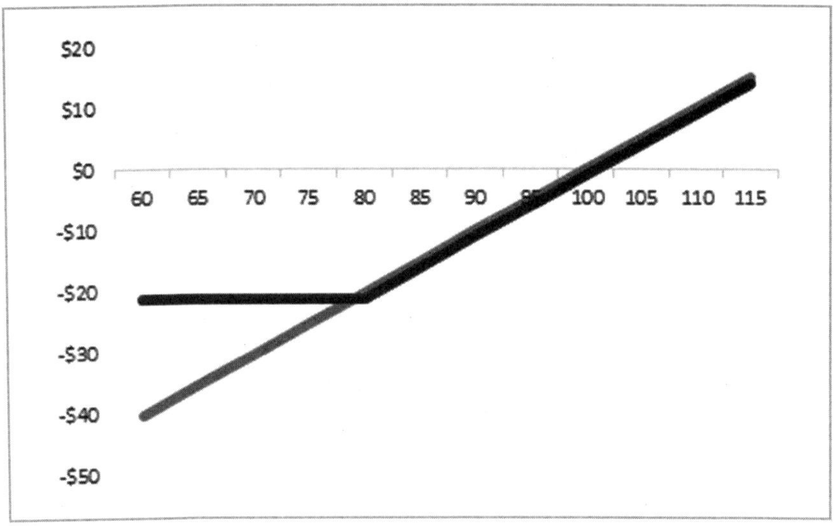


From $80 and above, it's nearly impossible to tell the two curves apart. Again, that's because this option is behaving far more like shares of stock rather than an option. But you still get a little insurance below $80 if the tide goes out.

## A Risky Reputation is a Matter of Perspective

Let's say you're willing to buy shares for $100, but in order to guarantee you can't lose more than $21, you decide to buy the $80 call for $21. Now you have $79 sitting safely in your money market. If the tide goes out and you lose $21, do you see it as doing exactly as intended because you guaranteed a maximum loss of 21%? Or do you see it as a complete disaster since you lost 100% on the option? This is yet another reason why options have a risky reputation. Traders have the wrong perspective. If the stock falls to

$60, they look back and wish they had bought the shares because they could continue to hold. But they lost 100% on the risky option and will never trade options again. Is that really what happened?

On one hand, if you want to say you lost 100% on the option, that's fine. But don't forget that also means you insured 79% of your cash. You only paid 21% of the stock's price, so the better way to see it is that you lost 100% of 21%, or just 21%. If you have regrets about not buying the stock, that's easy to fix. With the stock at $60, take $60 of your $79 cash and repurchase the stock. There, now you have your stock back—and another $19 to boot. Your average cost is $60 + $21 for the call, or $81. With the stock at $60, you're down $21 while the stock trader is down $40. However, if you don't like the stock at $60, you can walk away and keep your $79 cash. The stock trader doesn't get that choice. The stock trader is down $40—not $21—and has no choice but to either continue to hold or take the $40 loss. Options do an amazing job at managing risk, but some traders will say they lost 100% on the option, and everyone takes it as one more piece of evidence that options are risky. Options just give you many choices. Stock gives you one. If you don't like the risk-reward profile of the $80 call, now you know what to do. Consider the $75, or the $70, and on down the line until you find the strike you like. Lower-strike calls will cost more total dollars, but you'll pay less for the insurance (extrinsic value). The choice is yours, and you get so many choices with options.

## Put Options: Playing the Downside Plus Insurance

Put options can be used as insurance against long shares of stock, and we'll look at an example in Chapter Three.

However, put options can also be used to speculate. What if the markets are melting down, and you want to speculate they're going to melt further? The only choice you have with stock is to *short* shares. Short selling means you borrow the shares from the broker but sell them as if you owned them. If you short 100 shares of stock at $100, you have an obligation to return 100 shares at some time in the future. The goal is to buy them back at a cheaper price, and that's what allows you to capture a profit. Short sellers are still buying low, selling high, just in the reverse order. Below is a risk graph for short shares of stock:

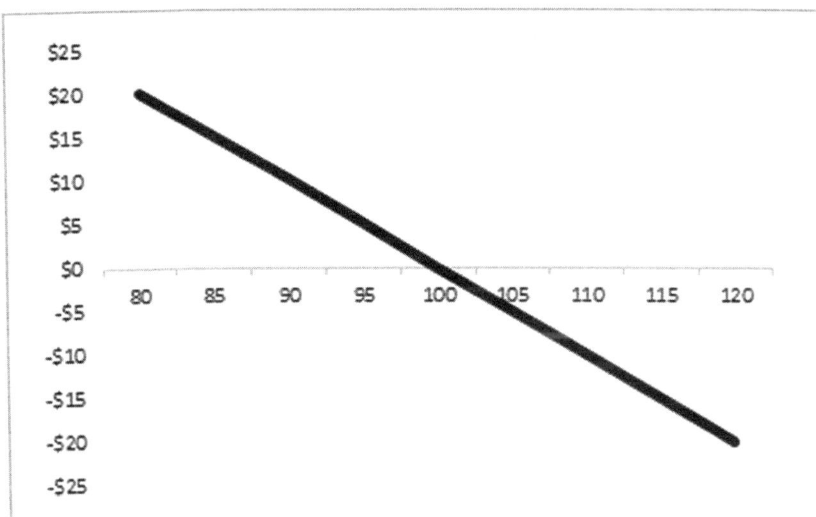


The risk graph is exactly the opposite of long shares, so now the risk is if the stock rises. Theoretically, a short stock position is riskier than long stock, as there's no limit on how high a stock's price can rise. That's true, but there's another side to consider. Markets can melt down, but they rarely melt up. In other words, when the tide goes out, it's often fast and furious. So, the downside risk can still be more devastating even though the risk is theoretically limited. For the same reasons, it can also be super profitable. It may take years for the market to rise 30%, but if traders think it's the beginning of the zombie apocalypse, it may take a matter of days to fall that same percentage. So, if you wish to speculate that prices will continue to fall, how can you accomplish that without all the upside risk? This is where put options come into play. Remember, a long put gives you the right to sell shares of stock at a fixed price. If you buy a $100 put, you have the right to sell shares for $100—no matter how low the price may be. So, put options increase in value as the underlying stock falls. The chart below shows a long $100 put purchased for $5 (black line) compared to short shares of stock at $100 (gray line):

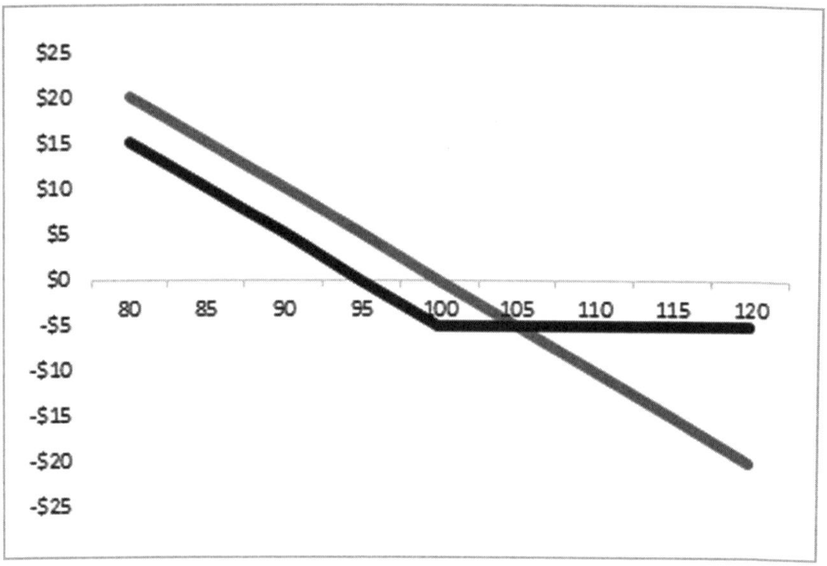


Just like with call options, put options create a bend at the strike price. That's the insurance policy. To find a put's breakeven price, subtract the premium from the strike, so in this example, $100 - $5, or $95. If the stock falls to $95 at expiration, you'd just break even on this put whereas the short stock position would gain five dollars. The put buyer needs the stock to make a fast, aggressive fall before profiting. So, the short stock position outperforms the long put if the stock price falls. However, the reason for paying the $5 premium is risk management. It's in case the stock rises. The put option guards against all the uncertain upside risk that short sellers must accept.

Everything that applies to calls applies to puts—just in the opposite direction. If you want to decrease the breakeven point and make the position behave more like short shares, use higher-strike puts. On the other hand, if you're looking for fast, aggressive moves, you may choose out-of-the-money strikes. Again, because markets can fall fast and furiously, many traders use out-of-the-money puts for speculation. Okay, let's now put these concepts to use, and we'll show you one of our favorite strategies for managing longer-term positions. As market makers, it helped us survive some of the most catastrophic events in stock market history, and it'll help you—and your money—survive too. Zombies included.

## The Stock Replacement Strategy

The stock replacement strategy is a unique twist on a long call that makes the option behave far more like shares of stock, so it's a great strategy for long-term investors. The strategy allows you to be more cash efficient, but also automatically adjusts the downside risk if things go wrong. Call options won't let you get caught in the psychological deer-in-headlights trap and hold all the way to the bottom. When Pete and I were market makers, we used this a lot when we needed long shares of stock as a hedge but wanted to preserve cash.

It allowed us to diversify risk across more positions, or just have cash to buy when everyone else was selling. It's one of our favorite strategies, especially for experienced stock traders who are new to options. It's easy to understand, but that doesn't make it any less powerful. What's the strategy, and how does it work?

Most traders buy options with strikes near the current stock price, as that makes the options relatively cheap in terms of dollars. For stock replacement, however, you'll do the opposite: You'll buy a deep-in-the-money call, usually with a delta around 0.80 to 0.85. By pushing the deltas so high, the call will behave far more like straight-line shares of stock—but for a lot less money. For instance, in early August 2023, the S&P 500 ETF (SPY) was trading for $450. The $360 call with 413 days to expiration was trading for $112 with an 0.85 delta. When traders first see this, they think it's an expensive option. Who'd want to pay $112 for an option? Remember, however, that the "option" is found in the extrinsic value. With the SPY at $450, the $360 call has $90 of intrinsic value, so the remaining $22 is extrinsic value. However, with interest rates near 5%, there's a cost of carry equal to about $20 ono the $360 strike, which is theoretically what you're saving by not buying the shares. In other words, because you're not paying $450 today to buy the shares, you can let that money sit in your money market and earn interest. So, the true extrinsic value is just a couple of bucks. It's a really cheap insurance policy. Remember that as we move through the example.

If you buy the shares, you'll spend $45,000 and make dollar for dollar as the index rises but lose dollar for dollar as it falls. That's a lot of money to place at risk. However, if you buy the $360 call, you'll spend $112, or $11,200 total. That's only 25% of the cost of the shares.

You're now more cash efficient, as you now have more money to spread around in other positions—possibly even other hedges. The chart below shows the current curve for the $360 call purchased at $112 (black line) compared to long shares of SPY purchased for $450 (gray line):

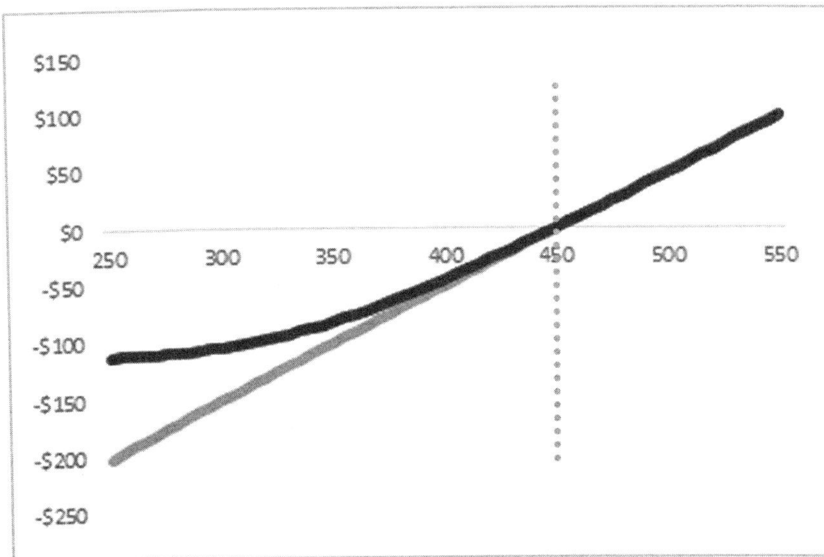


The SPY is currently $450, as shown by the dotted line. From a stock price of $400 and higher, the black and gray lines just about perfectly overlap, and that means the call option will perform about like the shares, provided the stock stays above $400. They're nearly impossible to visually tell apart, and that's why it's called the stock replacement strategy. While the lines are close, they're not identical. The black line sits $22 below the gray line at $450, but it's just hard to see in the chart because $22 is less than 5% of $450. Remember, the true insurance policy is only a couple of dollars. So, the stock replacement strategy underperforms a tiny bit if the index rises. If the index rises to $500, the stock trader makes $50. However, with the index at $500, your $360 call would be worth $140, so you'd make $140-$112, or $28—exactly $22 less. Well, why buy the call?

The reason for spending $22 of extrinsic value is if the index falls. That's the price of the insurance policy, and the price to walk away. Sure, it's unlikely for the index to fall from $450 to $360 in a little over a year, but that's why the insurance policy is relatively cheap. If the index falls below $400, you can see the difference between the shares and call begins to widen, as the black and gray lines begin to spread apart. The stock continues to lose dollar for dollar while the call losses begin to taper off toward a maximum $112 loss. That's the insurance. The call automatically reduces your exposure as the index falls. It won't allow you to continually be exposed to such downside risk. The stock, however, doesn't change course. It just continues to lose dollar for dollar as the tide goes out. If the index falls to $360 at expiration, the stock trader would be down $90 while your call would expire worthless, and your maximum loss is the $112 spent—exactly $22 more than the stock trader. Again, that's because you were effectively buying shares plus a $22 insurance policy. Well, if you're worse off by $22, where's the insurance?

That $22 extrinsic value is the insurance policy if the index *falls below* $360. You're not paying $22 to outperform the shares if things go well. For all index prices below $360 at expiration, you'd take no more losses while the stock trader would. The $22 fee is to manage risk if things go wrong. The breakeven point would be $360 strike - $22, or $338. If the index falls to $338, the stock trader and you are down $112. For all index prices below $338, you'd lose less at expiration. As covered in the previous section, if you think 22 sounds like too high of a price to pay for the insurance, you know what to do. There are lots of strikes on the menu, and each one changes the risk-reward relationship. By moving to a lower strike call, you'll pay a greater total price, but you'll pay less extrinsic value, and that means a lower insurance value. For instance, at the same time, the SPY $300 call was trading for $167. It has $150 of intrinsic value, but only $17 of extrinsic value. Yes, $167 is more expensive than the $112 you'd spend on the $360 call, but it's still a small fraction of the share price—just 37%. That lowers your breakeven to $467. However, now the insurance doesn't kick in until $300 - $167 = $133. Remember, there are no right or wrong answers—only answers that are right for you. Options give you so many choices over shares of stock, and they'll automatically manage risk if things go wrong.

No matter how hard you try to convince some people that options are just hedging unwanted risk, they'll say they want nothing to do with options and will just stick with good ol' safe shares of stock. Well, now that you understand some basic option pricing properties, sit back and get ready for something really mind bending.

## Surprise! Stock Traders Are Options Traders

We've shown that as you move to lower and lower strikes, call options behave more and more like shares of stock. Now let's ask an interesting question: What's the lowest strike price you could ever have? Well, obviously zero. There is no such strike, but what if it did exist? To make it more interesting, what if it had no expiration date? In other words, you could exercise it at any time, pay nothing, and get 100 shares of SPY. Sounds too good to be true. In the financial markets, however, you must pay for all benefits, so if it sounds like a good benefit, it'll have a steep price too. It turns out, that a zero-strike call would trade for exactly $450—identical to the shares. It wouldn't trade for one cent more, or one cent less, no matter how much time remained. No call option can trade for more than the current price of the underlying stock, so if you push the strike to zero, it will trade for exactly the same price as the shares.

So, for anyone who still thinks options are dangerous, stock traders are mathematically trading options with a zero strike and unlimited time to expiration. Stock traders pay no extrinsic value—or insurance value—but they run the risk of riding the stock to significantly lower levels than the options traders. If you don't want the risk of possibly riding the underlying stock all the way down to zero, you can select any in-the-money strike and limit risk. It's a question of how much you want to spend and how much you want to insure. The lower the strike, the more you'll pay for the call, but the less you pay for the insurance. So, if you're willing to ride the stock price all the way to zero—and spend a lot of money to hold the shares—you're still free to do it. Understanding options doesn't lock you out of the stock club. Remember, when trading options, you're ultimately trading shares of stock. But what if you don't want to potentially take the elevator all the way to the ground floor? Then choose a stock replacement call, which again means a call with an 0.80 to 0.85 delta. If you don't like the insurance value of the $360 call, check the $355, the $350, the $345 and all the way down. If you want to limit your insurance to something small, say $10, a strike price will be there, and it'll still cost less than the stock. Once you understand options, you'll see the menu has lots of choices that you don't get with shares. For this SPY expiration, there were 110 strikes but about 40 that would be good choices for the stock replacement strategy. Now that's a lot of choices. Each strike offers a slightly different risk-reward profile. Options allow you to structure positions and portfolios to weather future storms—the ones nobody will see coming. Options allow you to define your risks and rewards before you enter the position. If you're fearful of the tide going out, options give you options, and that makes it more likely for you to follow the most important Wall Street maxim of all: Buy low, sell high.

# Chapter Three:

## Manage Your Risk, Not Your Profits

People are wired to have an extreme fear of losses. It's coded into our DNA from the Stone Ages when cavemen learned costly lessons about risk. Sure, Zog could dive headfirst into rustling bushes and snare a gourmet long-eared rabbit, but it may be the waiting jaws of a saber-toothed tiger. Always remember the Golden Rule of Risk Management—avoid extreme outcomes. Ending up a winner—or dinner—is about as extreme as it gets.

Professional traders have an innate behavior that's genetically hardwired from the Stone Ages, and they survive by using similar approaches. Sure, some market opportunities are just begging for you to dive headfirst into the bushes, like buying all the shares of Enron you can afford because Fortune just voted it "America's Most Innovative Company" for the sixth consecutive year. How can you go wrong?

No matter how tempting they may be, professional traders have learned it's always better to live to play another day, and they do that by reducing any unwanted risk. As one of our world-class coaches and former market maker Stuart Dorfman reminds our students, "Know your risk." It's a simple way to say, if you don't know what's behind the door, don't open it. Retail traders, however, still haven't caught on. They approach trading as a guessing game, Wall Street's version of *Let's Make a Deal.* They may choose Door #1 because they *think* it has the prize—and hope it's not the goat. Their time is spent predicting the future. When will the stock move, and by how much? That's a common approach retail traders call "analyzing the market." Professional traders call it guessing. Just tune in to novice conversations, and they'll go something like this:

**Homer:** "What do you think Outta Cache Technologies will do next month?"

**Hubert:** "I think it's going higher. I just feel it's overdue for a run."

**Homer:** "Me too. It's been flatlined for a year but showing signs of a pulse. If it moves, it could really go. I'm buying more!"

**Hubert:** "Do you think it's going up a little or a lot?"

**Homer:** "Listen...ya hear that sound, Hubert? That's opportunity knocking. This stock is off to the Moon—then Mars!"

**Hubert:** "Yes, I heard it, Homer! I thought it was you knocking on the desk. It must be a sign from beyond. I'm buying more too—on margin!"

It's easy to see how traders can get themselves talked into frenzied, reckless buying based on what they think. Well, here's the harsh, unsympathetic reality that we call the Second Golden Rule of Risk Management: The market doesn't care what you think. You can't use your thoughts to raise a stock's price. Comedian Steven Wright once joked, "Everyone who believes in telekinesis, raise my hand." It works great for jokes—not for markets. A similar but equally bad idea, or to put it more respectfully, ridiculously stupid, is to think you can control the markets with your eyes. We'll hear traders say, "Yeah, I know this short stock position is like TNT on a hot grill, but don't worry...I'm watching it closely." If you can control stock prices with your eyes, we'd be eager to talk to you. Warren Buffett would too, and probably the Federal Reserve. Predicting the market is easy—being right is hard. So, it's not a good risk-management system to place trades based only on what you think—or think you see. How can retail traders avoid jumping into the hungry jaws of a market meltdown? Buying shares of stock entails many types of risks, but you don't have to accept them all. Options were designed to reduce, or hedge risks, so you can choose the risks to remove—and get paid for risks you're willing to accept. Sure, you must have some opinions, such as bullish or bearish, stocks or bonds, yin or yang. But the focus of conversations and actions should center on risk management. Here's how our conversations would go:

**Jon:** "I see Tequila Mockingbird went up five points yesterday, and we have 20 calls."

**Pete:** "Yep. Based on the opening prices, we can sell half and roll half for a 75% guaranteed return but still have unlimited upside."

**Jon:** "This stock is hot enough to sear an iguana. It could come crashing down. Our goal was a double."

**Pete:** "A double tequila?"

**Jon:** "No, a double in price."

**Pete:** "Ok, well then maybe we should do an over-roll to lock in more money—but still have unlimited gains?"

**Jon:** "Good idea, but the volatility is still higher than their alcohol content. Maybe we should spread five contracts off vertically? We can collect another $4 to further hedge the downside risk."

**Pete:** "That would give us a 120% guaranteed return, and we'd still have unlimited potential upside on five calls. Whaddya think?"

**Jon:** "BANG!"

Notice how the conversation dealt with facts—not guesses. The stock went up five points. We can sell half and roll half to lock in a 75% return. Volatility is high. We can collect $4 and increase our returns to 120%. We'll still have unlimited upside potential. None of these statements are hopes, dreams, or aspirations—they're facts. We're looking at what has happened and what we can do at current prices to stay in the game for more profits—but reduce risk. Now go back and read the conversation between Homer and Hubert. How many facts are there? Just one—they're guessing. The entire conversation was about what they think—no respect for the Second Golden Rule of Risk Management. As new information hits the markets, whether news, changing prices, or volatility, you're free to alter your outlooks—and you should. You have more information today than yesterday. Each day is like a new deal of cards. As each card is turned over, you're gaining new information. How do you keep from being overwhelmed with information?

Information only has value if it can alter a decision. So, only pay attention if the information is something that would make you change your mind. If you hear someone on CNBC say, "I think Curl Up & Dye Hair Salons will be next year's hot stock," that's not new information, at least any information you want to react to. The words "I think" are a good clue. But if the Federal Reserve says it's about to put hydraulics under interest rates, that's something you'll want to pay attention to. If new information makes you keep your same hand, that's fine, but at least consider what's changed. However, if new information makes you change your view—for better or worse—it's best to make changes to your positions. The core of our conversations is always about reducing risk based on new information. Are there times we add to the risk? Sure, if the information warrants it. As traders, we're always looking for new opportunities, so that means we must add to current positions, which is to take more risk. We're always looking for the trades to give us the best chances to meet our goals.

## Set a Goal—And Stick to It!

The most important thing about risk management is setting a goal. In fact, you can't even define risk without a goal. An investor who wants to double his money in 10 years can probably buy the S&P 500 index and hold on for the ride. At an average rate of 7% per year, the goal will be met in ten years, and that's not a bad estimate for that index. However, a short-term trader trying to double his money by Friday can forget about using the same strategy. Neither goal is wrong—they're personal preferences. While the first trader has a higher probability of success, goals have no measurement scale. You can classify goals as high probability or low probability, but you can't say they're good or bad.

However, each strategy would be wrong for the other trader. One trader would be taking too much risk to meet the goal, and for the other, too little.

Former Dallas Cowboys' coach Tom Landry said, "Setting a goal is not the main thing. It is deciding how you will go about achieving it and staying with that plan." Considering his 29-year career had 20 consecutive winning seasons and his 20 career playoff victories are the second most of any coach in NFL history, they're words worth remembering. Goals make decisions easy. If you're trying to earn 10% on your entire portfolio by year end, each trade should be invested at roughly a level to earn 10%. It makes no sense to place a trade that can earn 100% when 10% is the goal. While 100% sounds 10-times better, it's just 10 times riskier. If that's not the risk you set out to take, don't do it. A variation of Murphy's Law says, "If there's a possibility of several things going wrong, the one that will cause the most damage will be the one to go wrong." That's the problem with taking too much risk to meet a goal. You don't want to find out your financial plan has been altered so that you can afford to retire exactly 10 years after you die. Placing trades where you expect to earn more than your goal—or earn less—doesn't make sense. Keep risk in line with goals. Goals should also be specific and measurable, so saying you

> **Setting a goal is not the main thing. It is deciding how you will go about achieving it and staying with that plan.**
>
> **– Tom Landry**

want to make a lot of money isn't a goal. Goals should also be realistic, so while aiming to earn 30% per month is specific and measurable, it's not realistic. It's not what markets are expected to return.

Below is a chart of the S&P 500 (SPX) monthly returns from 1900 to June 2023:

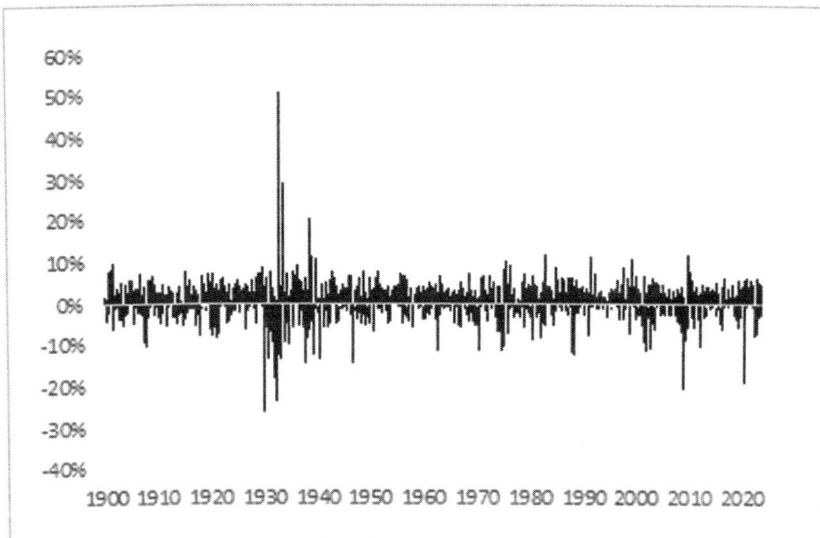


Only one time—July 1932—did the index ever beat 30% for the month, and that's when it shot up 51.4% for the month. That's only one time out of 1,482 months, or .07% of the time. To be fair, it got close in April 1933 when it returned 29.3%. But aside from those two times in a 123-year history, it never got close. The long-term average is 0.87% per month, or about 10.5% per year. Don't expect to consistently earn 30% per month. Now, you may think you can do it with leverage. If you can earn about 1% per month, then 30-times leverage would earn 30% per month. True, but if the market doesn't consistently return 1% per month, it means some months will be down. Look at the above chart, and there's nearly a mirror-image below 0%. If you have 30-times leverage and get caught in just one of those months, it may take years to dig out, and there goes your goal. Create realistic goals, and risk management becomes easier.

## What Does Everybody Else Think?

It sounds like obvious advice, but it's hard to put into practice. Just because you have a "realistic" goal, doesn't mean you'll automatically achieve the goal. It just means there's a high chance. So, just thinking of a goal—no matter how realistic—isn't enough. Remember the Second Golden Rule of Risk Management: The market doesn't care what you think. It's the crowd's collective opinion that drives the market. Once you realize that, it adds another layer of appreciation to managing risk. Markets are formed by the collective opinion of all traders—not yours. It's what everyone else thinks that matters, and this is why professional traders aren't surprised when market bubbles form. It doesn't matter how "overvalued" *you* may think a stock price may be. If you think that everybody else thinks it's going higher, it's rational to buy. Think about the 2007-2008 financial crisis. From about 1995 to 2005, housing prices had been in an upward spiral, and many financial professionals—including bank presidents and lenders—felt the market had been overvalued for some time. So, why did people continue to buy houses? And why did banks continue to lend?

Because professionals felt that everyone else felt that prices were going higher. An individual opinion doesn't matter. The collective opinion does. Every year prices did go higher, so it fueled beliefs that the trend would continue. If you were a bank president back then, you may have been convinced housing prices were outrageously high in 2005 and decided to stop making home loans. But how could you justify your actions to the Board of Directors when your competitors were setting record-breaking earnings because of their home loans? It only proves they're right—and you're wrong. Savvy bank presidents must make decisions based on what is likely to happen based on what the crowd thinks—not what they think.

For example, let's say you, as a bank president, thought prices couldn't go higher, but now discover other mortgage lenders created 2/28 loans. These loans offered a super low fixed rate for the first two years, but then moved to a higher floating rate for the remaining 28 years. That was done because of the demand for speculation. People are more likely to buy and flip houses if rates are low. So, how should you respond?

No matter what you think about current home prices, you should realize the new 2/28 loans would make home buying easier and will put *upward* pressure on prices. The better idea was to make loans, or buy real estate, no matter how overvalued you thought the market may be. And that's exactly what happened. Buying continued, housing prices continued to rise, which reinforced beliefs about home prices rising, which caused more buying—and the bubble continued. Tons of money can be made from bubbles, which is why it's rational to participate in them. It doesn't matter what you think about today's prices. It's what everyone else thinks that matters. However, all bubbles must eventually burst, which is why they're called bubbles. How did this bubble pop?

Buyers of 2/28 mortgages believed they could just continue to refinance and maintain the low two-year rates. However, after home prices began to fall, it became impossible to refinance the homes. And that's when the bubble began to burst. So, if you feel Tequila Mockingbird is overvalued, feel free to short it. But if everyone else thinks it's going higher, you're going to be holding a short position with a chart that looks like a SpaceX rocket launch. Sure, your opinion counts, it just doesn't count much. If you buy 100 shares of Tequila Mockingbird, you'll put a tiny bit of upward pressure on its price, but that's like pouring a cup of water into the Atlantic Ocean to raise the water level. What you'd really like to know is when the tides are moving—and in which direction. For traders, it's better to follow market trends—the collective opinion of the crowd—but hedge your bets.

## Trade the Market–But Hedge Your Opinion

As a trader, you're free to have an opinion on the market, but remember, it's what everybody else thinks that matters. What if you're wrong? This is where you become a risk manager. Risk management is eliminating any *known* risks you don't want and reducing the remaining risks to acceptable levels—just in case you're wrong. But because of the intricate web of globalization, it's impossible to identify what the remaining risks are. As economist Elroy Dimson said, "Risk means more things can happen than will happen." It's a great way to remember that no matter how many risks you account for, there are still more possibilities. If you think there are only three things that can go wrong and hedge them all, a fourth will mysteriously

> ***Risk means more things can happen than will happen.***
>
> ***– Elroy Dimson***

appear. So, we tell people to trade the market—but hedge your opinion. What does it mean to hedge?

Hedging is the most important concept for traders. After all, remember, you're risk managers. *Hedging means you're giving up some potential gains in exchange for limiting losses.* A hedge is the purchase or sale of a position that will move in the opposite direction of another. If one position gains, the other loses, so they tend to offset each other. Buying car insurance is a hedge. The premium is relatively small compared to potential expenses should you get into a wreck. The policy reduces your overall wealth, but guards against potentially large losses that could destroy it. If you want to photograph great white sharks in a feeding frenzy, purchasing a safety cage would be a hedge—and a pretty good one at that. You may not get the up-close photos you wanted, but you won't end up as sushi either.

As risk managers, your goal is never to eliminate all risks. That's easy to do—don't trade. Put your money in a coffee can and bury it in the front yard. If you want to diversify, bury one can in the front yard and one in the back. Inflation will have a feeding frenzy on your money, and no cage will save you, but at least you'll never have to worry about market risk. Well, that's not a good solution either, so you must take some risk, and the stock market is your best bet. However, it comes with a wide choice of risks. That's why you must choose a goal, select the risks that provide the best chance of reaching that goal—and hedge the remaining risks. Options were designed as hedging tools, so if you want to manage risk, you must use options. Remember the Golden Rule of Risk Management: Avoid extreme outcomes. Never put yourself in a position where you can make it all—or lose it all. Or end up as sushi. Never. Regardless of how you go about hedging, how do you choose the risks to accept—and which to hedge?

## Hedging Made Easy: The Score Dictates Action

Trading decisions are always based on meeting goals. Managing trades is a lot like coaching football. Professional coaches aren't hired to predict scores. They're hired to win games—that's the goal. To do that, they must make decisions at each down of the game, or in other words, as new information arrives. Depending on the score, time remaining, previous plays, how opponents will likely respond, weather conditions, team standings, and many other factors, different plays may be called. One thing you'll notice, however, is that the plays are based on the score relative to the clock. Professional coaches are score managers. They're managing the score compared to the time on the clock, and that's what drives their decisions. For instance, if the team is ahead with 10 seconds on the clock, it's a simple decision. The quarterback will down the ball on the snap, and the clock will run out. It's a guaranteed win, so why risk any other play for more points? Extra points don't count toward your goal of winning the game. In fact, they jeopardize it. Because that's the best play, all players—even the other team—know it's coming. The score dictated the play.

What if that same team is behind by five points with three seconds on the clock? The decision is easy again—it's a Hail Mary pass. It's the *only chance* the team has to win, so you might as well go for it. A 10% chance of winning is better than a 100% chance of losing. Everyone knows it's coming, and everyone runs downfield on the snap. Again, the score dictated the actions for both teams. Coaches know when the final buzzer rings, it's the "W" or "L" that matters—not the number of points. Coaches manage points relative to the clock to gain the highest chance to win. Of course, those are extreme conditions, so the answers were easy. But it's the same idea at each play of the game. What's the score, and how much time is on the clock? It's a little art, a lot of science, and experience provides the best answers. In the NFL, it's decades of past experiences that makes a coach, not what he thinks the final score will be.

Professional traders make decisions the same way. What's our goal, and what do we have to do today, if anything, to give us the best chance of reaching it? Hedge fund manager Ray Dalio nailed the idea for traders: "What is most important isn't knowing the future — it is knowing how to react appropriately to the information available at each point in time." If you're ever in doubt about a trade to enter or exit, go back to your goals, and ask what you need to do to give yourself the best chance for meeting them. The goals dictate the play. That's where you'll find the answer. Now that you understand the basic concepts of managing risk, how do professional traders hedge risk? This is where options come to the rescue, and there are countless ways to hedge with options, but let's get started with some basic, but powerful, hedges.

> ***What is most important isn't knowing the future – it is knowing how to react appropriately to the information available at each point in time.***
>
> ***– Ray Dalio***

## Hedging Long Shares of Stock

Previously, we've said a put option is like an insurance policy for long shares. A long put makes money if the stock price falls, whereas your long stock position loses money as the stock price falls. So, if you own shares of stock, buying a put option is a hedge. The two positions tend to offset each other thus making the put act like an insurance policy for your shares. In the chart below, you bought 100 shares of stock at $100 (gray line). Because of the unlimited downside risk, you may decide to buy a 120-day $100 put for $5. The combined position of stock plus put creates the black line:

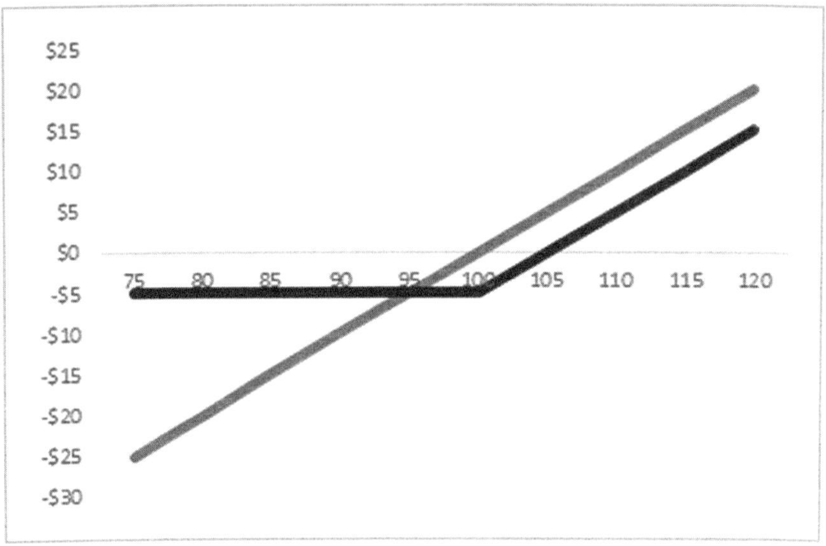


You can see the hedge at work: For all stock prices above $100, the long stock position outperforms the hedged position, as the gray line sits above the black line. In fact, it sits $5 higher, which is the cost of the put, or insurance policy. If the stock price rises, the long shares will outperform the hedged stock position by $5, and you'd have been better off not buying the put. But that's like saying if you don't wreck your car, you'd have been better off not buying insurance. The put was a hedge, and you expected to give up some of the upside in exchange for something. So, what did you get for the $5 premium?

The black and gray lines cross at $95, which is the breakeven point for both positions. If the stock falls to $95, you'd lose $5 by holding the shares, and you'd lose $5 for buying the put. With the stock at $95, you could exercise your $100 put and collect $100 cash. However, you paid $5 for the put, so that's why it also ends up losing $5 too. However, for all stock prices below $95, the benefit of buying the put appears. Now the black line sits higher than the gray line. The hedged stock position loses less than the long shares by limiting losses to $5—even if the stock falls all the way to zero. Buying a put hedges the risk of holding shares. When you hedge positions, you're working in the middle of risk and reward rather than at the extremes of making it all—or losing it all. So, when risk changes, professional traders will do something to guard against new risks. When trading only shares of stock, you don't get these choices. You simply hold 100% of the risk in exchange for 100% of the gains. If those gains aren't necessary to reach your goals, they need to be hedged.

## Synthetic Positions: Hedging Made Easier

*Scan the QR code*
*to watch our video*
***"Synthetic Positions"***

After seeing the previous graph, you may be saying, "Hey, that stock plus put position looks just like a call option risk graph." If you spotted that, congratulations, you just opened the door to a deeper level of understanding—and power—of options. The combination of long stock plus a put is called a *synthetic equivalent* of a long call. Synthetic positions are combinations of assets that behave like others. By "behave," it means they produce the same risk graphs. Just like synthetic wool looks, acts, and feels like regular wool, it's made from different stuff—synthetic sheep, of course. That's the idea behind synthetic option positions. You can buy 100 shares of stock plus a $100 put, but you could also buy a $100 call by itself—for a lot less money—and accomplish the same thing. So, stock plus a put is synthetically the same as a long call. It sounds like a strange concept but think about saying ½ is the same as 0.5. They're two different ways of "constructing" the same idea. They look different and use different numbers, but they're exactly the same. That's what synthetic positions are all about. Which hedge should you choose? Options give you many choices, and this is where understanding synthetics gives your hedging powers a boost. If you already own 100 shares, buying a put is the easier, cheaper hedge. But if you don't own the shares, buying the call accomplishes the same thing for a lot less money since you don't have to buy the stock. If you now can see that buying shares plus a put is identical to buying a call, it's a beautiful way to understand that call options are insurance too. All options—calls and puts—are ways to hedge, or reduce, risk. It's completely unfair to say the option is risky. Let's try another hedge, and it's one of our favorites we used as market makers—and still use today. If it helped us survive, it can help you too.

## The Powerful Stock Swap

Traders often think that you're either a stock trader or an options trader. You're neither. You're a risk manager. Sometimes, stock is a great choice. Other times options will be. But here's a great example where stock traders can instantly become better risk managers by understanding options—even if they start out buying shares. Let's say you own 100 shares purchased for $100 and it's risen to $120. You have an unrealized $20 gain, which you'd like to protect. At the same time, you feel the stock price will climb higher, so you'd like to hold out for bigger profits. What can you do?

First, don't forget the Second Golden Rule of Risk Management: The market doesn't care what you think. Don't base your decision to buy, sell, or hold based on the strength of your convictions. Instead, think like a professional. It's okay to have an opinion that the stock will continue to rise, but hedge that opinion in case you're wrong. Trade the cards you've been dealt. Next, turn the cards over and look: You have $10,000 into the trade and $2,000 of an unrealized gain. Those are facts and must be dealt with first before you gaze into the crystal ball. Trade the market in front of you, but create some type of hedge in case you're wrong. If you only have shares of stock in your toolbox, there's not much you can do, other than sell off some shares. If you sell 50 shares, you'll only have 50 shares left. You won't capture as many gains if the stock does continue higher, and you'll only get one more shot to sell 50 shares.

This is a great dilemma to have, and fortunately, options make it easy to solve. Anytime you have a sizeable unrealized profit in shares, it may be a great time for a *stock swap*, which is another simple, but powerful strategy. The stock swap is done by selling your shares but swapping them for an in-the-money call with a high delta, say 0.70. Recall that delta measures how sensitive your option is compared to shares of stock. If your call has a 0.70 delta, it means it's picking up 70% of the changes in the stock. If the stock rises one dollar, your option will pick up 70 cents. Recall that the stock replacement strategy usually uses 0.80 to 0.85 deltas, so it's close to the same idea. The reason for reducing the deltas a little more is that you're more focused on getting money off the table—hedging risk—rather than making the call option behave like shares. If you wanted to make the call behave more like shares, you could certainly select higher deltas. The choices are yours—and there are many. Regardless of which delta you pick, you'll still capture significant profits if the stock continues to run. As the stock continues to climb, or as time passes, that call's delta will rise toward 1.0 and behave exactly like the stock. However, if the stock falls, the option will automatically reduce your deltas, just as if you were selling shares. In other words, the call will continue to hedge the position if the price falls. If the stock falls below the strike, the call expires worthless, and you can't take any additional losses beyond that. So, the reason for keeping a high delta is that you want the call to behave reasonably close to the shares—but at a fraction of the cost. That's your hedge.

With the stock at $120, let's say the 90-day $100 call is trading for $22, or $20 of intrinsic value plus $2 extrinsic value. So, you can sell your shares and simultaneously buy the $100 call for an overall net debit of $2. Here are the trades:

1. Buy shares = -$100
2. Sell shares = +$120
3. Buy $100 call (open) = -$22
   Net debit = $2

That means you've recouped your initial $100 invested, less the $2 insurance policy. So, if the stock has a meltdown temper tantrum, the stock swap recovered $98 of the initial $100 paid for the shares. After the swap, you've moved from long shares purchased at $100 (gray line) to the long $100 call (black line):

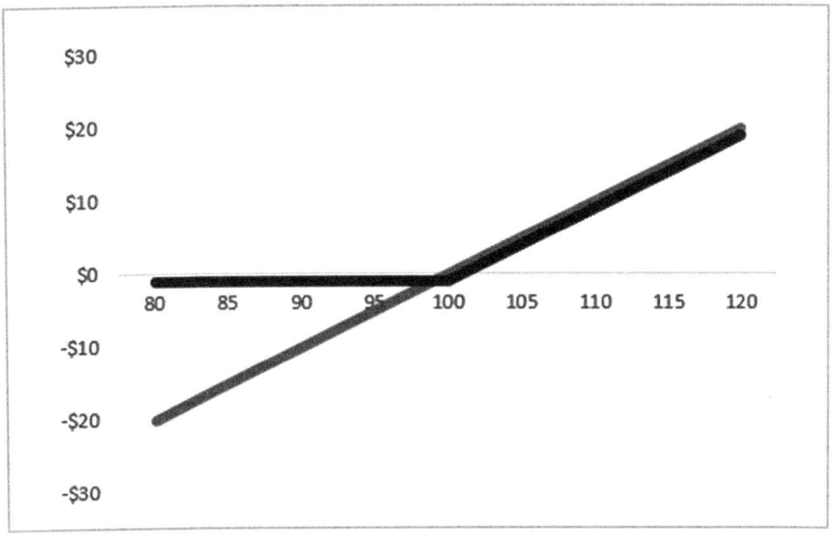


Remember, you'll always bend at a strike price for options—that's your hedge. For all stock prices above $100, the two positions behave nearly identically, and it's difficult to tell the two positions apart. Had you not done the stock swap and continued to hold the shares, your profits would be $2 greater. That's the $2 of extrinsic value in the option—the cost of the insurance policy. If you look closely, the gray line sits a tiny bit higher than the black line for all stock prices above $100. It's exactly $2 higher, which is the cost of the hedge. Why reduce your profits by $2 if things go well?

Like all insurance, the benefits are only revealed when things go wrong. In this case, if the stock price falls below $100, the call expires worthless, and the most you can lose is the $2 paid for the stock swap. Do you see the hedge? You've given up $2 of potential upside in exchange for knocking out $98 of the downside. If you see that as a benefit, is it fair to say options are risky?

At the start of this swap, we assumed the stock was $120, and the swap recovered $98 of your $100 principal. What if you wanted to hold on for more profits but also wanted a guaranteed gain? If there's a big enough unrealized gain in the shares, it's easy to do. Just use a call with a higher strike. Assuming the same expiration date, higher-strike calls will be cheaper since they give you the right to pay a higher price, so they're not as valuable as lower strikes. Because it's a cheaper option, you'll recoup more of your initial $100 paid for the shares. So, rather than swapping your shares for the $100 call, you may decide on the 90-day $110 call trading for $12.50. That's only $10 of intrinsic value but $2.50 of extrinsic value. Now your transactions look like this:

1. Buy shares = -$100
2. Sell shares = +$120
3. Buy $110 call (open) = -$12.50

   Net credit = $7.50

Notice you now have a $7.50 net *credit*—that's your guaranteed return. In other words, you got your $20 unrealized gain off the table but then spent $12.50 for the call, which left $7.50 in your pocket. When you bought the shares at $100, you started on the gray line below. After swapping the shares for the $110 call, you moved to the black line:

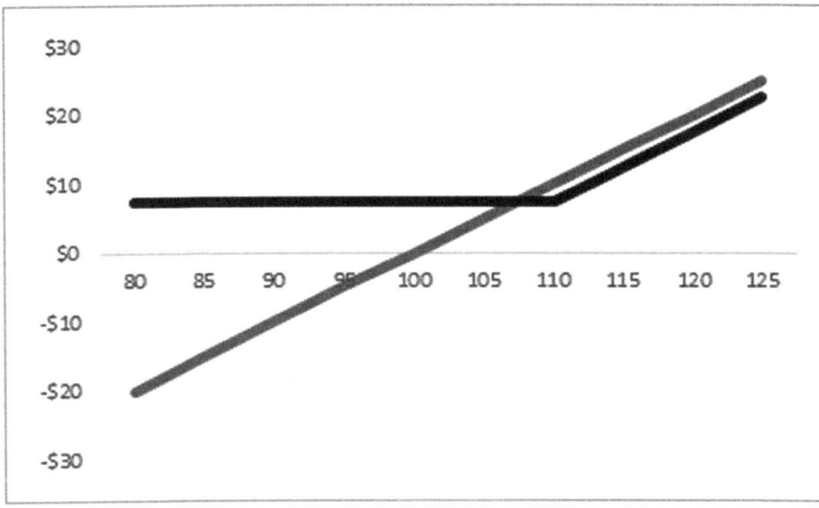


Now you've created a bend at $110, which means the insurance can kick in sooner. That's why there's more extrinsic value on the option—the insurance value is greater. By doing the stock swap, if the stock continues to rise, you'll continue to have unlimited profit potential, but your profits will be $2.50 lower than had you just held the shares. As with all hedges, you'll underperform if things go well. But if things don't go well, you're guaranteed a $7.50 return, or 7.50% on your money. Why choose either strike? Why not take the guaranteed gain plus unlimited profits? Each choice in strikes creates a tradeoff in risk and reward. Yes, the $110 call guaranteed a profit, but the $100 call will be more profitable if the stock continues to rise. So, it comes down to risk tolerances, which are dictated by goals. Don't ask whether a hedge is right or wrong. Ask if it's right for you.

We just saw how a stock swap is a great hedge for long shares of stock that have risen in price, but it requires that you first buy—and hold—*unhedged* shares of stock. So, before the strategy can be used, you must take a lot of risk up front. Before that, we say how buying a put option is a hedge for long shares of stock, but you must pay for the put. What if you want to hedge long shares, but you don't want to pay for the insurance policy, or the put option? Can options help? Options can help with any hedging question, so yes, they can. And it's done with a strategy called a collar.

## Collar Your Risk

A *stock collar* is a popular strategy for stock traders looking to hedge risk, but without having to spend a lot for insurance. How is that done? Well, remember the definition of a hedge: You're giving up some gains in exchange for reducing a risk. If you buy a put to hedge long shares, you give up gains because you had to buy the put. Well, what if you could sell some of the *potential gains* from your shares for a fee and use that money to buy a put? Go back to the basics of rights versus obligations. If you buy a call, you have the right to buy shares, so if you sell a call, you have the potential obligation to sell shares—exactly what you're looking for. So, if you sell a call, you'll collect some cash, and you can use that cash to pay for a put. By selling the call, you'll cap the stock's upside potential, which is the same thing as saying reducing the potential gains. By purchasing the put, you'll block off some risk. Therefore, the collar is a way to hedge risk without having to pay for the insurance policy.

For example, on July 26, 2023, Nvidia (NVDA) was trading for $450. The stock was trading around 50% volatility, so the options were relatively expensive. The 30-day at-the-money $450 call was trading for $34 while the 30-day at-the-money $450 put was trading for $32, which annualizes to 85%. Considering that stocks are expected to move about 8% to 10% per year, that's far too much to be paying for insurance. The reason the put premiums are so high, however, is that there's a lot of room for Nvidia to fall—there's a lot of risk—so traders are bidding up the cost of the insurance. What can you do? Let's say your goal is to earn at the rate of 12% per year, which means all dollars should be invested at that level of risk. If you bought the shares, a 12% annual goal is a gain of 1% per month, which means the stock price would have to rise to about $455 to meet that goal.

By owning the shares, however, you have *unlimited* upside potential gains—far more than the 1% goal. So, one thing you could do is sell the $455 call, which was trading for about $31. Doing so, you've sold off all rights above $455, but that shouldn't matter, as those are gains larger than what you're trying to capture. Your real concern is the downside risk. If the stock crashes, it could take months—or years—to recover those losses. That's where the damage comes in for long-term investors. If you sell the $455 call for $31, how much insurance will it buy? The $450 put, remember, was $32. You could buy that put, but you'd have to pay the $1 difference ($32 cost vs. $31 received from selling the call). Another choice is to think about how much risk you're willing to take. Let's say you're willing to allow the stock to fall $10 to $440. The $440 put was trading for $26, so another choice is to sell the $455 call for $32 and buy the $440 put for $26 for a net credit of $6. If you buy the shares, sell the $455 call, and buy the $440 put, you'll end up with a collar, which is shown in the risk graph below (black line) with the original long stock position (gray line) for comparison:

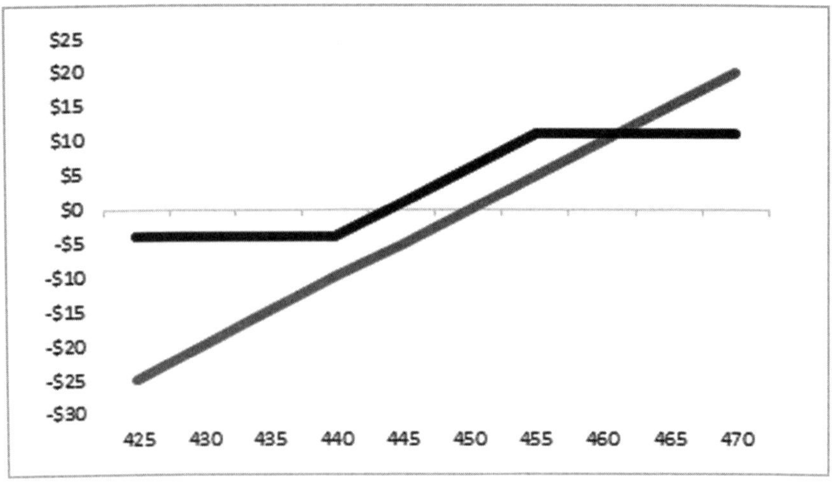


The chart shows if the stock falls to $440, your maximum loss is $4—far better than unlimited risk with such a risky stock. Remember, Nvidia was trading at 50% volatility. The math is a little tricky, but that means if you had thousands of stocks like this, 68% of them would move +/-$65 within 30 days, and 95% would move +/-$130 within that same time. That's a big range, and yet the collar allows you to guarantee that your maximum loss is $4—for no out-of-pocket expense.

On the upside, if the stock rises to the $455 strike, your maximum gain is $11, which is from the $5 gain in the stock moving from $450 to the $455 strike plus the $6 credit from the collar. That $6 credit boosts the potential return to $11/$450, or a 2.4% maximum gain.

Notice that the black and gray lines cross at $461. At that price, both strategies produce the same $11 gain. The collar produces $11 at a stock price of $455 while the stock must reach $461, so you're more likely to receive the gain with the collar than the long shares. The main reason for the collar, however, is to guard against the downside risk. Your downside breakeven is $444, so the stock can fall $6 from the current $450 price, and you'd just breakeven. No matter how low the stock price may fall, your maximum loss is $4. Many traders think credits are better than debits, but if you execute a collar for a credit, it just means you're allowing for more downside risk—and smaller upside gains. Credits or debits aren't good or bad, they're just different choices. It all depends on your goals as to which is right for you.

Even more interesting, if you switch the strikes—sell a lower-strike call and buy a higher-strike put—you'll reverse the position to a bearish bias. For example, if you sold the $440 call and bought the $455 put, the risk graph switches to a bearish bias:

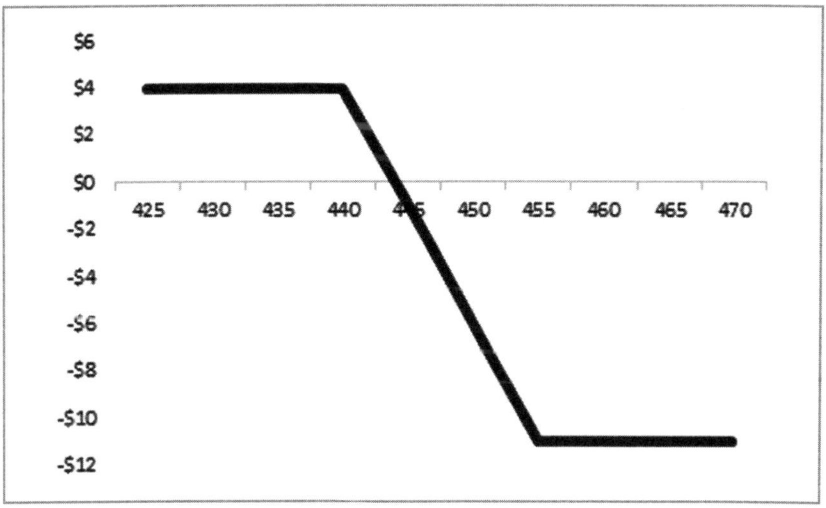


So, if you had shares and wanted to speculate on a short-term bearish move—but guard the upside risk—it's easy to do with collars too. Nvidia had over 70 strikes for this expiration, but if you consider just 10 strikes on either side of the current stock price, it results in 110

combinations of trades, and each one either shifts the entire risk curve up or down—or bullish to bearish. That's a lot of choices, and certainly more than you'd get from just holding the shares. The stock also has LEAPS options, which go out nearly three years, so you can find nearly any time frame to suit your goals. The choice is yours.

## Going Vertical

Another popular options strategy is the *vertical spread*, and it's one of the most versatile of all options strategies. You can create vertical spreads with bullish or bearish outlooks and can also establish them for debits or credits. The choices are nearly endless with this strategy, which is why it's a staple for professional traders. For example, if you were bullish on a stock, you may buy a vertical bull spread. You'd buy one call at one strike and sell another call at a higher strike with the same expiration. You'll be long and short options at the same time. For instance, perhaps you buy a May $100 call and sell a May $105 call. In trading terms, this is the May 100/105 vertical spread. Vertical spreads get their name from the quote boards on brokers' platforms. Vertical spreads are listed vertically in the same monthly columns at different strikes.

By purchasing the 100/105 vertical, you have the right to buy shares at $100 and the potential obligation to sell for $105. So, the spread can increase in value to a maximum of $5—the difference in strikes—and that means you must pay for it, which traders call a *debit spread*. The market price will be something less than $5, so debit spreads will trade at a discount to their maximum value. Who'd want to pay $5 for something that might lose but can, at most, be worth five dollars? Here's where vertical spreads can be a risk manager's—that's you—best friend.

For instance, let's say Pineapple Computer is a super-charged, high-flying stock trading at $500 and around 70% volatility, which is really high. You'd like to own it for the next 90 days, but with that kind of volatility, it's so risky. Who'd want to buy a stock that could lose half its value by Friday? Well, that's the wrong way to look at it. It may also zip past Mars and you've missed an awesome opportunity. The better way is to manage the risk according to your goals. Options allow you to turn problems into opportunities.

Let's say the 90-day $500 call is trading for $70. Even though it's cheaper than the $500 stock, it's probably not too appealing either. You could lose $7,000 quickly with a stock like this. However, let's say the $510 call is trading for $66. If you buy the $500 call and sell the $510 call, it'll cost $4 on a net basis. You have the right to buy shares for $500 but the obligation to sell for $510, so the most the spread could be worth is the $10 difference in strikes. In trading terms, you bought the 500/510 vertical spread for a net debit of four dollars. You paid $4 but could possibly make $10, or 150% return on your money. Below is the risk graph for the long 500/510 vertical spread purchased for $4:

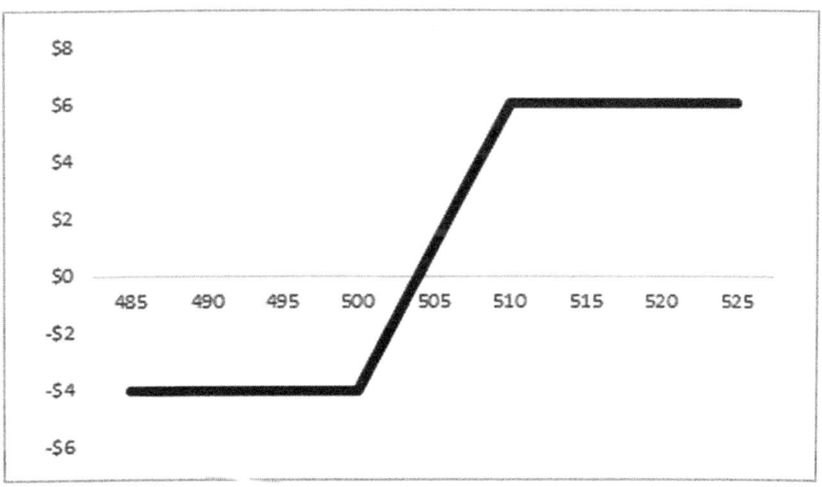

The risk graph shows your breakeven point is $504, which is found by adding the $4 cost to the long $500 call. If the stock rises to $504 at expiration, you'll just break even. If the stock is between $504 and $510, you'll make some kind of profit with the maximum profit occurring at $510. If the stock is $510 or higher at expiration, you'll make the full $10 difference and more than double your money. If the stock is below $504 at expiration, you'll have some kind of loss, with a $4 maximum loss for all stock prices at $500 or below.

So, while paying $50,000 for 100 shares doesn't sound too appealing, the vertical spread is only $400. If you wanted to put that much into the stock, you couldn't even get one share. You're completely locked out of the opportunity. But now, for $400, you're controlling 100 shares. Granted, you're only controlling those shares between the stock prices of $500 and $510, but it's better than zero. You could also buy two spreads for $800 and possibly make $1,200, or three spreads for $1,200 and possibly make $1,800, and so on. Vertical spreads allow you to take smaller bites at potentially amazing opportunities you never would have dreamed of doing in the past. Options allow you to manage risk you were unwilling to take. But what if they were the most amazing opportunities—and you missed them? Vertical spreads have limited risk and limited rewards, and that's one of the things that make them so versatile. However, in this example, to get the full $10 gain, you need the stock to rise from its current $500 price to $510, which is a 2% move in a month. What if you wanted to be a little more conservative? Perhaps you could buy the $490 call for $75 and sell the $500 call for $70, for a $5 net debit.

The chart below compares the previous 500/510 vertical purchased for $4 (gray) to the 490/500 vertical purchased for $5 (black):

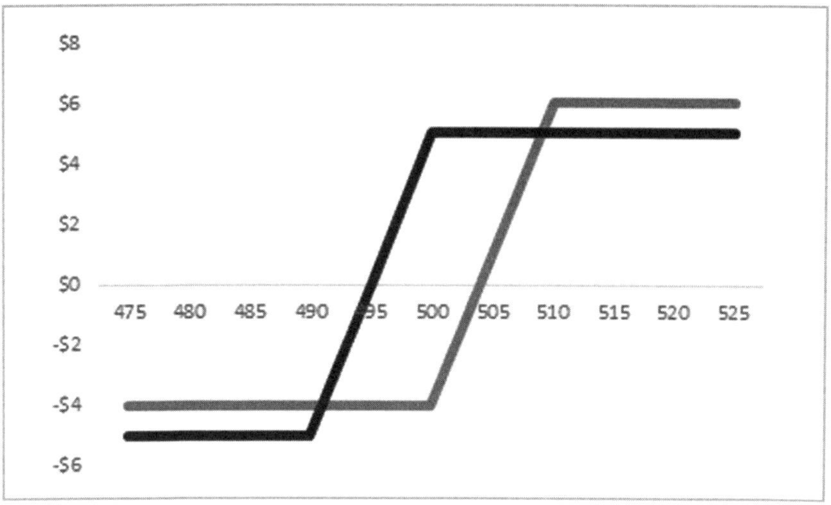


The 490/500 costs a little more because it's deeper in the money and therefore has a better chance of making money, including the maximum. Consequently, traders will bid up the price of that spread. Remember, lower-strike calls are worth more money, so if you create a vertical spread using lower-strike calls, it'll cost more money too. Notice with the stock currently at $500, this 490/500 spread doesn't even need the stock price to move, and it will still make the $10 difference in spreads, for a $5 gain, or 100% return. The breakeven price is the long $490 call plus the $5 cost, or $495. With the stock at $500, you can afford to have it fall $5 by expiration and just break even whereas the 500/510 vertical needs the stock to rise $4 just to break even.

Like all options strategies, each of these vertical spreads is just a tradeoff in risk and reward. Each is priced according to risk, and one isn't better than the other. They're just different. Always be sure to keep risk and reward in proper perspective, and it's easy to lose sight of with vertical spreads. In this example, you could spend $50,000 to control 100 shares, or you could spend $400 with the vertical spread. Stock traders think nothing of buying the shares and losing $5,000 because it's "only 10%" but if they trade the vertical spread, they'll freak if the spread is down 50% and they lose $200. Always remember that the calls are insuring the cash in your account that's not being spent on the shares. Call options are hedged positions. Vertical spreads hedge them further by making them even cheaper. No matter how much you continue to hedge hedges, you're going to have some price to pay, and that can always be down 50%. Keep risk and reward in the right perspective.

You may think you can never be too safe, so why not put the spread super deep in the money? Well, there is such a thing as being too safe. Each increase in safety has a cost, whether in dollars or opportunity costs. If you push this spread too deep in the money, it'll eventually reach a point where you'll pay $10 to make $10, and after commissions, it isn't such a good deal. In the financial markets, as you use options to make things safer and safer, you'll eventually reach a position that'll earn the risk-free rate. Options hedge risk. They don't allow you to get more rewards for taking less risk.

## The Art of Morphing

Morphing is a technique where you'll make a single trade, or possibly a small series of trades to alter the current risk graph. Morphs are usually done when your outlook changes, say from bullish to bearish. Or, possibly from bullish to even more bullish. Because options allow you to easily bend and alter risk graphs, morphs are a powerful and common tool for options traders. For example, let's say you bought a $100 call for $5, but the stock has been falling and volatility rising. Your outlook has changed from bullish to bearish, and you're now able to sell the $95 call for $7. Once you do, you'll switch, or morph, from the long $100 call (gray line) to the vertical bear spread (black line):

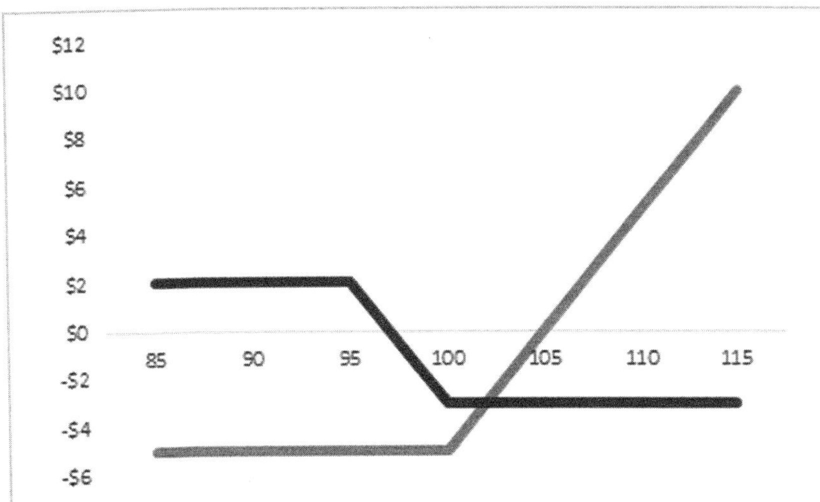


When holding the long $100 call, you had the potential for unlimited gains, but you needed the stock to rise. However, once it began falling, your outlook changed, and by selling the $95 call, you can now make profits if the stock falls far enough, but it comes at the expense of taking losses if the stock rises. Traders not familiar with morphing may, instead, sell the $100 call, and once that order fills, buy the 95/100 put spread. By understanding morphing, however, the identical risk profile is quickly captured in one trade—selling the $95 call.

Like most options topics, an entire book could be written on morphing. For now, we just want to introduce you to the idea, as it's a handy tool for maneuvering through risky markets. Let's try one more and assume you bought the 95/105 strangle for $5. A strangle is a strategy where you buy a call and put with different strikes but the same expiration. So, perhaps you buy the $95 put and buy the $105 call. The *strangle* is usually used when you're expecting an explosive move but unsure about the direction. It requires a large move up or down to become profitable. The expiration breakeven points are found by subtracting the total premium from the put's price and adding it to the call's price. In this example, the lower breakeven is $95 - $5, or $90 and the upper breakeven is $105 + $5, or $110. That's a wide range of prices. If the stock is between those breakeven points at expiration, you'll have some kind of loss. If the stock is between the strikes, you'll lose the entire premium. However, let's say volatility is on the rise, perhaps coming into a critical earnings report or FDA announcement, and the $100 straddle is now selling for $7. A straddle is similar to the strangle, except the call and put use the same strike price. If you own the 95/105 strangle and sell the $100 straddle, you'll morph from the 95/105 strangle (gray line) to the 95/100/105 butterfly spread (black line):

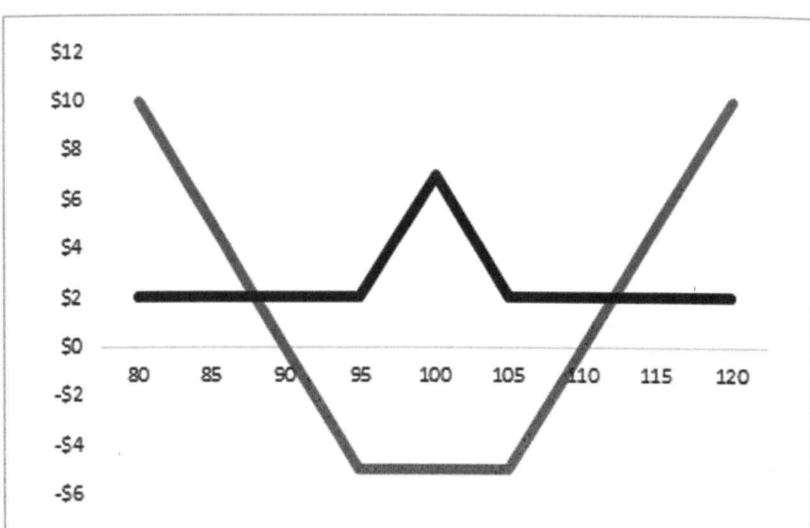

Notice, however, that you paid $5 for the strangle but sold the straddle for $7, so your entire risk curve is now sitting at a guaranteed $2 minimum gain. You can't lose. However, if the stock sits at $100 at expiration, you could make a maximum of $7 or anywhere in between. But the idea is that because market conditions changed, you were able to find a new strategy that locked in gains but still allowed you to hold out for more profit. Once you're in the butterfly spread, new morphs become possible, and the process can continue as market conditions change. To find these morphs, however, you must understand options. It's yet another way to show that options manage risk—not create it.

Options allow you to alter risk-reward profiles unlike anything you can do with shares of stock. Think about the risk profiles we've shown just in this chapter, and they're a small fraction of the things you can do, and it's all possible by understanding just two types of options—calls and puts. More importantly, they're things you will never be able to do with shares of stock. So, if you think options are risky, you'll only continue to manage your profits—not your risk. No matter which option strategy you choose—and there are many—you'll be managing risks. The alternative is to buy shares of stock and let the risks manage you. Before you set out to beat the odds, be sure you can survive the odds beating you. The best way to do that is to hedge, and the only way to hedge is with options. Manage your risk, and the profits will take care of themselves.

# Chapter Four:

## It's Easier Said Than Done

What's the difference between perception and perspective? It depends on how you look at it. Sorry for the bad joke, but perception and perspective are the difference between profits and losses—and that's no laughing matter. As traders, you must understand how risks change as time, stock price, volatility, and other conditions change. As things change, your risks change too—but how? If you can't answer that, you're not trading—you're guessing—and exposing your positions to potentially bigger risks. Retail traders miss this point all the time, and it's one of the reasons their past gains end up visiting Davy Jones' Locker when the tide goes out.

Hedging is second nature for professional traders, but for retail traders, it's hard to put into practice. It's not always from a lack of understanding or discipline but one key reason—differences in perceptions. Traders often think they're managing risk when they're not. Of course, you probably think these money mistakes don't' apply to you. Everyone thinks they're immune to making them, but all that does is reinforce the chances for making them. So, Pete and I want to share some insights from the field of behavioral finance—the psychology of financial decisions—that have contributed to our success by giving us different perspectives about risk. Look at the chart below. Is it a duck or a rabbit? It depends on how you look at it:

Risk works the same way. It's easy to look at something and think you've identified a risk, but it could be misperceptions about the way people see the problem. The human brain is super skilled at detecting patterns, but that very skill can also make it prone to illusions. You've probably seen optical illusions where two colors look different, or one line looks shorter than another, but they're identical. Or maybe a hypnotic spiral that appears to be moving, but it's not. If the eyes can be fooled, is it possible for other senses to be fooled too? Unfortunately, yes, and it's all in the way we perceive information. Remember GIGO—garbage in, garbage out. If we perceive the wrong problem, we come up with the wrong solution. So, let's start with a problem that has nothing to do with options and see how people shopping for cars with better mileage make bad judgments, and it's all from the way they perceive the problem.

## Misperceptions Are Easy–And Costly

Let's say you're shopping for a new car, and your goal is you want to get better mileage. Your car gets 50 mpg, and the salesman shows you the latest high-mileage model that gets 100 mpg. It's certainly a big increase. Do you make the switch?

Here's a second scenario: Your car gets 14 mpg, and the salesman shows you a similar car that gets 21 mpg. Do you make the switch now?

Most people would switch in the first scenario but not the second. Your brain says the first switch increased the mileage by 50 mpg while the second scenario only increases by 7 mpg. So, it's obviously better to switch from a car that gets an additional 50 miles per gallon than one that gets an additional seven.

## It's obvious, but wrong. But how?

Let's say you drive 100 miles. Switching from a car that gets 50 mpg to one that gets 100 mpg saves one gallon of gas. But switching from a car that gets 14 mpg to one that gets 21 mpg saves 2.4 gallons—more than twice as much. Your gas savings will be more than twice as much with the second car, but you probably turned down the deal. What happened? The problem was misperceived, and the goal was missed. When you set out to get a more fuel-efficient car, you thought the problem was to get more miles per gallon. But that's saying you want to drive further on one gallon of gas. The real problem is to use fewer gallons per mile. The problem isn't about high mileage—it's about low consumption. They sound like similar problems, but they're not, and that's why it's easy to get fooled.

This is why many car manufacturers now post fuel efficiency in "gallons per 100 miles" in addition to "miles per gallon" on the sticker to help consumers make better decisions. The very thing you were trying to accomplish—saving gas—backfired because of the way you perceived the problem. It's not because the math is hard, but it's the way we perceive problems. Imagine what can happen when you're dealing with money, dollars, percentages—and emotions. When it comes to money, where do problems begin? A fairly new field of psychology called behavioral finance, sometimes called behavioral economics, answers these questions. It's all in the way our senses detect changes. Whether it's our eyes, ears, or touch, our ability to detect an increase or decrease depends on what we started with. For example, look at the two boxes below. The first contains 10 dots while the second box has 20 dots. Without counting and just by glancing, you're probably quite confident the second box has more dots:

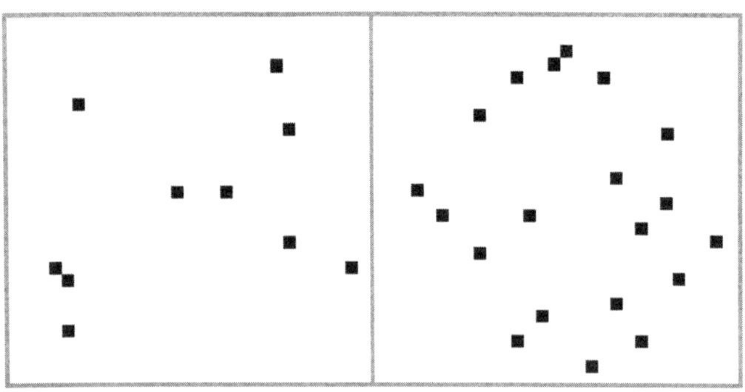

Now look at the next two boxes. The first box has 100 dots while the second has 110 dots, which is also 10 more than the first box. However, it's not so apparent as the previous example when increasing from 10 to 20 dots. Instead, both boxes look nearly identical:

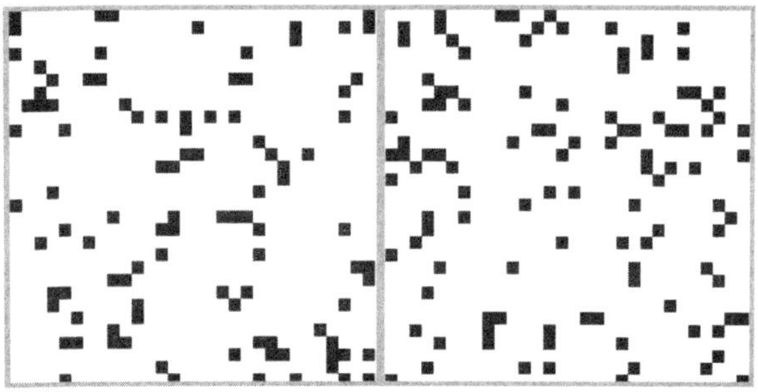

The idea is that you can sense a change of 10 dots in the first example because it represented a relatively large increase—a 100% change. But when you add 10 dots to 100 dots, the 10% increase isn't large enough to perceive. The idea that your ability to visually detect changes depends on the starting point was first pioneered by German psychologist Ernst Weber (1795-1878). More importantly, he discovered it applies to all other senses.

If you pick up your cell phone and a friend's cell phone, you'll most likely detect a difference in weight, even though they may vary by only an ounce or two. But if you pick up two suitcases that vary by an ounce, you'll never feel it. You may have noticed this at the gym. An exercise machine may count by 2.5-pound increments at lower levels of weight but by 10-pound increments at higher levels. At higher weights, equipment manufacturers know you'll never feel it.

Ernst Weber wanted to know the smallest change that could be made before it was readily detected. He called these changes a just-noticeable difference, or JND. And what he found is that they all depend on the starting point, which was later stated as a mathematical formula called Weber's Law. It simply says that if you need to double the number of dots from 10 to 20 before most people can easily detect it, you'll need to increase 100 dots to 200 dots to have the same change in perception. That proportion remains constant. If it takes a 100% change in the number of dots in boxes before you can detect a change, it'll always take that same proportion no matter how many you begin with. That's Weber's Law.

It doesn't just apply to things you can count. If you turn up a dimmer switch so you feel the light appears twice as bright, it's probably closer to four times as bright. What scientists can measure as four-times as bright, our eyes detect as twice as bright. What about our ears? No exception there either. If you turn up your headphones so they sound twice as loud, it's closer to four times as loud. Well, nearly 100 years later, two pioneering researchers discovered this same principle applies to money.

Daniel Kahneman and Amos Tversky are two notable researchers in behavioral economics, and Mr. Kahneman won the Nobel Prize in 2002 for his work. One of their key findings is that people perceive money just like they perceive dots in boxes—*it depends on the starting point.* This becomes critically important for traders.

If you have $10 in your wallet and add another $10, it's noticeable. But if you had $1,000, adding another $10 isn't readily detectible. It's the same $10 increase, but you don't "sense" it in the same way compared to starting with a larger base. If you had a million dollars land in your lap, it would probably be life changing, or at least worth a Facebook post. However, if that happened to Bill Gates, he'd be happy too, just not as happy. That doesn't mean he doesn't value an extra million, but it wouldn't create the same sensation of happiness as it would for most others. In other words, money has diminishing returns. The more you have, the less a fixed increase is appreciated. Graphically, this means people's perception of money isn't a straight line: Twice as much money doesn't make you twice as happy. Instead, it depends on how much you start with. Researchers have studied this effect and were able to quantify it, and the "feeling" of money looks more like the chart below:

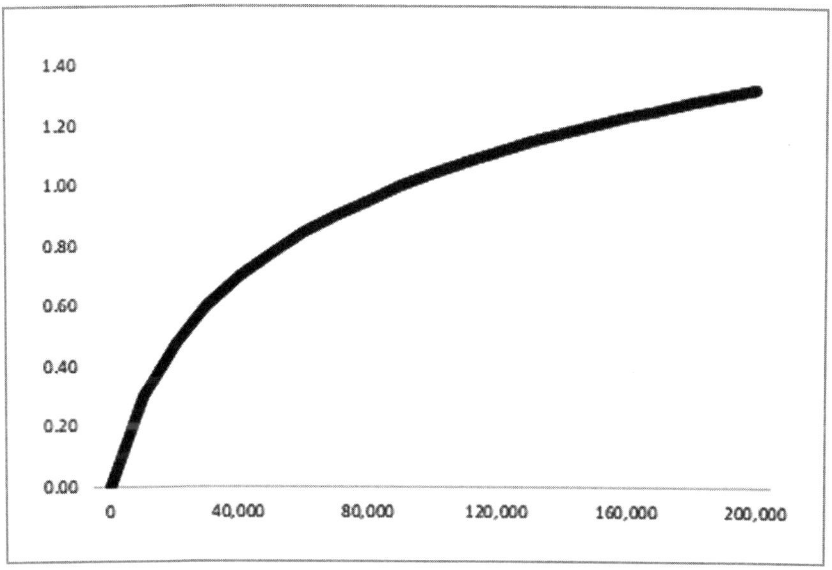


If we make the horizontal axis your starting point with money and the vertical axis a rating scale of "happiness" or "satisfaction," we'd get this curved line. So, if you start at the left side of the chart with no money, but suddenly get $10,000, the "satisfaction" value jumps almost vertically. On the right side of the chart, things are different. If you have $200,000 and add the same $10,000, it adds happiness, just not as much, so the graph begins to flatten out. While it never goes completely flat, it approaches a totally flat line as you move to higher levels of money. Now here's where things get critical. Money works the same way in reverse. If you have $200,000 and lose $10,000, you won't feel the same regret as if you had $10,000 but lose it all. The way our senses process changes is very interesting, but what does it have to do with trading? Absolutely everything.

## The Range Effect: It Depends on the Starting Point

Behavioral economists have found that your sensitivity to financial decisions depends on the range of dollars we're talking about, which is called the *range effect*. For example, let's say you're shopping for a tablet that costs $200, but discover you can drive 30 minutes across town to buy it on sale for $100. Do you make the trip? Now imagine that it was, instead, a flat-screen television for $2,000 but you can drive 30 minutes across town to buy it on sale for $1,900. Do you make the trip? You probably said yes to the tablet because it's 50% off but no to the television because it's only 5% off. That's a financial misperception because of the range effect.

Just like with the car example where you thought the problem was about miles per gallon when it was really about gallons per mile, people fall into a similar trap here. It sounds like the problem is about percentages when it should be about dollars. You're not trying to save a certain percentage—you're trying to save money. Interestingly, after surveying thousands of people, Kahneman and Tversky found that most would make the same decision. They'd drive for the tablet and trade time for money but not the television, where they chose to trade money for time. The tablet covered a $200 range, so even a $10 or $20 savings sounds like a lot. Saving

$100 is a no-brainer—make the trip. The television, however, spanned a $2,000 range, so the same $100 off doesn't have the same impact. In essence, people were valuing $100 differently. The real question is whether 30 minutes of your time is worth $100. If it is, you should take the drive for the tablet and the television. After all, a hundred bucks is a hundred bucks, but that's not the way people see money. Instead, they see $100 as having different values depending on the range of prices in question. Kahneman and Tversky made many amazing discoveries that apply to trading, but here's one that is perhaps the most disturbing of all.

## Gambling Your Way from Losses

The range effect causes people to make bizarre financial choices. Here's another typical question Kahneman and Tversky asked respondents. Imagine I owe you $500, but I give you two choices:

A. I'll pay you $500.

B. Flip a coin. If it lands heads, I'll pay you $1,000. If tails, you get nothing.

Which would you choose? Both choices have an expected $500 value. That is, if you were allowed to take both choices hundreds of times, you'd be expected to end up with the same $500. The difference is that Choice A is worth $500 *for sure*, while Choice B is worth $500, *on average*. So, both have the same average, but Choice B has risk: You may get $1,000, but you may get nothing.

Think back to the curved graph at the beginning of the chapter. If you can go from zero to $500, it has more value than going from $500 to $1,000, so you should take Choice A. That's what most people took, and exactly what Kahneman and Tversky expected. The surprise came when they reversed the question. Let's say you owe me $500, but I give you two choices:

A. Pay me $500.

B. Flip a coin. If it lands heads, you owe me $1,000. If tails, you owe me nothing.

Which would you choose? The researchers believed if people don't like risk, they should take Choice A. Why risk owing more money? Most respondents, however, chose to gamble with Choice B. Why be risk averse with gains but risk seeking when facing losses? Once you understand the perception of money, it makes sense. Again, think back to the curved graph. If you owe me $500 and take Choice A, you're guaranteed to go from a starting point of $500 to zero. In other words, you have $500 in your pocket now, but if you pay the debt, you're guaranteed to go to zero. Remember, going from zero to $500 creates more "satisfaction" so going in reverse causes more "pain." Those dollars are more valuable, so they're more painful to lose. So, if you're already faced with losing $500, why not gamble to get out of the debt? The first $500 is worth more than the second $500, so it makes sense to gamble those dollars to save the first $500. Losing $1,000 is painful, but it's not as painful as losing the first $500.

If it's hard to imagine, stretch it out a bit. What if you owed $10,000 but could flip a coin for a loss of $11,000 or nothing? Losing $11,000 is painful, but not nearly as painful as the first $10,000, so it makes sense to take the gamble. That's why people choose to gamble. If it sounds like pretzel logic, it doesn't make any more sense why you need to make a light four times as bright to make it appear twice as bright, or why the volume needs to be four times as loud before you perceive it to be twice as loud, or why you'd make the drive for the tablet but not the television. Believe it or not, like it or not—that's how we're wired. It's like the Microsoft blue screen of death: It's just a massively corrupted file in our brains, but that's how we're programmed to interpret gains and losses.

In fact, researchers have tried to quantify just how much money would be required before people would accept the bet. Would you bet $100 to win $100 at the flip of a coin? Probably not. But what if you could win $150? What about $200? At some point, you'll eventually say yes, and for most people, it turns out to be a factor of two. If people can win twice as much as they can lose at the flip of a coin, they're willing to take the risk. That's another way of saying the money they currently have is more valuable than the money they may win.

Research consistently shows that people are risk averse. But here's the real danger. People despise taking losses so much that it overcomes their aversion to risk. *In other words, people are willing to gamble their way from losing situations.* They're willing to take more risk than they're normally comfortable taking if it means they may escape a loss. When that mentality is used for trading, it becomes destructive—not profitable. However, avoiding a loss doesn't just apply to the most recent trade. It means for all trades at any time. Imagine you paid $10,000 each for two different stocks. One is now worth $20,000 while the other is worth $5,000. You need to sell some shares to put a downpayment on a car. Which stock do you sell? Behavioral finance predicts you'll sell the winner because losses are too painful to bear. You're thinking if you hold the losing shares, there's a chance the price will come back. In other words, you're choosing to gamble your way from a losing position. This is exactly why gamblers increase their bets when Lady Luck isn't in their favor. If they walk from the table, it's a definite loss. So, to avoid the loss, they continue to bet—and bet bigger. Maybe things will turn. Most of the time they don't, but they're willing to take the gamble to avoid the loss. It's exactly this idea that led to the stock market joke: What do you call a short-term investment that failed? A long-term hold. It's just not that funny when it happens to you. How can options help you avoid this costly misperception?

## Speculation—With Discipline

On August 19, 2023, Microsoft (MSFT) was trading for about $319. Let's say you wanted to buy shares to speculate on the next earnings report in about two months. However, you also feel the stock could rally between now and the report, so you want to take a position now but also limit losses to a $1,500 maximum. Buying 100 shares will cost nearly $32,000, and you could easily lose more than $1,500 with that much invested. If that happens, it'll be easy to convince yourself to continue holding the shares since losses are so painful to accept. Can options make you more disciplined?

The October $320 call with 62 days to expiration will get you through the earnings, and was trading for $14.40, or $1,440 total, so you're assured of not losing more than your $1,500 limit.

Below is the risk graph for the $320 call (black line) compared to the shares (gray line):

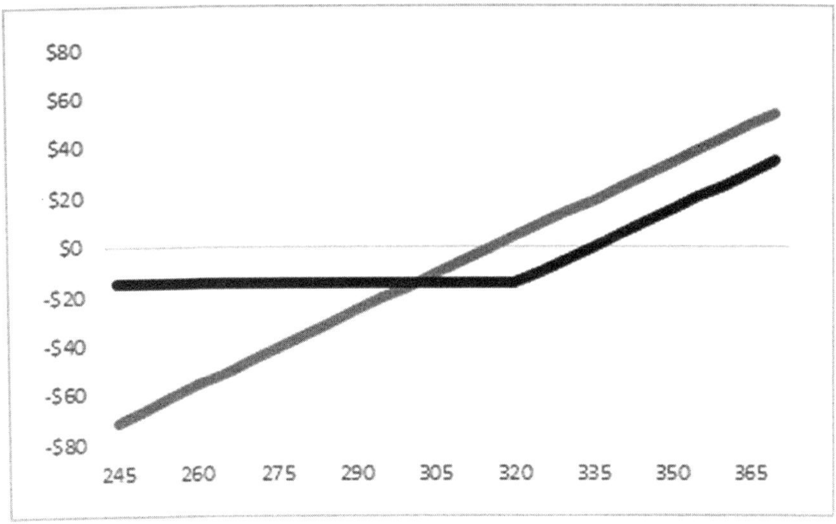


The $320 call is out of the money, so it's all extrinsic value. The breakeven point is $320 + $14.40, or $334.40. So, the stock must climb to $334.40 just to break even on the trade. However, that's in line with your outlook for a fast, aggressive move into earnings. More importantly, it guarantees you won't lose more than $1,500, which was the goal. If the call expires worthless, you'll have more information at that time to see if you still want to buy the shares—or another call. *Remember, part of the benefit of the call option is that it's insuring the cash that's not being spent on the shares.* Why don't more traders hedge like this? Because they see a potential $1,500 loss as 100% for the option but less than 5% for the stock. It's the range effect applied to options, and it's a costly misperception. In both cases, it's roughly a $1,500 loss. The option guarantees this limit. Shares of stock don't. If you want choices, you have no choice but to use options.

## The Sunk Cost Fallacy: Money Down the Drain

Imagine you bought a ticket to a football game for $100, but you get to the game and discover you lost it. Do you buy another one? Now let's change it up. You were going to buy a ticket at the gate for $100, but discovered you lost $100 cash. Do you buy a ticket?

When respondents were asked these questions, most said they *would not* buy another ticket if they lost a ticket because the game would then cost $200. However, if they lost $100 cash, they *would* buy a ticket, and the game would cost $100. It may sound logical, but it's the *sunk cost fallacy* at work. A sunk cost is any expenditure that's made and not coming back. So, whether you lost a $100 ticket or $100 cash, you lost $100 in value. It's gone, it's not coming back, and shouldn't have anything to do with your decision to buy a ticket. Decisions should always be made on differences in choices, not similarities. So, whether you buy a ticket or not, you lost $100 in value, one in the form of a ticket, the other in the form of cash. If you go to the game, you lost $100. If you don't go to the game, you lost $100. It's a $100 loss that's common to both decisions, so shouldn't be part of the decision to go to the game. The question is whether you want to pay $100 to go to the game.

Investors make the same mistake. Let's say you invest $10,000 into Sam & Ella's restaurant chain, but for reasons unknown, it's not taking off, and the price just continually sinks. So, you invest another $10,000, and another, and another. It'll be hard to shut it down for such a big loss, so you're more likely to continue throwing money at it until it "turns around." You're more likely to gamble your way from such a large losing position.

Traders feel like the money wasn't lost if it was "recovered" from the same stock. That's why losing a $100 football ticket but buying another for $100 makes it feel like it cost $200. It's two of the same things, so it seems the values should be added. Instead, the question at each stage should be, "Do I want to invest $10,000 into Sam & Ella's based on what I know today?" The previous money invested—no matter how much—has nothing to do with the decision. They're sunk costs. So, if sunk costs cause such misperceptions, how can options help you avoid this fallacy?

You must get rid of any emotional attachments to investments and realize that lost money is lost. You only get new choices each day based on current information. In the previous example, if the Microsoft $320 call goes bust, it's easier to see that it's not coming back. An option that expires worthless forces you to take a good hard look at the position. You can choose to buy another call—or abandon the plan—but it won't allow you to continually hold the shares and hope. Options don't have emotional attachments. Traders do. If you buy an option to help you meet a goal, you'll have a decision to make at expiration—whether you want to or not. Options force you to reassess your view at each expiration regardless of how much money you've spent. They'll force you to make better decisions by avoiding the sunk cost trap.

## Risk Changes as Price Changes

Sunk costs cause another misperception for traders too. Once you've spent money for shares, it's easy to think that's the amount of "risk" you have in the position. Imagine that you just bought 100 shares of stock for $100 per share and the stock has now risen to $120. What's your maximum risk? Retail traders will say it's $100 per share because that's the amount paid. Professional traders, on the other hand, will say the maximum risk has increased to $120. After all, if the stock falls from $120 to $100, would you feel like you lost nothing? Or would you feel like you're down $20?

If you still think the risk is the $100 purchase price, how would your answer change if you sell the shares for $120 and immediately buy them back for $120? Since that's your new purchase price, isn't that the new risk? If yes, why does it matter if you don't go through the motions of selling and instantly buying? The answer is, it doesn't. The price you paid has nothing to do with the amount at risk. It's a sunk cost, so it shouldn't enter future decisions. What matters is the opportunity to sell for $120 was there. Turning down the opportunity to sell for $120 doesn't leave your risk at $100.

Remember, each day is a new deal of the cards, and you'll always have more information today than you had yesterday. If you choose to hold the shares at the higher $120 price, it's no different from buying the shares for that same price. For professional traders, the current stock price dictates the risk—not the price paid.

Unrealized gains are potential profits, and if you don't guard unrealized gains, you'll never have any profits to harvest. Whether you earned it, inherited it, won it, or found it, the source of the gains doesn't matter. As price rises, risk rises. So, how can you trade the market but hedge ever-changing risk? This is where one of the most beneficial types of option hedges comes to the rescue—rolling.

## Rolling Away from Risk

Rolling is another technique traders use to remain in a position—but reduce the maximum loss. Remember, as the stock price rises, your risk rises, so you should continue to hedge. The most common types of rolls are the roll up and the *roll down*. As prices rise, you'll roll call options up, and as prices fall, you'll roll put options down. These trades always produce credits to your account, which further reduce your maximum loss but allow you to hold out for bigger profits. Remember, lower strike calls are worth more money, so if you roll up, you're selling the more valuable strike, which means you'll get money back—a credit—from the roll. The opposite is true for put options: Higher-strike puts are worth more money, so rolling down produces credits.

For example, let's say you buy a $100 call for $10. As the stock price rises, the price of the $100 call rises, so to reduce the newly created risk, you could roll to a higher strike, say the $105 call. Perhaps the $100 call is now worth $15 but the $105 call is worth $11, so you could roll for a net credit of $4. Here are the trades:

1. Buy $100 call = -$10
2. Sell the $100 call = +$15
3. Buy the $105 call = -$11

   Net credit = $4

All you're doing is closing the $100 call, which generates $15 cash, and you're using that cash to buy the $105 call for $11.

The risk graph below shows the result of the roll. The original $100 call (black line) has shifted higher to the $105 call (gray line):

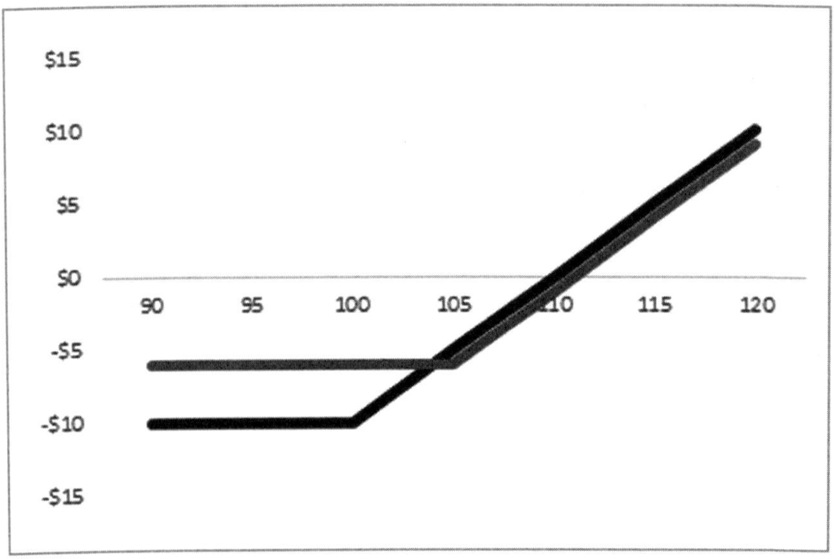


The $105 call initially cost $10, but after collecting the $4 credit, you have effectively reduced the initial $10 cost to $6. By rolling, you're collecting credits, which reduces the amount of money exposed to downside risk. From here forward, you'll just continue to roll the call, collect more profits, and still have unlimited profit potential while always hedging the downside risk. Each roll slightly reduces the maximum profits had you not rolled, but reducing profits isn't the issue. Rolling locks in gains—and still holds out for more. Try that with shares of stock. So, time to think again: *Are options risky?* Those are some basic, but powerful hedges used by every professional trader. Rolling put options works the same way, just in the opposite direction.

## Anchors Aweigh: The Anchoring Bias

Anchoring is the subconscious use of an arbitrary benchmark, or reference point, for value. It has applications everywhere, but in the stock market, it's the costliest. For instance, experimenters would show respondents some item, and they were supposed to guess the selling price. But before showing the item, the researchers had people write down their phone number. Respondents whose phone numbers started with higher numbers tended to place higher values than those with phone numbers starting with lower numbers. In other words, just seeing—or even thinking about—higher numbers tend to make people guess higher numbers. It's hard to believe because it makes no sense, but that's exactly why it's an interesting behavior, and it's been confirmed by many studies.

Kahneman and Tversky conducted another study where participants were shown a small wheel, like *Wheel of Fortune*, which was spun, and participants saw the number where it landed. Then they were asked to guess if the number was higher or lower than the percentage of African nations in the United Nations. It was designed to be a question where most people would have no clue. Group A saw an arbitrary number of 10, and Group B saw an arbitrary number of 65. The median estimate in Group A was 25, and in Group B it was 45. Yet, when asked if the wheel had any effect on their guesses, they said no. It's hard to imagine, but arbitrary numbers influence decisions. Do people fall for the trap?

Let's say you're shopping for clothes and find a shirt selling for $50 that's "reduced from $100." The higher price is there for a reason: It serves as an anchor for value. It feels like you're saving money, even though your bank account sees the math differently. Always remember that something is only worth what another will pay. If nobody was willing to pay $100, it's not worth $100, which is why it's on sale for $50. So, you could also interpret the price tag as nobody thought $100 was a good deal, so maybe I'm getting ripped off. Instead, you'll see it as a way of saving money, and anchoring is the reason.

To make better decisions, you should also compare $50 to zero, since you could walk away and spend no money. But that price is there, acting like a beacon in the background of your mind, influencing you to think it's a much better deal than it is.

Anchoring affects sellers too. Let's say you paid $500,000 for a home but now must sell, and the market price has dropped to $480,000. You'll be tempted to want to list if for the purchase price or "wait for" the price to get back there. Sellers often forget that if they're selling their home to buy another one, the one they're buying is probably cheaper too. If they wait for theirs to get back to the purchase price, other homes will be more expensive too. However, it'll still be hard to let it go for $480,000 because your purchase price serves as an anchor for value. But when you bought the house, did you ask the sellers how much they paid? Did it matter? The purchase price—yours or the seller's—is a meaningless, arbitrary anchor. How does the anchoring bias affect traders? In the chart below, the last closing price is $115. Do you see the stock as a good deal since it used to trade at a high of $222?

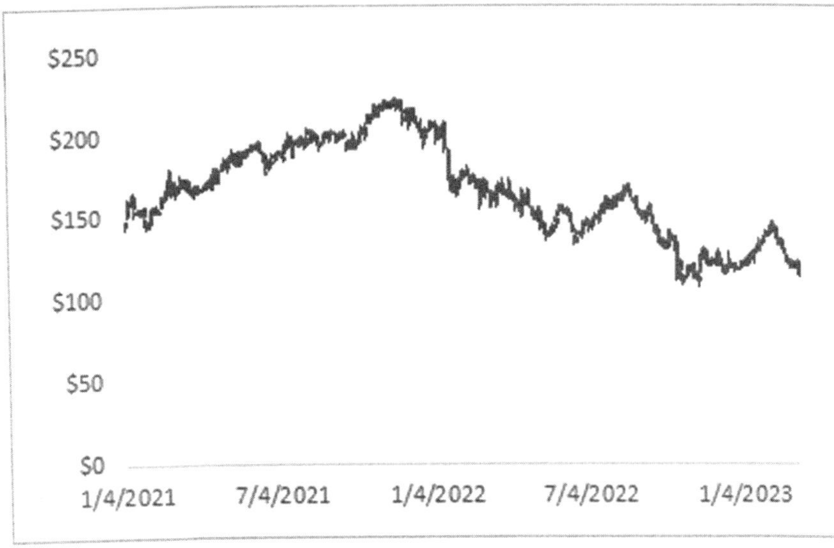


It's tempting to think the stock is "on sale" since it traded much higher within the past 12 months. Investors felt it was worth well over $200 less than a year ago, so it's a matter of time before it gets back up there, right? Nope, that's anchoring. That high price is a meaningless, arbitrary benchmark. That was the price then and nothing more. The chart is First Republic Bank (FRCB) in April 2023 just before the FDIC said it was considering seizing the bank, which caused a 43% meltdown to $3.50 in about a month. The price fell another 42% in after-hours trading. On May 1, the California Department of Financial Protection and Innovation closed the bank, and the FDIC seized all assets, making it the second-largest commercial bank failure in American history (the first being Washington Mutual in 2008). JP Morgan bought the assets at auction for nearly $11 billion, and that was the end of First Republic—along with any chance for the "anchor" to pull the stock price back to $222.

If you're comparing to the high, the chart made the stock look like a good deal, but it was only two months later when the stock was trading below a dollar. Traders make a similar mistake when opening or closing positions. If an option appears to be a good deal at $5, they'll place a limit to buy at $4.90 since it used to be that price not too long ago. Or they'll get filled at $5, watch it climb to $10, but then drop back to $9.50. They place an order to sell at $10 since that's where it used to trade. This is the anchoring bias at its worst. One of our traders and former market maker Greg McDermott always reminds traders, "There are only bids and offers." It means that professional traders make decisions based on current prices, not prices you want—or ones that existed in the past. During this banking crisis, if you wanted to speculate that FRCB was going to rebound and avoid bankruptcy, you could buy an out-of-the-money call for relatively little money. Once the stock collapsed, your losses were limited to the cost of the call. There's no temptation to hold on and gamble your way out. You paid for the right to walk away—and that's exactly what you did.

## The Endowment Effect: I'm Not Willing to Sell

The only reason for investing money today is to get a return on that money. To do that, however, you must eventually sell. It sounds easy to do, but there's another behavioral finance problem at work—the *endowment effect.* It says when you own something—part of your endowment—you'll think it has more value than everyone else. Why? Because it's yours, and if you own it, it must be worth a lot. At least, that's the perception.

An interesting study was done at Duke University where basketball tickets are allocated to students through a lottery. Some students were interviewed before a championship game and asked how much they'd be willing to spend on a ticket. The median answer was

$150. However, when the winners were interviewed, they were asked the price they'd be willing to sell a ticket, and the median price was $1,500, or 10-times the amount their perceived value to buy. Even though the tickets were allocated randomly, once they landed in the hands of lucky winners, the subjective value skyrocketed. Why would someone think the ticket's now worth $1,500 when they were only willing to pay $150? That's the endowment effect. To make good financial decisions, you must be patient enough to trade at the right times—and the right prices. This effect isn't new and was even observed in 300 B.C. by Aristotle who wrote, "For most things are differently valued by those who have them and by those who wish to get them: what belongs to us, and what we give away, always seems very precious to us." The endowment effect is very real, and it poses a big problem for traders. Options can help.

Traders often demand a higher price when they sell compared to what they'd be willing to pay at the same time. If you buy shares of stock for $100 that have risen to $120 and allowed you to meet goals, it's tempting to think they're worth more just because you own them. Rather than selling to lock in your gains—and goals—you'll be tempted to continue to hold the shares because of the endowment effect.

A common solution is the covered call strategy, where you own 100 shares but sell a call on the same underlying, which gives you the potential obligation to sell the shares. Because you sold a call, you'll receive cash, which gives you a limited downside hedge. What are the benefits?

On August 8, 2023, Microsoft (MSFT) was trading for $330, and let's say you buy shares with a goal of earning 5% over the next three months or so, which means the stock must reach $346. That's a fairly low probability, and it's filled with downside risk, but selling a call can help. The November options had 102 days to expiration, so they closely fit with your 90-day goal. There was no $346 call, but there was a $345, which was trading for $17. By selling the call, you'll collect the option premium, so your effective cost basis drops to $330 - $17, or $313. If you effectively pay $313 but sell for the $345 strike, it's 10.2% return—far bigger than your goal. That means you can sell a lower strike call and be better off. Lower-strike calls are more valuable, so you'll receive more money, and that gives you a bigger downside hedge. However, you'll also have the obligation to sell at a lower price, so your return will be lower. You've reduced your gains in exchange for reducing the downside risk. It's a hedge. Let's see if it works.

The $310 call was trading for $36, which has $20 of intrinsic value and $16 of extrinsic value. If you sell this call, your cost basis is $330 - $36, or $294. If you effectively pay $294 but sell for $310, your return is 5.4%-just what you wanted. However, notice that you now have a $36 downside hedge. The stock could drop to nearly 11% to $294, and you'd just break even. Even more important, this $310 strike is an in-the-money call, so there's a very high chance you'll get assigned and sell the shares—also exactly what you wanted.

Below is a chart comparing the stock plus short $310 call (black line) compared to the long shares at $330 (gray line):

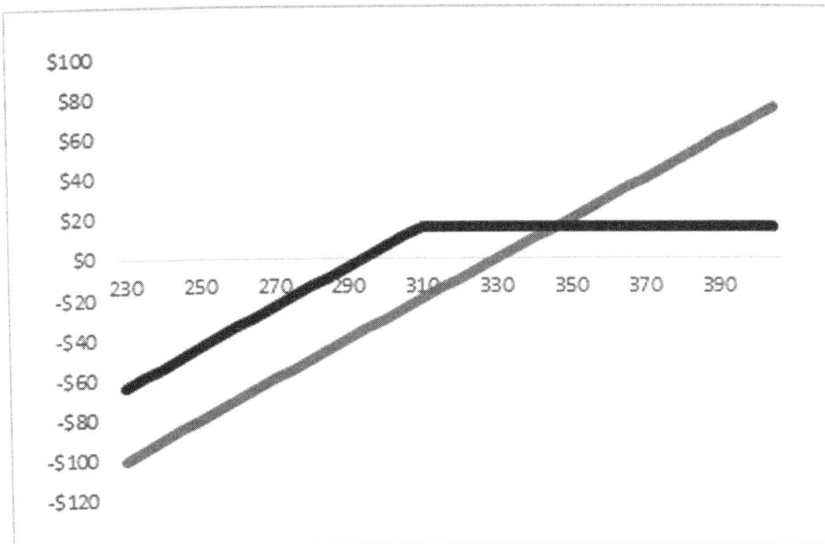


There's a massive difference between these two strategies. The chart clearly shows the downside hedge, as the black line sits $36 below the current $330 stock price, which was created by the sale of the call for $36. The black line also shows your gains are capped at $16, which is the extrinsic value from the call. That's the price the call buyer paid you to hold the downside risk. The chart also shows the two lines cross at $346, which is where both strategies produce the same $16 gain. However, this is the most important point to see: You've changed the strategy from very bullish to "not bearish." In other words, as a stock trader, you need the stock to rise from $330 to $346, or 4.8%, to earn $16. By selling the call against the shares, you don't need the stock to rise at all to capture the same $16 gain. In fact, the stock can even fall to the $310 strike, or 10.4%, and you'll still collect $16. By selling the call, a much wider range of stock prices will meet your goal, which is saying you have a higher probability. If the stock is above $310 at expiration, you'll get assigned and sell the shares, which removes the risk of not wanting to sell—the endowment effect—as the shares will automatically get called away.

Of course, you could buy back the call at any time, but that creates another advantage: You'll be making decisions based on new information that you don't have today. Traders sometimes think the "risk" of the covered call strategy is that you may get assigned, or "called out" of your shares because the price is higher. Risk is never defined as missing out on some reward. That's a missed opportunity, not a risk. The better way to understand the advantage is to see that the call's extrinsic value provided a much higher chance of meeting your goal—and gave you an 11% downside insurance policy to boot. In the stock market, you can't have it all. You can't have all the gains and all the downside protection. Instead, you get choices, and options give you more choices than anything else you can trade. If this blend of stock and a short call gives you a very high chance of meeting an otherwise low probability trade, then potentially selling the shares at $310 is the tradeoff. It's another great example of why it's wrong to say options are risky. They only alter risks and rewards. And yet, some traders will see the stock trading at $320, they'll get assigned and sell the shares—and then claim they got burned on the strategy. Selling the $310 call is just one of many choices. If you don't like these risks and rewards outlined here, you could sell the $290, $300, $315, or $320 call and get different risks and rewards. The choices are yours, but they're far more than just buying shares—and hoping they rise enough to meet your goals.

## You've Been Framed: It Depends How You Say It

Is the glass half empty or half full? It depends on how you look at it, and that's the idea behind *framing*, which is sometimes called *reference dependence*. Psychologists have shown that everyone makes decisions based on a reference point, or frame. You may think you don't, but that's why it's a psychological trap. It means we can be fooled into making bad decisions depending on the reference point we choose—or are forced to see. Our perceptions can be influenced just by how a question is worded.

Marketers use this tactic all the time. For example, advertising beef as 90% lean versus 10% fat changes purchasing habits. It can be the same beef in the identical package, but if one is labeled "90% lean" while another is labeled "10% fat," the "lean" label will have greater sales. A similar, almost comical, version of this framing effect happened in the 1970s when credit cards were becoming popular. Credit cards collect a small piece of each purchase—about 2%—from merchants. If you swipe a credit card for a $100 dinner, the restaurant may receive $98, and the credit card issuer takes $2 for a processing fee.

Well, back then, there was a heated debate. Gas station owners wanted to charge a premium for using credit cards to offset the processing fees, but the credit card companies thought it would reduce the use of credit cards. So, credit card companies took aggressive action and said station owners weren't allowed to charge premiums if they wanted to accept their cards. But was it fair for station owners to eat the cost? The argument continued and eventually made its way all the way to Congress. That's a heated argument, so how was it resolved? Congress said gas station owners could advertise a "base price" that was available to everyone—even those using credit cards—but offer a "discount" to anyone paying with cash. But that's exactly the same thing as saying credit card users will be charged a premium. It's just framed differently. If a gas station advertises $3.50 per gallon with a five-cent discount for cash, why is that different from advertising $3.45 plus a five-cent premium for using credit? It's not. It's the same problem framed differently.

Many of these behavioral finance misperceptions overlap, and this credit card debate can also be tied to risk aversion. If you word a problem in a way that you may take losses (pay a premium for using a card), it's more painful than saying you've given up some gains (gave up a cash discount for using a card). No matter what you call it, how you word it, or how you frame it, people pay more for using a credit card. Interestingly, even to this day, credit card companies, station owners, and customers are all satisfied even though the problem was never resolved. How can framing destroy investing returns?

Researchers have studied millions of online poker games, and the results were astonishing. Players who won most often also lost the most money. The reason, apparently, is that players get excitement from the wins, and that pushes players to bet aggressively even if their hands aren't that good. Again, it's a classic case of people trying to gamble their way from losing positions. Aggressive betting also means the opponents are more likely to fold if their hands aren't too good, so there's an incentive to bet aggressively. But those players only fold if their hands aren't too good, so the stakes are small. The aggressive bettor ends up winning a lot of small bets, and that feeds the excitement. However, that same player will bet even more aggressively when he has a really good hand, but unfortunately, when another player has an even better one. The result is that the player ends up with a very big loss. The long-run result is a lot of small wins—but a few really large losses—for an overall performance that's only slightly worse than Enron. Why keep playing?

Because for gamblers, it's the number of wins—not the amount of money—that seems to count. It's the frame of flashing lights, ringing bells, and spinning wheels that creates the excitement and fuels the drive to continue. Conversely, professional poker players will usually lose more hands than they win, but when they win, they win big.

This same behavior occurs between the retail and professional traders. Retail traders feel excitement from a lot of small wins, but they usually don't keep track of the total dollars won or lost. If they win 10 trades but lose only one, they feel good about trading—even if they've lost more money than they've won. Professionals, on the other hand, are focused on the dollars. Those are, after all, the reason for trading or investing in the first place. Professionals manage risk, so they often incur many small losses, but just like professional poker players, when they win, they win big. So, don't get caught up in the reference point of having "many wins" but only a "few losses" when it really means you're losing money. Keep track of dollars. Don't settle for winning 80% of the time if it means you've lost 80% of your money. How do options help to correct for framing?

Traders are hooked on using percentages to measure performance, and it's okay to use percentages when comparing one investment against another. However, percentages also create illusions. If you have a million-dollar portfolio, it's easy to say it's "only" down 20%. But that's $200,000. The percentage is small, but the dollars are large. However, if you trade options, the total cost is much lower than the stock, so the measurement that matters most—dollars—is kept relatively small. However, traders panic when they see their $3 option down 50%. Yes, but it's only $150. When trading options, be careful of how you frame your goals. Be sure you're speaking the universal language of investing—dollars. No matter how little you invest, you can always lose 50%. Options can provide a clear answer to the difference between perception and perspective—no matter how you look at it.

# Chapter Five:

## It's DDA or the Highway

They're a market for rights. They're a market for obligations. But for professional traders, options are also a market for discipline. Options are used for setting goals—and staying with the plan. Goals may be easy to set, but as the last chapter showed, it's easy to get sidetracked. Retail traders say they have goals, but once the market turns against them, the goals go on autopilot and fly straight into the Bermuda Triangle, never to be seen again. And if there's one thing the market does guarantee, it's that it will, at some time, turn against you. To invest, trade, or speculate successfully, you don't need to pick the perfect stocks at the right time. You need discipline.

When Pete and I were kids, our father instilled a powerful sense of discipline. He said it was the key to success, no matter what you do. He'd tell us, "It's DDA, guys—discipline dictates action." Discipline means different things to different people, but all definitions share a common thread: It's behaving in a controlled way to conform to a certain set of rules or standards. It's self-control. It's restraint. It's doing things you don't want to do if you want to accomplish a goal. Anything worth doing is worth doing right. And if it's worth doing right, it's not going to be easy. Discipline is the key.

Pete and I became professional football players, and without a fierce sense of discipline, we never would have made it—no player would. Fans always think how fun it would be to be a pro athlete—the glitz, cameras, money, and fame—but it's the stuff fans don't see that makes professional football players wish they were the ones sitting in the stands. Professional football games may only have a 60-minute clock, but how much time is dedicated to preparing for a single game?

It's 10 to 12 hours per day, six days per week of rigid diets, stretching, running, workouts, and intense practice sessions. Rinse and repeat. When you're not being physically pushed to your limits, you're studying playbooks and game films. It's a smorgasbord of physical and mental challenges. The problem is that for every extra hour you squeeze from the day to prepare for a game, the competition does you one hour better. It's a constant battle to fit 25 hours into a day. And when you absolutely, positively think you've reached your limits, when you can't push any harder, faster, or longer, the coach will push you to new limits. Once you mentally push through to that next level you never thought possible, you're about halfway ready for the next game. That's the part fans don't see. They see a thrilling 40-yard touchdown run. They don't see the amount of training, skill, and athleticism required to run a 40-yard dash in 4.4 seconds. That'll make a cheetah look slow. And the guys trying to tackle him were running it in 4.5 seconds—still lightning fast—just not fast enough. No player wants to go through this type of training, so why do they? It's the drive to win that drives discipline, and discipline dictates action. It's DDA or the highway.

Well, if pro football sounds like it requires DDA, try trading. It may not be physically challenging—a 4.4 40-yard dash isn't going to help—but you're competing on a field much bigger than 100 yards—it's the entire world. The money's bigger too.

In 2022, the most valuable NFL team was the Dallas Cowboys, estimated at $8 billion. The most valuable stock market ticker was, and still is, the S&P 500 ETF (SPY) with a market cap of $405 billion. It traded about $34 billion—per day. The total notional value of open option contracts was $400 billion, and the SPY was just one of about 8,000 tickers to choose from. In 2022, the estimated total value of all NFL teams was about $132 billion. The total value of all publicly traded companies was a staggering $40 trillion—or 300 times the size of the NFL. Not only that, the stock market is 60% larger than the *entire* U.S. economy.

Stock market competition is stiffer too. Pro football players are lucky to have a five-year career, which is why they say NFL means Not For Long. Warren Buffett, on the other hand, is still considered the world's greatest investor—at 93 years of age. Trading isn't about moving fast. It's about thinking fast. And the world is full of super-smart, fast-thinking people. However, you're not only competing against them. Today, you also have AI computers, bots, and ECNs to contend with too. One thing the NFL and options traders have in common is that for every winner, there's a loser. The only way you make money in the options market is if another trader loses. It's the most competitive environment in the world where the score isn't kept in bright lights on a jumbotron—it's kept in dollars. And yet, retail traders think they're competitive by watching CNBC, reading *MarketWatch*, and placing trades based on what they think. The competition is ahead of you, willing to put in that extra hour, to do you one better.

Thinking a stock is moving higher doesn't make you a trader. It doesn't even make you competitive. That's conviction—not discipline. If you're after conviction, check out YouTube or Reddit, and you'll find plenty of charismatic P.T. Barnums who are convinced their picks will be the greatest performers of the year. Just remember, we saw similar people proclaiming their convictions about Enron, Worldcom, Bear Stearns, Lehman Brothers, Washington Mutual, Silicon Valley Bank, and others who said these stocks were going to set trading records. And they were right—the largest bankruptcies in history. So, the counterpart to DDA is CDC—conviction doesn't count. When it comes to trading, it's DDA or the highway.

Trading requires more than conviction. Everyone's trying to do the same thing, at the same time, with the same information that everyone else is using. You can read, research, and analyze all you want, but if you're using the same information that everybody else is using, why would that give you an advantage? Would you feel you had an advantage at a professional poker game just because you know the rules and can see how much money is being bet? Everybody at the table knows that information too, so it's not giving you an edge. You can't beat the averages by doing what the average person is doing. And yet, that's the approach retail traders take. They read what everybody else is reading, gain conviction a stock is moving up or down, bet a bunch of money—and hope for the best. So, if you want to know one of the big secrets of professional traders, it's understanding how to set up strategies that help you maintain discipline.

## Discipline Dictates Action

Profitable trades are more often the result of managing risk than correctly guessing the market's direction. Unfortunately, as Chapter 4 explained, DNA gets in the way of DDA. Emotions will make you second-guess yourself. Losses will make you take more risk. Small gains will make you take quick profits. And framing will just make you see things the wrong way. Successful trading comes from forming a plan—and sticking with it—but making sure emotions don't get the better of you. That's where discipline—and options—come in. Options can be used as risk management tools, but they can also be used to put your plan on autopilot. Options can turn your ideas into an emotionless computerized trading system. When you remove emotions, it doesn't make trading easy, but it makes it easy to stick with the plan. In this chapter, we want to share some of the most powerful strategies that can help you stick with your plan. That's the most important part. After all, it's DDA or the highway.

## Hold Out for the Long Term: Call Option + Zero-Coupon Bond

Let's look at a strategy that can help longer-term traders stay disciplined. Stock prices tend to drift higher over time, so there's an added benefit from holding stocks over longer periods. However, it can also work against you. Remember, as soon as prices rise, you'll be tempted to take profits. Or, if prices fall, you'll want to hold and hope. Neither will help you accomplish your goals. You won't be able to fight it. It's in our DNA, but here's how options can help.

Let's say you're considering a $100 stock trading at 30% volatility. You think the company has great prospects over the next three years, but with that volatility, the risk is too great to blindly hold that long. If you're just trading shares of stock, you don't have much of a choice other than to buy the shares and hope you can remain disciplined. Here's where the call + zero-coupon bond strategy can help. Let's say the risk-free interest rate is 5%. A pricing model shows a $100 call with three years to expiration, 5% interest, and 30% volatility is worth $27. Rather than taking your chances with the stock, you could take the $10,000 cash you were going to use for the shares and, instead, buy a three-year zero-coupon bond. A zero-coupon bond, also called "zeros," is a government bond that pays no interest. Instead, it's sold at a discount to face value. When you receive the face value at maturity, the difference acts as your interest. At 5% interest, a three-year $10,000 face zero will trade for $8,639. If you invest that amount but receive $10,000 in three years, the $1,361 difference acts as your interest. So, to buy the bond and call today you must invest $8,639 + $2,700, or $11,339.

If the stock falls below $100 at expiration, you'll lose $2,700 on the call, but gain $1,361 in interest, for an overall $1,339 loss. However, if the stock is above $100 in three years—and you still want to own it—take the $10,000 from your matured zero-coupon bond and exercise the call for $100. Remember, no matter how high the stock's price may be, you're guaranteed to pay the $100 strike and receive the shares.

The chart below shows the risk graph of the zero-coupon bond plus $100 call strategy (black line) compared to buying shares at $100 (gray line):

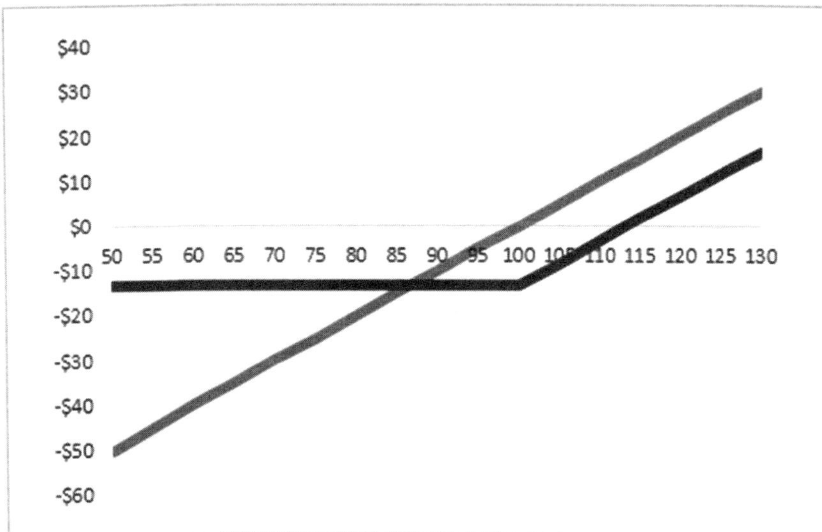


For all stock prices below $100, the black line shows a $1,339 loss—that's it. So, for the next *three years*, you can sit back and forget about the day-to-day oscillations, occasional bad earnings, or your emotions getting in the way. The option strategy allows you to remain disciplined and stick to your goals. Both strategies break even at a stock price around $87, so this strategy insures any losses below $87 for three years but allows you to capture unlimited upside gains. Again, you can see the hedge at work. The stock must climb nearly $14 to break even on the call, so you're giving up $14 of potential upside in exchange for reducing all losses below $86—that's a classic hedge. Some traders may wonder, why bother buying the call? Can't you just buy the shares and use a stop order at $87—for no cost?

## Stop Orders Are Not Insurance

It sounds like a good idea, but there's a big difference between options and stop orders. If you use a stop order and the stock trades at—or below—your stop price, you'll sell your shares, but there are two big risks. First, the stock could gap well below $87, so you could end up with far less than expected. Second, if you do get stopped out but the stock rebounds, you've lost the shares. Stop orders work perfectly if the stock never touches $87, but at 30% volatility, it's nearly guaranteed to happen at least once. So, even though you may intend to hold for three years, using a stop order is nearly guaranteed to kill the deal.

The call option, however, will never trigger you out of the position. If the stock falls below the $100 strike—no matter how far—you still own the call. If the stock rebounds, your call is alive and ready to capture any gains. In trading terms, the stock's path doesn't matter to the call option. What matters is that the option is alive (hasn't expired) if the stock rises above the strike. In trading terms, stop orders are *path dependent* while options are *time dependent*. Stop orders need the stock to remain above the stop if you're to remain in the position. On the other hand, call options just need to be alive. No matter how many times the stock may trade below $87, it doesn't matter to your call option. It will always be there ready to capture any gains that may appear in the future. That's a big benefit and why you must pay for options but not stops. Stop orders offer no insurance. Call options do, so they allow you to maintain discipline over time. Stop orders can kill it.

## Call Options Are Put Options

Anything you can do with a call, you can do with a put. If we had calculated the three-year put option's value, after some technical adjustments, it would trade for $1,339 less than the $100 call. That means you could buy the shares and the three-year $100 put and have the identical risk profile. So, if you already own shares, consider puts. If you don't have shares, consider the call plus zero-coupon bond strategy. It's another way to show that call options are absolutely a form of insurance. Options are flexible, and they give you many perspectives, opportunities, and choices not found in shares of stock. Options help you stay disciplined.

## Giddyup! Momentum Trading Made Better

Many traders use *momentum strategies*, which is the idea that trends will continue. It's like Newton's first law, which roughly says an object in motion remains in motion unless acted on by an outside force. In trading terms, a stock that's trending higher will most likely remain on that path unless acted on by an outside force, which is usually news. So, momentum traders will buy when prices are rising—but sell as they're falling. That doesn't necessarily mean they sell all their shares, but instead, they'll scale back to reduce the risk. However, this is where momentum trading gets tricky. Sometimes there's no news, but instead, just a technical charting point where prices may reverse all by themselves. It may be a flat line resistance, moving average, or any number of bearish candlestick patterns such as doji, engulfing, or kicker patterns. It's as if the market has a mind of its own. One day prices are rocketing to the Moon, and the next day they're falling back to Earth. As Chapter 4 showed, trading plans are easier said than done because DNA gets in the way of DDA. You may plan to buy

50 shares each time the stock rises a certain percent or sell 50 shares each time it falls a certain percent. But what's likely to happen? Once the stock makes a small move in your favor, you'll be tempted to close to capture the for-sure profits. Or, when it falls, you won't want to sell to avoid taking losses. It's easy to lose discipline and exit for the highway. It's difficult to be a momentum trader unless you're super disciplined. Here's another great example of a well-defined trading plan where options can help.

If you're expecting higher moves, you could buy a slightly out-of-the-money call. The delta will be relatively low, but you will have some gamma. That means the call option will *automatically add* deltas to your position as the stock rises and *automatically sell* deltas as the stock falls. The option forces you to stick to your plan. Better yet, it treats every trader the same. If Pete and I buy a $100 call, it will treat us exactly the same as it does you. The option does the automatic hedging—not the trader. For example, on August 3, 2023, Apple (AAPL) closed about $190 before reporting earnings after the closing bell. The next morning, the stock traded nearly 5% lower and then lost nearly 2% the following day before stabilizing at $180. Let's say you felt it was about to begin a steady path higher, and you want to buy 100 shares now but continually add to your position as it rises—you want a momentum strategy. That's a nice strategy, but also a nice price tag. It'll cost $18,000. How can options help?

With the stock at $180, the $185 call with 101 days to expiration was $8. It has $8 of extrinsic value, but remember, that's the price you pay to walk away—just in case your outlook is wrong. The delta was 0.48, so it's behaving about like 48 shares right now. However, what if you bought two calls? That'll give an equivalent of 96 shares, which is pretty close to your 100-share goal. However, it'll only cost $1,600—about 9% of the cost of the shares. Could you lose $1,600, or 100%, of your investment? Sure, but that's also the range effect coming to play with your DNA. It feels like $1,600 is a bigger loss because it's 100% of the investment. That same loss on an $18,000 investment is only 9%, so it feels smaller. Always remember, percentages aren't money, and $1,600 is $1,600. It's far more likely to lose that amount—or far more—by holding $18,000 worth of stock. What's the benefit of buying two out-of-the-money calls versus 100 shares of stock? The chart below compares long 100 shares at $180 (gray line) to buying two $185 calls at $8 each (black line):

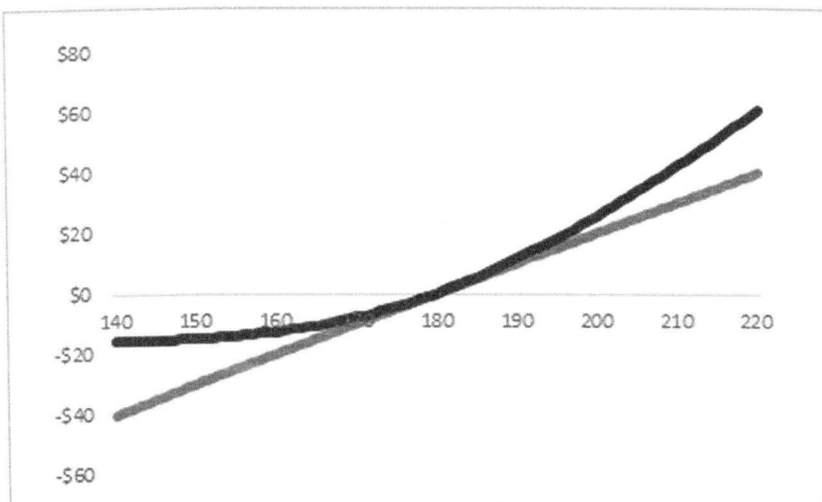


Notice how the black line is curved compared to the gray line. That curvature is *positive gamma*, and you always get positive gamma when you buy an option, whether calls or puts. Whenever you have positive gamma, the risk curve will slope upward, resembling a smile. Positive gamma is one of the best weapons you can have as a momentum trader. Long shares of stock have no gamma, which is why the risk graph is always a straight line. Positive gamma means you're effectively buying shares as the stock price rises but selling shares as the stock price falls—exactly what you want as a momentum trader. Notice in the above chart, as the stock price rises, the black line "pulls away" or rises above the gray line. That's caused by the option automatically adding deltas (shares) to your position. It's as if you have an emotionless private trader—say Mr. Spock—continually buying shares as the stock price rises. Because of the continued buying, the two long calls are more profitable, as they'll eventually become 200 shares as the stock continues to rise. What about the downside risk?

In this case, the long calls...also pull away! The two long calls lose less than the long 100 shares. That's gamma now coming to your rescue. The long calls automatically sell deltas (shares) as the stock price falls thus causing you to lose less. Again, exactly what you want as a momentum trader. In other words, the two long calls earn more if the stock rises but lose less if it falls. It'll treat you exactly the same as a professional trader. It's just the option playing the momentum—not your emotions. Does this mean you can't lose?

Unfortunately, that's the unicorn strategy—it doesn't exist. All strategies involve tradeoffs—and potential losses—but options give you a much wider choice of tradeoffs. When it comes to options, if you make money from stock prices moving, you'll lose money when they sit still and vice versa. Here, if the stock remains at $180 expiration, you'd lose $1,600 but would have lost nothing had you bought the shares. Even if the stock rises to $185, you'd still lose $1,600 at expiration whereas the stock trader would have made five dollars. At expiration, if the stock falls to $164 or rises to $206, both strategies break even. So, to use call options as part of a momentum strategy, you need the stock to make fast, aggressive moves. But isn't that the very definition of momentum? If that's your outlook, the options ensured you could never lose more than $1,600, which is a claim a long stockholder could never make. Unfortunately, if that happens, retail traders would likely say they lost 100% of their money and therefore options are risky. They never consider the amazing benefits of gamma applied to a momentum strategy and forget that you must pay for all benefits—especially amazing ones. This momentum option strategy did exactly as it was told according to your outlook, which happened to be dead wrong. And yet, traders see that as the option's fault. To be successful, you must have discipline, but you must also have the right perspective. If you have the right perspective, you'll see amazing ways that options create opportunities not possible with stock—all while hedging risk.

## Fading the Market

For every strategy, there's a counterpart. After all, if you buy a call, someone must sell a call, and that trader's outlook will be exactly opposite of yours. So, if you're using a momentum strategy, the trader on the opposite side must be using the opposite, which is called *fading the market*. When fading, you'll want to buy as prices fall but sell as they rise—buy low, sell high. This is the Warren Buffett approach, which is highlighted by his quote, "Be fearful when others are greedy, and greedy when others are fearful." In other words, as prices are rising, be fearful and lean toward selling into the momentum. If prices are falling, realize it's a buying opportunity,

> ***Be fearful when others are greedy, and greedy when others are fearful.***
>
> ***– Warren Buffett***

so buy when everyone else is fearful. Just like with momentum trading, fading is easier said than done. As the stock rises, you'll naturally want to abandon plans and hold out for bigger gains. If the price falls, you won't want to buy for fear of adding to losses. It's easy to say you'll buy as prices fall, but following through is another story. However, because option risk profiles have curvature—gamma—you can automatically fade the market just as easily as pursuing a momentum strategy.

Fading is the opposite of momentum, so just do the opposite—you'll sell options. Whenever you sell an option, you'll create *negative gamma*, which means the risk graph will slope downward, resembling a frown. Using the previous example, let's say you thought Apple would rise but want to fade the market. Now you could buy 100 shares at the current $180 price but perhaps sell the $185 call and collect the $8 premium. The risk graph below compares long shares (gray line) to long shares plus a short $185 call for $8:

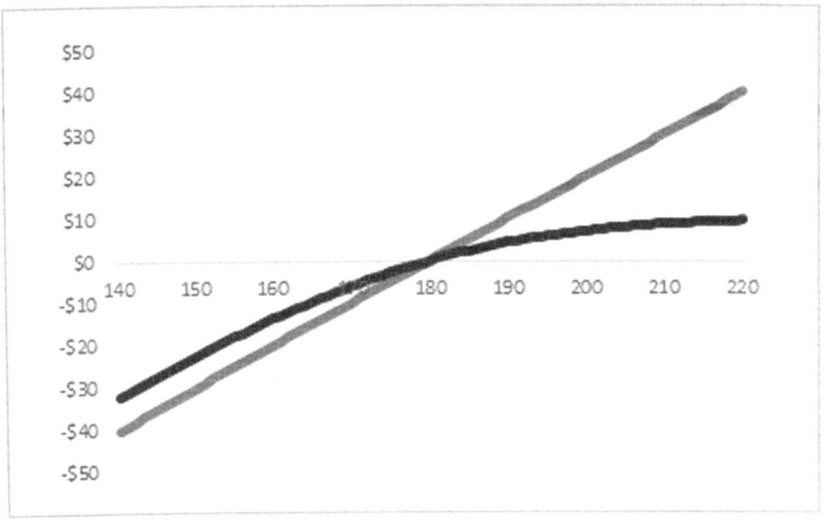


The chart clearly shows the fading effect. If the stock price rises, the black line begins to taper off and produce fewer profits. That's caused by the negative gamma automatically selling deltas (shares) as the stock price rises. However, if the stock price falls, the black curve gets steeper, which is the equivalent of buying shares as the price falls. The benefit is that by collecting the $8 premium, the black line sits above the gray line for all stock prices below $180. That's your hedge, or insurance policy. When you buy shares and sell calls, it's a popular strategy called a *covered call*, which was introduced in Chapter 4, and the Appendix provides even more details. Unfortunately, too many traders see the strategy as an "income generator," which is certainly okay, but it misses the bigger point that it allows you to fade the market. Once you have a goal of momentum or fading—or perhaps both—you can select option strategies that allow you to accomplish that without emotions. In both cases, it was the option's property of gamma that makes it possible. Options are great hedging tools, as that's what they were designed to do, and that's what makes them great for maintaining discipline. Whether you're playing momentum or fading the market, options allow you to do it with discipline.

## Selling Straddles Against Stock

If you like the idea of fading the markets, options offer a host of appealing strategies. Another similar strategy is selling *straddles* against shares of stock. Recall that a long straddle is a strategy where you buy a call and put with the same strike and expiration. Let's say you're interested in a $300 stock that has fairly high volatility at 30%. You want to buy 100 shares now but are willing to buy another 100 if the price falls further. Strategies like this sound appealing on paper, but it's easy to forget your discipline if the stock price falls, and that's where a good downside hedge can help. A pricing model shows with the stock at $300 and volatility at 30%, the $290 call is worth $23 while the $290 put is $13. If you sell the $290 call and put—a short straddle—you'll collect $36, which is 12% of the stock's price. If you buy 100 shares and sell the $290 straddle, you get the following risk curve:

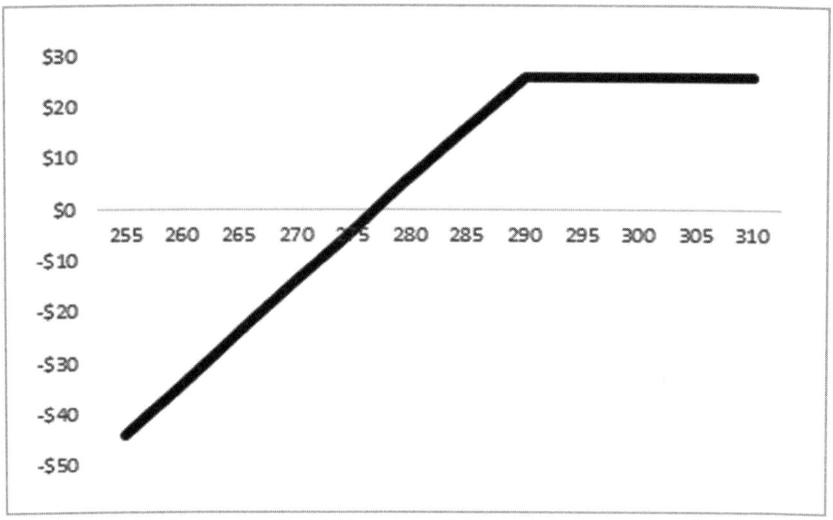


It looks just like the covered call, and it is, except that you're effectively holding 200 shares and selling 100 shares. If the stock falls below $290, or about 3.3%, you'll get assigned on the short put and buy 100 shares—exactly in line with your goals. However, if the stock price stays above $290, you'll get assigned and sell your 100 shares. With the stock currently at $300, the odds are on your side you'll get assigned and sell for $290. However, if you pay $300 for the stock and collect $36 from selling the straddle, your effective cost basis is $264. If you get assigned and sell for $290, the $26 gain represents a 9.8% return for 90 days, or 39% annualized. Selling straddles against shares of stock is another powerful strategy that allows you to stay true to your goals by maintaining discipline.

## Systematic Writing

The systematic writing strategy is a fascinating strategy for investors seeking to buy and sell shares of stock, but also collect option premiums to hedge downside risk. The strategy involves three steps, and each step is determined by the stock's closing price at expiration—not your emotions. At Market Rebellion, we normally don't advocate selling naked puts, but serious investors who are willing to take the assignment can certainly make use of the strategy. However, you can also substitute short vertical spreads for the first step. Like all strategies, you must have a goal in mind, so let's say you're willing to buy 200 shares of stock. Once that's figured out, the first step is to sell naked puts on *half* the position. So, if you're willing to buy 200 shares, begin by selling one put. If it's an out-of-the-money put, you'll receive less money, but also have a lower cost should you get assigned. You could also choose to sell an at-the-money put and receive more money but have a greater chance of assignment. Regardless of the strike you choose, sell the put and wait for expiration. If the stock is above the strike at expiration, the put expires worthless, and you'll sell another put. The idea is to continue selling puts *until you get assigned* with the goal of acquiring 100 shares of stock. Once you do, move to step two, which is to sell a straddle, which is the same as the previous strategy. (You can also substitute a strangle, which is selling a call and put with *different* strikes but the same expiration.) After selling the straddle, one of two things will occur at expiration. If the stock is above the call strike, you'll get assigned, and sell your 100 shares. If so, you've collected at least three option premiums to buy low and sell high. However, if the stock falls, you'll get assigned on the short put, which means you'll be long 200 shares, but that's still in line with your goals and risk tolerances. One you acquire 200 shares, move to step three, which is to continue selling *two calls* until you get assigned. If you get assigned, you'll sell the shares, and you've collected at least four option premiums to buy and sell shares you wanted to buy anyway. After the assignment, go back to step one and begin selling puts to acquire more shares. Can you lose? Of course, no strategy creates guaranteed gains. For this strategy to lose, the stock would have to do nothing but fall. If that happens, however, it's simply the wrong outlook—not the option strategy—that caused the losses. The strategy worked exactly as intended. You collected multiple option premiums to buy and sell shares of stock you were going to buy and sell anyway. The systematic writing strategy just helps to keep you focused by dictating which trades to enter—and provides sizeable hedges in case you're wrong.

## Adding Leverage Without the Risk—Or Cost

Stock traders often like to use financial leverage to increase returns. Financial leverage is done by borrowing money to purchase more shares of stock. If you sign a margin agreement with your broker, it's easy to borrow money to borrow shares. Every broker is set up to do that. However, if you own 100 shares but borrow money to buy another 100 shares, you've doubled the potential for profits—but also double the potential losses. Financial leverage usually cuts both ways. Can options help to solve this problem? Let's say a stock is trading for $300 at 40% volatility, and you believe it's about to break out into an aggressive run. You want to buy 200 shares and sell at a target of $330 over the next three months. However, that'll cost $60,000, which means there'll be large potential losses if you're wrong, and at 40% volatility, there's a good chance the price could be much lower. What can you do?

Here's a strategy Pete and I used a lot as market makers. We would buy shares, but also use a ratio call spread for no net cost, or at least very close to nothing. A *ratio call spread* is a strategy where you buy one call but sell two calls (or more) at a higher strike but the same expiration. For example, rather than buying 200 shares, you could buy 100 shares, which cuts the cost in half. Next, find the call strike you want to buy but continue looking at higher strikes until you find one that's trading for about half the price. That way, the net cost of the ratio spread will be close to nothing. At 40% volatility, the 90-day $300 call is worth $24, and the $330 call is worth $12—a perfect match. You can buy the $300 call for $24, but sell two of the $330 calls at $12 each, for a total of $24, so there's no cash outlay on your part. In the real world, it'll be tough to find a pair of strikes that'll exactly be a net zero cost. Even if you do find two, after commissions, there'll be a slight cost. Most of the time, you'll usually end up with a slight debit or credit depending on the strikes you choose. Now, if you only bought the $300 call and sold two of the $330 calls, that's a strategy called a ratio spread, and the resulting risk graph looks like this:

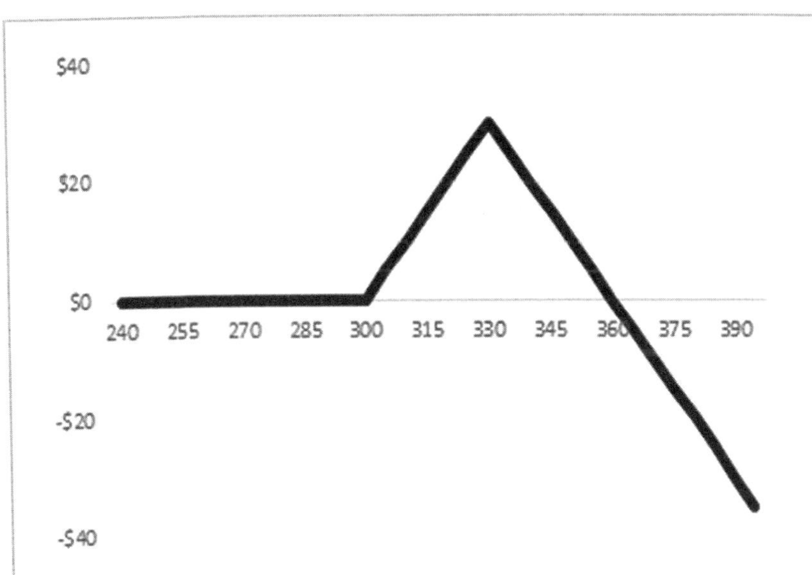

The strategy has unlimited upside risk since you're short one call on a net basis, so that's not a strategy we'd recommend, especially for new traders. However, in this example, we're also assuming you bought 100 shares of stock. The risk graph below shows the long 100 shares plus the ratio spread (black line) compared to only long 100 shares (gray line):

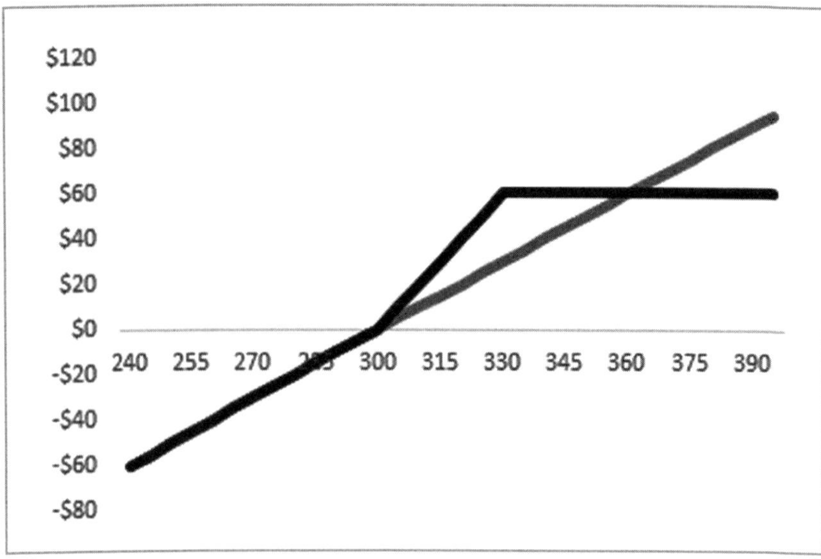


For all stock prices between the $300 and $330 strikes, the black line is twice as steep as the gray. That's because you're long 100 shares of stock plus you're long the $300 call, so you're effectively long 200 shares for all stock prices above $300. Your profits will therefore be twice as large compared to just holding the stock alone. For instance, if the stock is $330 at expiration, you'd be up $30 on the shares but $60 on the stock plus ratio spread. However, if the stock rises beyond $330—your goal—you've sold off any rights above that level.

The two lines cross at $360, which is where both strategies produce the same $60 gain. So, the stock would have to rise beyond $360 before the long shares outperform. Remember, though, your outlook is for the stock to rise to $330. Rising to $360 is another 9% higher. If you only held the shares, you'd need the stock to rise to $360 to produce the same profit as when it rises to $330 with the stock plus ratio spread combination. The downside has *no additional* risk beyond the long 100 shares that you were planning to hold anyway. If the stock falls below $300, all calls expire worthless, and you're just left holding 100 shares, which is exactly what you would have had without using the ratio spread for leverage. Since there's no 0ut-of-pocket expense, or very little, does this mean the ratio spread was free?

Remember, no strategy is free. Instead, each choice of options, expirations, and strikes creates tradeoffs in risk and reward. Here, you used some of the unknown stock profits beyond $330 to finance the cost of the $300 call. Speculators are willing to pay for that, so you got paid for selling two of the $330 calls, and you used that money to buy the $300 call. If you remember from the covered call, the idea was to sell a call to add a small downside hedge in the long shares. With this strategy, you're giving up some upside potential in exchange for increasing the leverage. Options are truly versatile.

Just as with the covered call, be carcful not to interpret your shares getting "called away" above the $330 strike as the "risk" in the strategy. That's a missed opportunity, not a risk. And yet, if the stock does shoot past $330, some traders will say they got "burned" on the strategy and options are therefore risky. The strategy did exactly what it was supposed to. This is why goals are so important, as they give you the proper perspective—and discipline—to allow a strategy to do what it's designed to do without you feeling regrets.

## Selling Vertical Spreads Against Stock

Throughout the book, we've talked about guarding the downside risk of the stock, but that usually requires that you spend money for a hedge. Let's say you own shares of stock that have risen in value, and you'd like to buy puts but without spending any money. Can that be done? Now that you're understanding the power of options, you should understand there's probably a way to create that risk profile. However, you should also realize that if you don't want to spend money, it means you'll have to give up some potential gains. But that's okay. If it meets your needs, it's a viable strategy, and it won't be available by using only shares of stock. So, what's a way this can be done?

Another favorite of our strategies is to sell *vertical spreads* against shares of stock. The strategy calls for you to sell two *vertical spreads* for every 100 shares of stock you own. The main idea is to buy puts to guard against the downside risk but to finance the purchase of the puts by selling vertical spreads. For example, let's say you bought 100 shares of Home Depot (HD) at $280, and the stock is now $295. The following option quotes are available with 16 days to expiration:

| STOCK = $295 | | |
|---|---|---|
| **Strike** | **Calls** | **Puts** |
| 290 | 9.10 | 3.30 |
| 295 | 5.80 | 5.10 |
| 300 | 3.40 | 7.70 |

Here are the three trades:

- Sell 2 $295 calls for $11.60
- Buy 2 $300 calls for $6.80
- Buy 1 $290 put for $3.30

The first two trades create two short 295/300 vertical call spreads. By selling the $295 calls for $11.60 and using that money to buy the $300 calls for $6.80, you ended up with a $4.80 credit. With that credit, you'll buy the $290 put for $3.30, which leaves you with an overall $1.50 net credit. The sale of two vertical spreads more than covers the purchase of the put, so there's no cash outlay on your part. The $1.50 credit represents an 11.4% annualized return on your money compared to the current $295 stock price. That's a nice bonus, but it doesn't always work out that way. Depending on the strikes you choose, you may end up with a slight debit or credit, but that's not the important point, as a credit isn't the goal. Instead, the goal is to purchase a put to guard against the downside risk by spending relatively little money. So, if you sell two vertical spreads and buy the $290 put, what's the result? The chart below shows the original 100 shares at $280 (gray line). After selling the two vertical spreads and purchasing the $290 put, you move from the gray line to the black line:

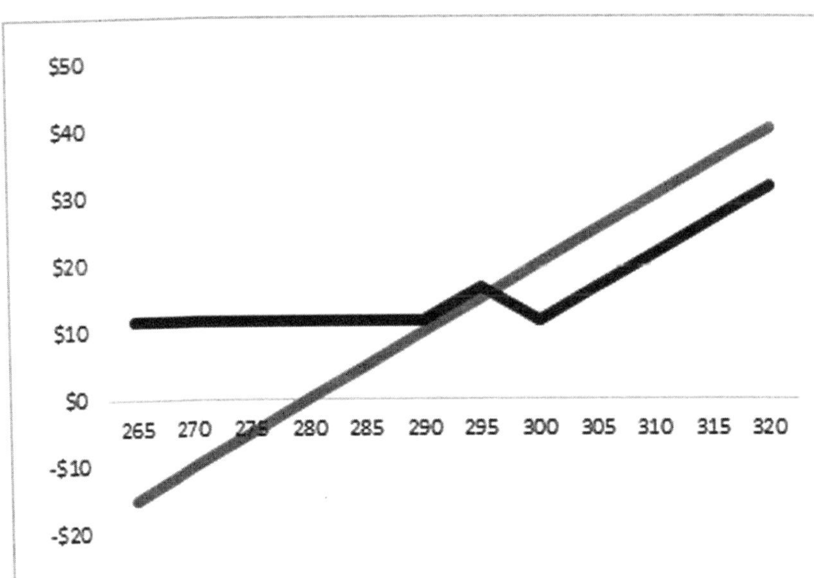

The big benefit of these trades is that they created a guaranteed gain of $11.50. That's because you bought shares at $280, but the $290 put gives you the right to sell for $290, which locks in a $10 gain. When that's combined with the $1.50 credit, it results in a guaranteed $11.50 gain. However, if the stock remains at $295—the short call strike—you can make even more. At that point, the put and credit spreads expire worthless, which leaves you the $15 unrealized gain you had before the trades. When that's coupled with the initial $1.50 credit, it's a total gain of $16.50. But it gets even better. If the stock rises beyond the $300 call strike, you begin making dollar for dollar at expiration—just as if you only held the shares. So, you're not giving up all upside in the stock. Instead, you're just giving up gains until the stock hits $300. As with all option strategies, hedges aren't free. For all stock prices above $295, the gray line sits above the black line. For example, if the stock rises to $300, you make $11.50 with the hedged position, but would have made $20 had you just held the stock. The difference is $8.50, which is from the $10 loss in the two vertical spreads less the $1.50 credit. In other words, for all stock prices above $300, you'd have been better off by $8.50 had you not done the hedge. But with the hedge, you're giving up $8.50 in potential profits in exchange for locking in a gain of $11.50—and possibly making more. But that's the exact definition of a hedge. Remember too, these options expire in 16 days. If the stock continues to climb, or sits still, you can do the same sequence of trades, which will just shift the black diagram upward. Over time, you'll continue to lock in gains, guard the downside, but still have unlimited upside potential.

This chapter shows a new side of options. You can sell options to help finance a hedge, but you can also sell them to create additional leverage at no out-of-pocket expense. You've now opened another door to the benefits of options. If you're feeling overwhelmed, that's good because we want to show the power and flexibility of options. There are hundreds of other doors to open, and each has a little different twist on risk and reward that you simply can't get from shares of stock. The good news is there's no need to be overwhelmed. Most traders—even professionals—only use a handful of strategies. This chapter was written to show how options not only maintain safety, but they also help to maintain discipline. Explore all option strategies and pick a few that will help you to reach your goals while taking less risk. Any time you can achieve a goal with less risk, you're better off. Options give you choices. *Discipline dictates action.* Take advantage of the choices. Take an interest. Take your time. Just don't take the highway.

# Chapter Six:

## Blurring the Lines—Hedging vs. Speculating

Bigfoot is blurry. The Loch Ness Monster is blurry. And every UFO that created crop circles in Kansas is blurry. The rarest of chance encounters are always captured in blurry photos. Despite ignoring the staggering odds that when these paranormal creatures appeared, they just happened to be crossing paths with the world's worst photographers, there's not much harm in believing these stories. But just for the record, you'd have better luck getting struck by lightning—twice. However, for options traders, there is something else that's always blurry, and unfortunately, there is a price to pay for not seeing clearly. It's the blurry line between hedging and speculating.

Many traders learn options through sketchy sources such as YouTube, Investopedia, Reddit, or more specifically, anywhere on the internet. There's nothing necessarily wrong with these sources. It's the people posting and, to put it politely, some don't have the brainpower to toast a crouton. Sure, you can learn good stuff from the internet, but you can also find sites that teach the Earth is flat, Halloween will fall on Friday the 13th this year, or that Bigfoot isn't blurry—he's just not photogenic.

At Market Rebellion, one of the things we make sure our traders know is the distinction between hedging and speculating. Hedging allowed us to be successful floor traders, but if you don't know the difference, you may end up speculating when you think you're hedging, which is like confusing the gas pedal with the brake. Since we're introducing you to the benefits of options, we want to make sure you know the difference too. So, what's the difference between hedging and speculating? Let's find out, and we'll try to make this as clear as possible.

## Hedging vs. Speculating

Hedging is any trade that reduces potential gains in exchange for reducing some type of risk. You're giving up some potential gains to avoid some, or all, of the losses. Buying car insurance is a hedge. Buying a put option against long shares of stock is a hedge.

Speculating is just the opposite: You're accepting greater risk to pursue greater profits. You're putting more money into a trade, increasing leverage, or some other action to increase potential profits while accepting greater possible losses. Speculating increases risk. Hedging reduces risk. Like all options strategies, don't think of one as good and the other bad. Even if you consider yourself a conservative investor, just by having money invested—even at low levels of risk—you're still speculating to some degree. The better way to approach decision making is to get the right blend of hedging or speculating for you to meet your goals. But this is exactly where the problems begin.

When traders learn about hedging, they like the idea but end up overdoing it. They run on the philosophy if one aspirin is good, two must be better. The irony is, in the process of "hedging" and trying to make things safer, they're actually making them riskier. They end up doing the opposite. It's a common mistake, and it all begins by misunderstanding the blurry hedging-speculating boundary line. This is another application where risk graphs can bring things into focus.

For example, if you buy 100 shares of stock, you have unlimited potential for gains, but you're also exposed to all the downside risk. If you buy a put, it's a hedge. Let's say you buy a $100 put for $5, which will now offset some of the downside risk. As the stock price falls, the put's price rises, and the two positions tend to offset each other. The risk graph below shows the stock plus $100 put purchased for $5 (black line) compared to the long stock at $100 (gray line):

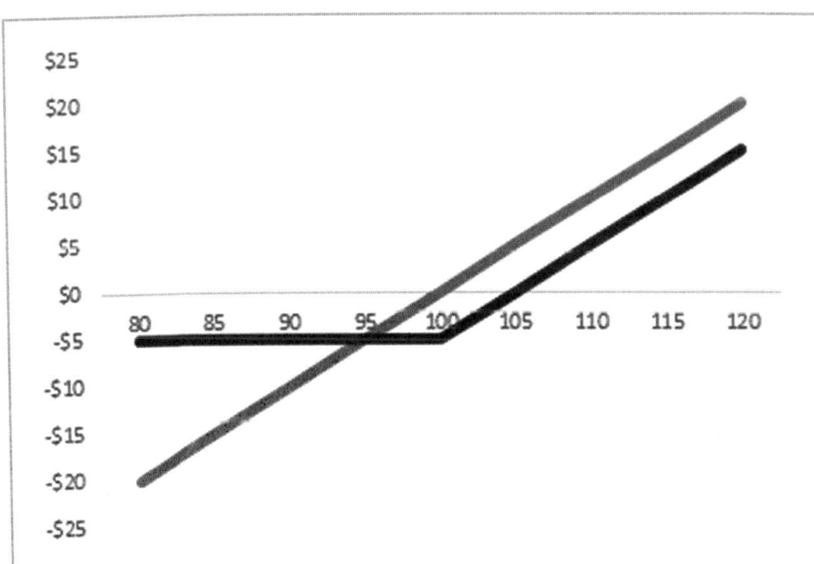

This is a classic hedge and shows what options were designed to do. The best way to see the hedge is to start at the $95 crossover point. That's where both strategies produce the same profit or loss. In this example, a $5 loss. For all stock prices above $95, the gray line sits above the black line, which means the long stock position will outperform the stock plus put combination, so the stock plus put combination gives up some of the gains. Why give up gains?

In case the stock price falls. For all stock prices below $95, the advantage has switched. The black line now sits above the gray line and outperforms the long stock. That's not necessarily saying it's producing profits. In this case, it's losing less. As the stock continues to fall below $95, long stock continues to lose, while the hedged stock position has a fixed loss. Those are always the key characteristics of a hedge—reduced gains and reduced losses. So, to see things clearly, always remember that hedging means you make less—and lose less. Now that hedging is in focus, what's speculating all about?

## Speculating for Profits

Speculating is just the opposite of hedging. Speculators intentionally increase risk in pursuit of greater profits. If you own 100 shares and buy another 100 shares, it's a speculative trade since you've increased the amount of money you can lose, but you've also increased the amount you could make. Gains and losses are potentially greater. Options were created to hedge unwanted risk, but this is where lines begin to blur. Just because you buy an option doesn't necessarily mean you're hedging a position. It depends on the position you're trying to hedge. As we just showed, if you have 100 shares but buy a put option, it's a hedge. But if you own 100 shares and buy a call, it's not a hedge.

The chart below shows 100 shares plus a long $100 call purchased for $5 (black line) compared to long 100 shares (gray line):

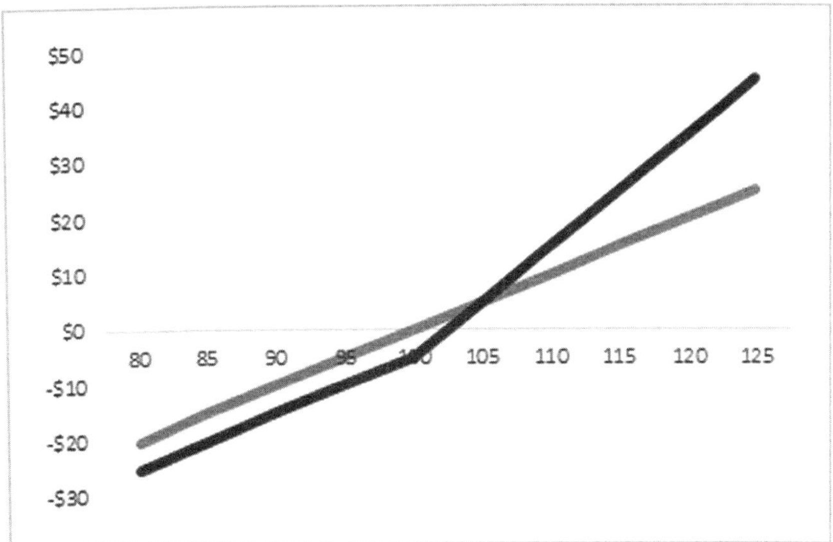


If the stock falls, the long shares plus call lose more, but if the stock rises, it earns more. You spent money to increase the gains if the stock rises. That's speculation. So, buying a put against long shares is a hedge, but buying a call against shares is speculation. Even though you bought options in both cases, one's a hedge, and the other's not.

Traders make mistakes by trying to over insure, and in the process, unknowingly make positions riskier. Knowingly accepting risk is one thing. Thinking that you're hedging but loading the boat with risk is another, and that's where traps are formed.

For example, let's say you've purchased a $100 call. If you buy a $100 put too, will that hedge the long call? After all, buying a put is a hedge against long shares, so won't it protect a call too? The chart below shows the combination of a long $100 call purchased for $5 combined with a long $100 put also purchased for $5 (black line) along with the $100 call purchased for $5 for comparison (gray line):

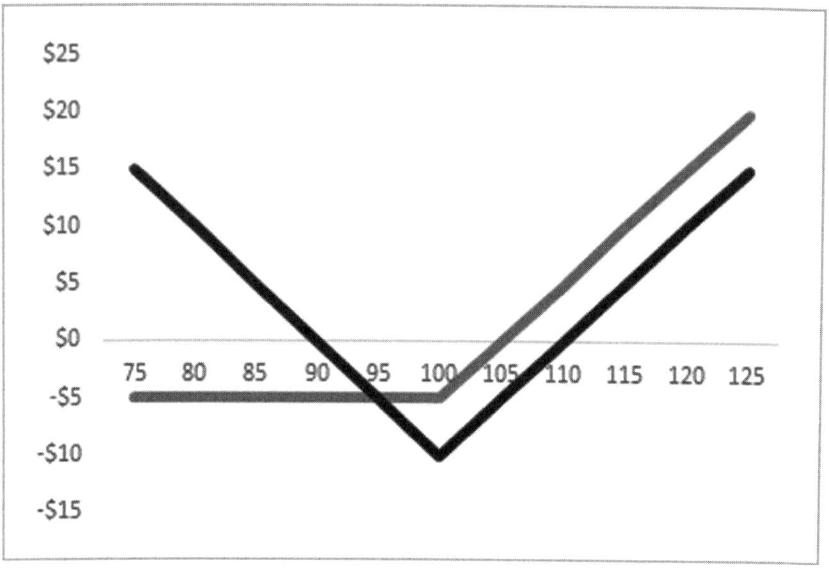


Did the long $100 put act as a hedge? The above chart shows the long $100 call had a maximum loss of $5. When the $100 put was added, the maximum loss *increased* to $10. Notice that the long call's risk graph is flat for all stock prices below $100. It doesn't make any money. However, when the $100 put was added, profits are now possible to the downside. By adding the $100 put, the maximum loss increased and so did the potential profits. So, while buying a put hedges long shares of stock, it doesn't hedge a call—it makes it speculative. Why the difference?

The long call is already hedged to the downside. Remember, a long stock position plus a long put is identical to long call. So, a long call has a built-in put associated with it. That's why the risk graph is flat for a long call for all stock prices below the strike. That's not true for shares of stock. Buying a put option on top of a call option doesn't hedge the downside. Instead, it increases the potential for gains.

In the last chapter, we talked about a short straddle where you'd sell a call and put with the same strike and expiration. The combination of a long call and long put with the same strikes and expirations is a *long straddle*. The straddle is designed to make profits if the stock rises or falls far enough. It needs a fast, aggressive move from the stock to get past the breakeven points, which are found by adding and subtracting the total price paid to the strike. In this example, you'd add and subtract $10 to the $100 strike to get breakeven points of $90 and $110. If the stock price remains between these two points, the straddle will lose money. That's a simple example where buying a put in one instance (against shares of stock) is a hedge, but in another (against a long call) it's speculative. Even though a put was purchased in both examples, that's not what defines a hedge, and you must be aware of the differences before you start trading options. Don't associate buying puts with hedging. Sometimes it is, but other times it's not. This is yet another reason options are sometimes seen as risky. Traders overdo their hedges and end up placing highly speculating positions, so an option's power can be destructive if you don't know what you're doing. Here's another one to try.

Let's go back to the long stock plus long $100 put combination that was a hedge. What if you bought a second put? Will you have doubly hedged it? Some traders think so, again, on the belief if one aspirin is good, two must be better. However, if you buy a second $100 put, the risk graph will look exactly like the $100 straddle above. So, if you buy shares of stock plus two puts, it's no longer a hedge—it's speculation. Remember, if the stock plus put combination is a call, then buying a second put makes it a straddle. No wonder traders make hedging mistakes. The real power of options comes from being able to add, subtract, hedge, or speculate as conditions change. Whatever you can do with calls, you can do with puts. It's a seemingly endless universe of choices, but because of the many choices, education is key.

Let's go back to long shares of stock purchased for $100. Now let's say you entered a covered call by selling a $105 call for $3 (black line). The long shares of stock purchased for $100 (gray line) is shown for comparison. Does the sale of the call provide a hedge?

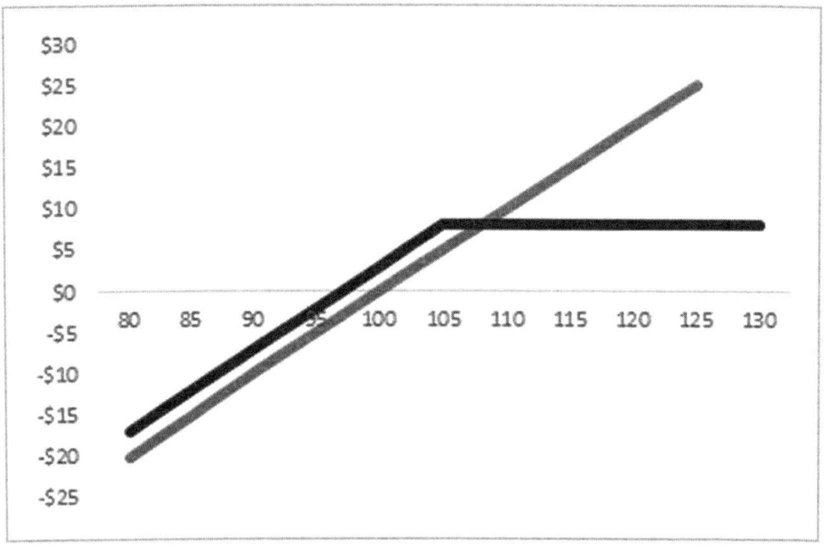


The above chart shows you've reduced the gains by completely flattening the black line for all stock prices above $105. However, you also reduced the downside losses, which can be seen by the black line being shifted a little to the left of the gray line. By selling the call, you've reduced the gains and losses, so it's a hedge. In many cases, the covered call isn't the best hedge, as you completely seal off all gains above the strike but only slightly reduce the downside risk, but it still fits within the definition of a hedge. Now think about this. If selling one call provides a small hedge, will selling two calls provide a better hedge? After all, you'll receive more money. What do you think? If you sell a second call, you create the risk profile below (black line below) with the long shares for comparison (gray line):

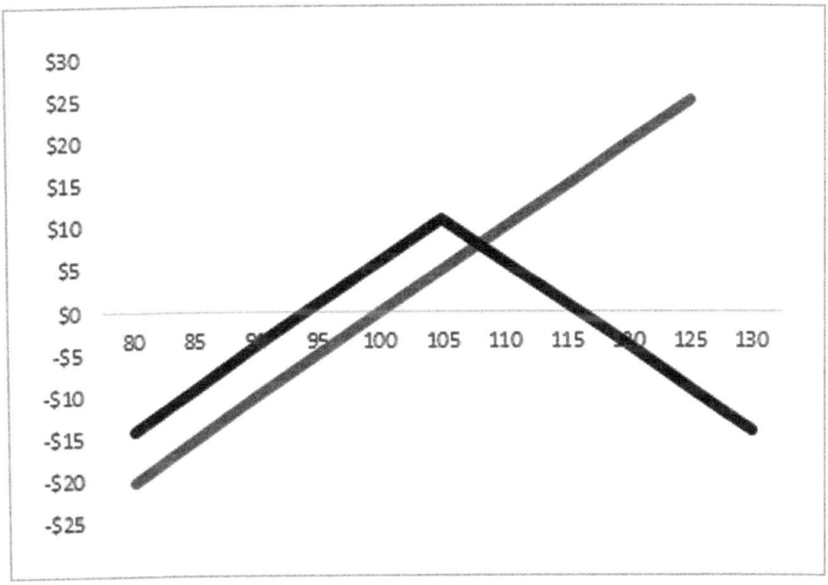


What a difference the sale of a second call makes. By selling the second call, you created a *short straddle*, which is one of the riskiest positions, as it has unlimited potential losses in both directions. However, you did increase potential profits by selling the second call, so you increased potential profits by accepting more risk. The sale of the second call changed the position from a hedged position to a speculative one. One of the main points to see is that buying an option doesn't necessarily qualify as a hedge, but neither does selling an option. Again, many traders think it does, so they just continue to sell. Okay, here's a last example to try.

Let's say you bought 100 shares. Rather than selling a call, which would hedge the position, you decide to sell a put. If selling a call brings in cash, which reduces risk, wouldn't selling a put also be a hedge? Many traders think so because they hear "selling" and "credit" and immediately believe it qualifies as a hedge. The chart below shows long shares plus a short $100 put sold for $5 (black line) compared to the shares of stock purchased for $100 (gray line):

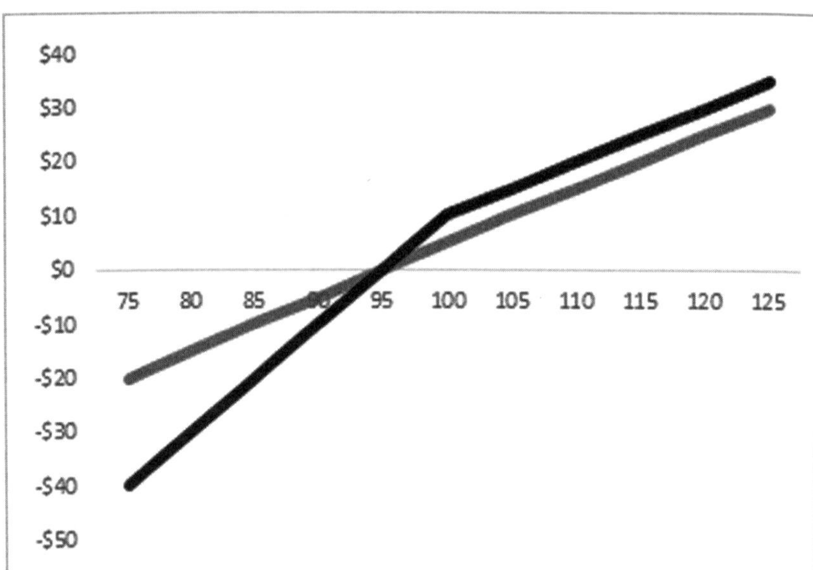


Again, start with the $95 crossover point. The black line sits above the gray line for all prices above $95, so you've increased potential gains. However, for all stock prices below $95, the position loses more money than just the long stock alone. By selling the put, you've increased the potential risk in exchange for greater potential rewards—it's a speculative position. Even though you sold an option and received a credit, it doesn't mean it was a hedge. In this example, it did exactly the opposite. The entire idea of misunderstanding hedging versus speculating is another reason why traders may think options are risky. They learn about a hedging strategy, but then try to over hedge, not realizing it's making the position speculative. The more they try to over hedge, the more speculative it becomes. Who would have guessed that being so safe could be so risky? Just because you're trading options doesn't necessarily mean you're hedging risk. It depends on how they're used. Hopefully this chapter helped to focus that blurred line between hedging and speculation. You don't want to be the person known for making things riskier by trying to make them safer. That's only slightly more humiliating than saying Bigfoot saw you but nobody believed him.

# Chapter Seven:

## There's Nothing Unusual About UOA

"That's where the money is." That's the legendary answer "Slick Willie" Sutton gave to a reporter in 1952 when asked why he robbed banks. The quote developed into *Sutton's Law*, a metaphor for anyone seeking answers to important questions—start with the most likely answer. In 1933, Sutton set out to rob a Philadelphia bank disguised as a postal worker. Why not rob a post office disguised as a bank teller? Sutton's Law provides a good starting point.

When Pete and I were market makers at the Chicago Board Options Exchange (CBOE), we'd often see strange activity, trades that made as much sense as robbing a post office. Traders from big firms like Goldman or JP Morgan would come to the trading pits and ask for a market in a little unknown, lightly traded stock like Small Street Journal trading for $20. We'd watch market makers provide quotes, and the traders would buy, to put in round numbers, an obscene number of call options. Now, by a lot, we don't mean 100, 200, or even 1,000 calls for a few $100k. It would be more like 30,000 calls at a cost approaching the Hope Diamond. Before the trader could walk off the floor, we could see the hyped-up happiness as the market makers were high fiving, breaking out the champagne, and calling yacht brokers. Who can blame them after selling a great big nothing burger?

"Who'd buy Skunk Street," I'd ask Pete, "it's a dog with fleas. "I know," Pete would respond, "their subscriptions were down 92% last year and their recent acquisition of a tire care chain makes no sense." And yet, the more we looked into it, the stranger it got. The options had five days to expiration. They were 10% out of the money. They had no volume, no open interest—and no chance for success. You'd have better luck bumping into Bigfoot picking a four-leaf clover. Who would do something so stupid, reckless, and wasteful?

Enter Sutton's Law.

After some thought, we realized that if the buyer had an IQ that was at least positive, the most likely answer is he knew that's where the money was. Maybe the buyer had inside information and knew the company was going to be acquired for a hefty premium? But isn't it illegal to trade on inside information? Yes, but it's also illegal to rob banks, but that didn't stop Uncle Willie or countless other gangsters. So, we'd watch the news, and sure enough, a day before expiration, the bright red breaking news banner

> ***The only way you can predict the future is to build it.***
>
> ***–Alan Kay***

would appear on CNBC: Small Street Journal was acquired by Main Street Journal for $50 per share. That giant trash heap of call options was now valued closer to the GDP of Peru. Pete and I routinely saw this and began calling it "smart money" because we realized it only appeared to be dumb before taking Sutton's Law into account. Start with the most likely answer: The reason we'd see massive orders on no-name stocks was because the traders knew something. So, we wondered if there was a way to follow the smart money. How could we get other traders in the pits to share the information? Willie Sutton said, "You can get more with a kind word and a gun than you can get with just a kind word." Well, we knew we couldn't take Willie's approach—kind words are never allowed on trading floors. But maybe we could build a computer program? Plus, it wouldn't be illegal, so there's no fear of having our pictures pinned up at post offices across America. What if we could scan the entire universe of trades—public information—for similar activity? We could search for short-term trades that far exceed the average daily volume and open interest, calculate the total dollars spent, and compare it to the time to expiration. Doing so, we could get a bird's eye view of all trades on all optionable stocks, across all exchanges, and all trading floors. So, we hired some big guns in the programming world and developed *Heat Seeker™*, the program that scans over 180,000 trades per second. If Willie Sutton asked us why we were building it, you should know the answer. It's obvious. That's where the money is. It's the closest thing we could imagine to a modern-day crystal ball. As computer scientist Alan Kay noted, "The only way you can predict the future is to build it."

So, we did.

While we call it *Unusual Option Activity*, or UOA, there's nothing unusual about it. When companies are making plans for big acquisitions, somebody knows about it. So, the second CEOs, CFOs, and other alphabet-soup people even begin talking about plans, the information is born, and it will circulate no matter how much they warn employees to remain tight-lipped. There's too much money up for grabs, and somebody's going to talk. However, at this stage, it's *non-public* information, or *inside information*, and it's highly illegal to trade based on this information. However, the very second someone places a trade, the rules change. It immediately becomes public information because it's printed to the tape, and now it's fair game. The SEC (Securities and Exchange Commission) isn't concerned about who can collect or analyze public information better. The agency isn't there to judge people's competency at interpreting information. The market is supposed to be a collective opinion of value, regardless of how each investor arrives at their conclusions. Accountants and CPAs have better abilities to analyze quarterly and annual reports than the rest of us, but the SEC doesn't prohibit them from investing. In fact, to have an efficient market, you need the opinions of accountants and CPAs, and that makes market prices better for everyone. If people could be excluded based on knowledge levels, the SEC would have to ban doctors from buying medical stocks, scientists from buying pharmacology stocks, and anyone in Silicon Valley from buying tech stocks. They'd have to ban Warren Buffett from buying Apple and Coca-Cola, moms from buying Kimberly-Clark, or pet owners from buying Chewy. The SEC's only concern is to ensure that everyone has access to the same information at the same time.

So, *Heat Seeker™* isn't illegal or even on the fringe of some shadowy area of the market. It's just a program that collects data that everyone else is free to grab. What makes it valuable is that it's difficult information to get—and expensive. However, our biggest advantage is that we have the ability to analyze the resulting scans better than nearly anyone on the planet. We understand markets.

We recognize how news will affect certain stocks and sectors. Most of all, we know options. Once we get scans from *Heat Seeker™*, we further filter out noise, which are those trades that may be large, but aren't meaningful for a number of reasons. For example, just because we see a massive trade doesn't necessarily mean it's something we should consider. While there are other services that scan for large trades, most won't further curate the trades to weed out the meaningless trades. We only select those that have the markings of smart money.

For example, we check to see if the trade is larger than the open interest, which tells us it's an *opening trade*. That's important. If traders are trying to capitalize on valuable information, they're not going to be closing positions. We may find it's the sale of calls against shares of stock—a covered call. No trader would use a covered call for a stock that's expected to skyrocket. So, we cross it off the list. The trick isn't in finding trades with large size. It's finding trades with large size that are meaningful, and that's what we do every day with *Heat Seeker™*. So, let's look at some examples, and once you consider Sutton's Law, you'll see that *Unusual Option Activity* is anything but unusual. Instead, the most likely answer is that somebody, somewhere, knew where the money was.

## Burford Capital Catches a Break

On March 28, 2023, *Heat Seeker™* found the purchase of 10,000 May $7.50 calls with 52 days to expiration purchased for $0.60 on Burford Capital (BUR) with the stock at $6.85. The trade size was well above the open interest of 1,236 contracts, so we knew it was an opening trade. The expiration breakeven point is the $7.50 strike + $0.60 premium, or $8.10. That means the stock must rise over 18%—just to break even. That alone is suspicious to say the least. Would you put $600,000 into an investment that requires an 18% move in less than two months—just to break even—and any stock price below $7.50 means you'd lose the entire investment? We hope not. It probably makes you cringe just thinking about it, and yet someone did. Considering that most stocks don't move 10% in a year, that's a massive move someone's confidently expecting within a short time. Why did they do it? The most likely answer is that's where the money is. The chart below is Burford Capital. Can you spot the day an unusually big announcement was made?

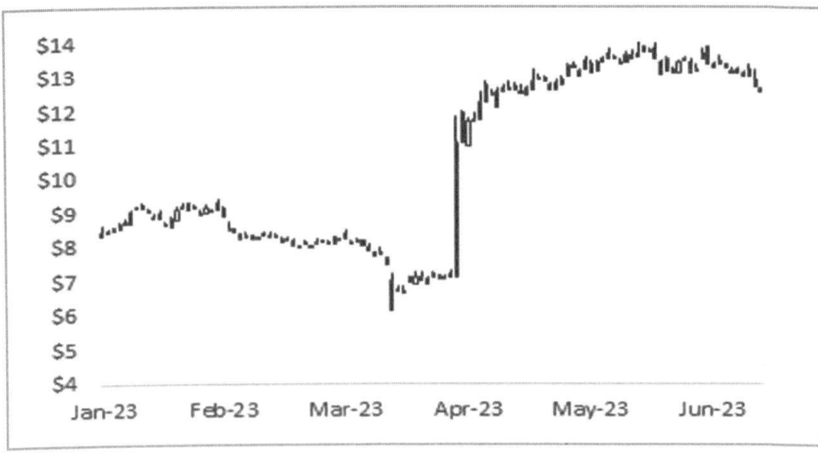


Stocks don't always make big moves just because of mergers or acquisitions. Burford Capital is a litigation funding company, which makes loans, usually to plaintiffs with strong cases, in exchange for a piece of potential awards. It's similar to venture capital firms but mostly limited to legal proceedings. This time, the stock pop wasn't from a buyout but, instead, the release of a case against Burford that could have been very costly. The news announcement was made on March 31—three days after the call options were purchased. Do you think that's a coincidence? The second the news was announced, the stock jumped 73%, and those calls traded for as much as $4.50, over 7-times their purchase price. A

$1,000 investment could have turned into $7,500. When you understand the idea of UOA, there's nothing unusual about it at all. We're just looking for trades that suggest a trader knows where the money is.

## Groupon Gets Upgraded

On June 27, 2023, *Heat Seeker™* spotted *Unusual Option Activity* in Groupon (GRPN) with 2,000 September $7 calls bought for $0.71 with shares at $5.21. The expiration breakeven price is $7.71, so the stock would need to jump 48% at expiration just to break even. The trader spent a total of about $142,000, so it's not the biggest UOA trade we've ever seen by a long shot. Why did it capture our attention? Because relative to other trades that typically take place in Groupon, it was big. It's all relative. The open interest was just 302, so it was clearly an opening trade. On August 11, just 45 days later, Credit Suisse raised the price target from $3.40 to $8. That's nearly as good as an acquisition. The stock rose 80%, as shown by the last candlestick in the chart, and the calls were trading for as much as $2.95, a 315% return. A $1,000 investment could have turned into $4,000:

These were big trades, but they can get bigger. It's not that unusual to see trades over 30,000 contracts, and once in a while, over 100,000 contracts. *Unusual Option Activity* doesn't just occur on the smaller, unknown stocks that may be poised for a buyout. It occurs on bigger names too.

## Capri Holdings Gets Purchased by Coach

On August 7, 2023, Capri Holdings (CPRI) had 6,700 September $42.50 calls purchased for $0.75 to $0.85 with shares at $35.78. That's over $500,000 dumped into an option with 39 days to expiration. The expiration breakeven is the $42.50 strike + $0.75 premium, or $43.25, so the stock must climb nearly 21% in a little over a month just to break even. The open interest was 1,523, so they were definitely opening trades. On August 11, just four days later, those calls changed hands for as much as $11.32, or a 1,232% return, while the stock rose 50%, which again illustrates the leverage with options. A $1,000 investment could have turned to $13,000. Take a look at the massive gap on the right side of the chart. What caused the price to skyrocket?

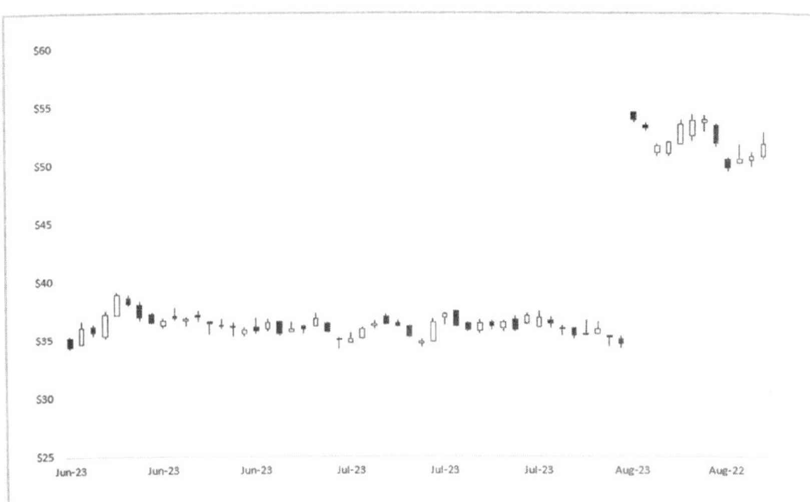

Capri Holdings was formerly known as Michael Kors, which distributes high-end women's apparel and accessories including Versace and Jimmy Choo. The company agreed to be acquired for $8.5 billion by Tapestry (TPR), the parent of the Coach brand. So, why do you think someone dropped $500,000 into an OTM option with 30 days to expiration? Because that's where the money is.

Now, just because a trade may be highly unusual and make the UOA trade log doesn't mean the stock is about to be launched into the ozone. Most of the time, it won't. How often can you recall big merger or acquisition announcements throughout any year? Not often. So, statistically speaking, you shouldn't expect them to appear on the UOA trade log a disproportionate number of times. The world has a lot of financial firms, asset management companies, hedge funds, and other institutional traders who place trades for hedging—not speculating. So, what's the best way to make use of the information?

This is another area where options strategies can work their magic. Options can be used in conservative ways by hedging, but they can also be used for speculation. By spreading money thinner and more efficiently, you can take part in many smaller positions and act like your own venture capital firm. Venture capital firms work by taking lots of small losses but holding out for really big wins. Options allow you to limit losses—shares of stock don't. By using options for UOA, you may take a lot of small losses, but you're also looking for the big gains, and they do happen, as you've seen. To make the most of UOA, however, you must understand why most traders use OTM options. Most of the time, they're losing deals, but they're used extensively for UOA. Why is there such a big attraction to OTM options?

## The Leverage of OTM Options

Long calls provide financial leverage because you only pay for a fraction of the stock's price today, but you control 100 shares. If you wish to buy the shares, you'd typically exercise at expiration and pay the strike price then, so you're floating the strike price over time. Remember, you're never required to buy the shares. Instead, you can sell the call to close and collect any value through the sale. Mathematically, buying a call option acts as if you're borrowing money—without actually borrowing.

Unlike buying shares of stock on margin, you'll never get a margin call for "borrowing" money. While all call options create leverage for this reason, there's an interesting property about OTM options that makes them extra special when expecting fast, aggressive moves, such as with UOA. It turns out you're borrowing more than 100% of the stock's price, and that's something you definitely can't do with shares of stock. Out-of-the-money options can create leverage found nowhere else in the stock market.

For example, let's say a stock is trading for $100 at 30% volatility. A pricing model shows the $110 call is worth $0.60 and the $110 put is worth $10.60.

If you borrowed $110, you could buy 100 shares of stock and still have $10 cash left over to nearly cover the cost of the put. Let's say you want to invest $1,000 in this call. You can buy $1,000/$60, or 16. Now let's say the stock quickly rises to $105. It's still out of the money, but that doesn't mean it won't respond to changes in the stock's price. Because the stock made a fast, aggressive move, the call option will pick up value. The pricing model says it's now worth $1.71. Even though the stock increased by only 5%, the call increased 185%.

If the stock rises to $110, the call increases to $3.77, or 528%. So, let's revisit one of the earliest questions in the book—are options risky? They can be used in risky ways, but if you're expecting fast, aggressive moves, OTM calls allow you to spread your money across more positions, and if the stock doesn't pan out, your losses are limited to just the call's price, which is extremely small relative to the stock's price. Using OTM options as a general practice would be very risky, as stocks normally don't make such fast, aggressive moves. But for UOA, it's exactly what you're expecting, so now you know why most of the unusual trades are done with OTM options. Traders get incredible leverage, but they can also manage the downside risk.

However, OTM options don't just provide great leverage. They're also extremely sensitive to changes in volatility, at least in percentage terms. So, to take your trading to an even higher level, you must understand some basic relationships between strike prices and leverage, and one of the most important is *normalized vega.* It sounds difficult, but it's designed to make things easy. Once you understand the leverage and volatility sensitivities of OTM options, you'll see why traders use OTM options for *Unusual Option Activity.*

## A Trader's Secret Weapon: Normalized Vega

In Chapter One, we outlined some of the "Greeks," which are outputs from an option pricing model. One of them was *vega*, which shows an option's sensitivity to changes in volatility. Volatility is ultimately what gives an option its value, so options are highly sensitive to changes in volatility. The more volatility, the greater the chance for the stock to make large moves—up or down—which means calls and puts both benefit. How sensitive are they to changes in volatility? That's the question vega answers.

As a recap, let's say a $100 call is trading for $5 with volatility at 20%. Your broker's platform shows the option's vega is 0.10. If volatility rises one percentage point from 20% to 21%, this option's price will rise by vega, or 10 cents, and trade for $5.10. On the other hand, if volatility falls one percentage point from 20% to 19%, the option's price will fall by vega, or 10 cents, and trade for $4.90. Remember, all Greek measurements assume all else remains the same. So, if volatility falls to 19% after the stock price made a sharp increase, your option won't be trading for $4.90—it'll be well above $5. But that's not because vega was wrong. It's because volatility fell *and* the stock price rose. Two things changed, not just one.

Most of the time, traders just want to know the vega number. However, it can also be helpful to know how much vega will increase or decrease the option's value in *percentage terms*, and that's what normalized vega shows. Normalizing is just a fancy term that means we're putting things on a standard scale to make easier comparisons.

It's like grocery shopping online where they may show a package costing $2.50 for 8 ounces and another priced at $1.25 for 113 grams. Which one costs more? It's hard to tell since they're in different units—ounces and grams. However, if you standardize the scale in pounds, they both cost $5 per pound. Much easier, right? So, if normalized vega sounds complex, just think of it as price per pound. To normalize vega, just divide vega by the option's price. If vega is 0.10 and the option's price is $5, normalized vega is 0.10/$5, or 2%. That means a one-percentage point change in volatility, up or down, will change your option's price by 2%. If you had a $5 option with a vega of .05, it's a different vega, but both options will change by 2% for a one-percentage point change in volatility. Let's go to a pricing model with the stock at $100, 30 days to expiration, 30% volatility, and zero interest rates. The table below shows a few strikes along with their prices, vegas, and normalized vegas:

| STRIKE | PRICE | VEGA | NORMALIZED VEGA |
|---|---|---|---|
| $90 (ITM) | $10.43 | .05 | 0.47% |
| $95 (ITM) | $6.42 | .09 | 1.4% |
| **$100 (ATM)** | **$3.43** | **0.11** | **3%** |
| $105 (OTM) | $1.57 | 0.10 | 6% |
| $110 (OTM) | $0.60 | .065 | 11% |
| $115 (OTM) | $0.20 | .033 | 17% |
| $120 (OTM) | $.06 | .013 | 22% |

What do you notice? The $100 ATM strike has the greatest vega at 0.11, but it's the OTM options that have the largest normalized vega, so their prices will see the biggest percentage moves from changes in volatility. The more OTM, the bigger the percentage change becomes. As traders, it's the percentage change in the option's price that matters to profits. Now that you understand normalized vega, let's see what happens to ATM and OTM options if volatility doubles.

## Doubling Down: What Happens to an Option's Price?

If you double volatility, an ATM option's price doubles. If you cut volatility in half, the ATM option's price is cut in half. *However, that's not the way it works for OTM options.* Remember, OTM options have much greater normalized vegas, so if you make changes to volatility—even small ones—their prices will be far more sensitive. You'll get much bigger percentage changes in their prices. For example, go back to the previous table. The $100 call is worth $3.43. If we change volatility to 60%, the call doubles to $6.86—exactly as expected. Now do the same with the $110 call priced at $0.60. If you double volatility to 60%, its price rises to $3.27—a 445% increase. What about the $120 call priced at $.06?

If volatility doubles to 60%, its price rises to $1.39—over 2,200%. So, if you're expecting a big increase in volatility, OTM options can be a great choice. However, if you're expecting the stock's price to plummet and a spike in volatility, OTM puts become one of the best plays in all of options.

## Bears on the Prowl

*Unusual Option Activity* isn't just limited to bullish plays. We often pick up unusual trades with put options, which suggests something negative is about to happen. Perhaps it's an upcoming earnings report that someone knows will be far below expectations. Or maybe it's a biotech stock whose Phase II trials will be announced next week as a bigger failure than Chernobyl. When playing the downside, OTM put options provide the same leverage benefits as they do with calls—but with an added bonus, and that's normalized vega. Why do put options get an added bonus but call options don't? Most of the time, if the stock price rises, volatility falls. So, your call options may gain intrinsic value but lose some volatility value. However, it's the opposite for puts. Remember, as shown in Chapter 4, people are far more sensitive to losses. The pain to the downside has been measured to be roughly twice that as the happiness received from the upside. So, when prices fall, traders rush out to buy puts, which increases their prices—and increases the volatility. When prices fall, put options pick up intrinsic value, but they also pick up volatility value. So, if you get a stock that makes a fast, aggressive move down, put options get a bonus, and that's a big spike in volatility.

For example, let's go back to the pricing model with the stock at $300, 30% volatility, and zero interest rates. The $260 put is worth $0.50. However, if the stock price falls, you'll gain a leverage benefit, just like with calls. Let's say the stock falls to $270. It's still out of the money, but the put's price has risen to $4.95, or 890%. However, what if volatility jumps to 40%? Now the put's price is $7.77—a 1,450% jump. What if volatility doubles to 60%? Now the put's price rockets to $13.60—over 2,600%. And yet, in all these examples, the put was out of the money.

This is why you must be careful about interpreting UOA with puts. Just because you may see someone buy a $260 put with the stock at $300, doesn't necessarily mean they think the stock's price will fall below $260. Instead, they may be looking for a fast, aggressive move. If you get that precipitous drop, you'll probably get a nice bonus with a pop in volatility. So, when you see UOA with far OTM puts, be sure to take a second look. That may be where serious money is hiding.

Pete and I talked about one of the more notable trades to ever hit the tape in our last book *Follow the Smart Money*. In 2007, Bear Stearns' stock fell from roughly $90 to $65 in a short time. *Heat Seeker™* picked up a trade where someone bought 55,000 $30 put options for $1.7 million dollars—with only 10 days to expiration. These puts weren't even listed, so someone had to call the exchange to request a listing. The trade made its way through the news and left everyone wondering why. Thomas Haugh, general partner of Chicago-based trading firm PTI Securities and Futures said, "It's not even on the page of rational behavior, unless you know something." Other bearish prints began to hit the tape, so we knew that somebody knew where the money was. Within the week, Bear Stearns' stock fell below $5, turning the $1.7 million-dollar investment into a $270 million windfall—a cool 16,000% in a week. Those numbers are hard to imagine, so to put the trade on smaller scales, a $500 investment would have netted you $40,000, and a $12,500 investment turned into one million bucks. When you understand UOA, you'll quickly realize there's nothing unusual about it.

## Consider the Leverage

One of the decisions you must make is the tradeoff between leverage and probability. An ITM option has a much greater chance of remaining in the money and providing some type of return. However, for the same amount of money, you could buy far more OTM options and gain even more leverage. In the previous table the $95 call was $6.42 while the $110 call was $0.60. If you wanted to invest $2,000, you could buy three of the $95 calls, but you could buy 33 of the $110 calls. So, not only does an OTM option create leverage on its own, but it also allows you to buy far more contracts for the same money. This is where using OTM options for speculation can be so powerful, and that's why you'll usually see them for *Unusual Option Activity*. Why buy an option that has a low probability of being in the money? Like all strategies, they're tools. You may not have a chainsaw readily available in your kitchen drawer, but that doesn't mean it's not useful. It just has limited uses. That's how professional traders see OTM options. They're extremely useful—and powerful—for the right times. Retail traders buy OTM options for the wrong reasons. They think they're limiting losses, but they end up using them for strategies that have little chance of making money. They're using chainsaws to carve a turkey. But when OTM options are used for the right reasons they're one of the best weapons for professional traders. One of the best reasons is when you're on the hunt for *Unusual Option Activity* because that's where the money is.

Despite his chosen profession that landed him on the FBI's "Ten Most Wanted Fugitives" list—and eventually life in prison—Willie Sutton did leave behind some great words of advice that also apply to trading. First, "Success in any endeavor requires single-minded attention to detail and total concentration." What's true for robbing banks is true for managing risk. And finally, "Go where the money is—and go there often." Now that you understand *Unusual Option Activity*, you should understand there's nothing unusual about that.

# Chapter Eight:

## Ignoring Technicals is NOT an Option

Some things are hard to ignore. Others are easy. And some, well, just don't deserve attention at all. As comedian George Carlin said, "Don't sweat petty things, and don't pet sweaty things." But when it comes to markets, there's one thing you can't avoid. Whether you're holding for years, looking for a swing trade, or flipping before the closing bell, ignoring technicals is not an option.

Technical analysis is the use of stock charts to analyze price and volume data. Analyses fall into many categories such as pattern formations, trendlines, channels, Japanese candlesticks, moving averages, and statistical oscillators. Traders who primarily use technical analysis are called "chartists," "technical traders," or just "technicians" for short. Chartists approach stock valuation differently from fundamental traders who mostly focus on financial statements, earnings, dividends, and macroeconomic data to determine if a stock is over- or undervalued. Chartists, on the other hand, study the history of price patterns to predict future stock prices. Technical analysis is described as an art and science that takes time to master.

Chartists believe the market price reflects all relevant information, so all fundamental information is included in the chart. If significant news hits the market, such as earnings, FDA announcements, mergers, acquisitions, or the CFO cooked the books and fled to Bolivia, you'll see it reflected in prices. So, according to chartists, if you're reading charts, you are using fundamental data. You're just letting others do the work for you. While you may not know what the news was, the charts will show where news—good or bad—affected the stock's price. Why bother with time consuming fundamental analysis when all that information is contained in the chart? Most of the time, quarterly earnings reports will have the biggest effect on stock prices, so those usually appear as gaps in the charts. For example, below is a chart for Lululemon (LULU). Can you guess where earnings announcements occurred?

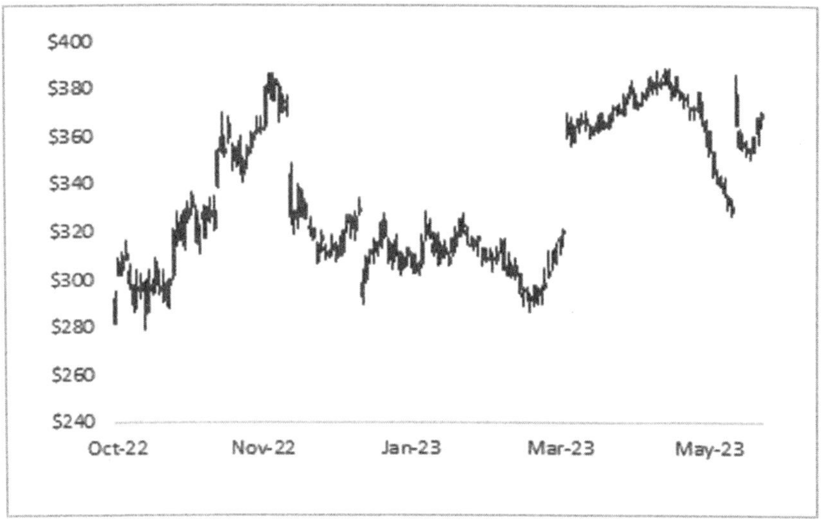

The large gap down in November was an earnings miss while the two gaps up in March and May were earnings beats. The current market price immediately factors in all relevant information, so ignoring technical analysis is ignoring information. This chapter isn't a technical analysis course, as it could take up a ton of terabytes. Instead, it's to convince you of the importance of technical analysis, especially when using options. Options have an expiration date. Shares of stock don't. So, time plays a role for options that's not critical for stocks. If you buy a 30-day call option, but the stock takes a nosedive first, the call may expire worthless, even though the stock may rebound later—long after the option expired.Basic technical analysis can reduce the chances of you stepping into financial black holes. At Market Rebellion, our traders and coaching staff are comprised of former market makers and specialists who made livings trading options—and using technical analysis. We thought it would be helpful to present a short list of the most common forms they consider important enough to use on a daily basis and how they help to make better decisions, at least, technically speaking.

## Japanese Candlestick Charting

*Scan the QR code*
*to watch our video*
***"Candlestick Charting"***

Throughout this book, we've used Japanese candlesticks for the charts, which is the most popular for traders. Years ago, Western bar charts were popular in the U.S., but regardless of which style you choose, they convey the four most important trading prices—open, high, low, and close.

While candlesticks convey the same information as Western bar charts, they make it easier to see this information. Candlesticks are formed by taking the opening and closing trades for the day and forming a box around them, which is called the *body* or *stick*. If the closing trade is above the opening trade, candles were originally drawn in white, but on computer monitors will usually be green. If the closing price is below the opening price, the traditional candle is black, but on computer monitors will usually be red. A vertical line is drawn through the body that lines up with the high and low trades for the day. These lines are called *shadows*, but many traders understandably call them *wicks*. Western bar charts work in similar ways. A Western bar is a vertical line connecting the high and low trades for the day. However, they use a small hash mark on the left and right sides to mark the opening and closing trades, respectively. Below is a chart of a bullish and bearish candlesticks compared to the corresponding Western bars:

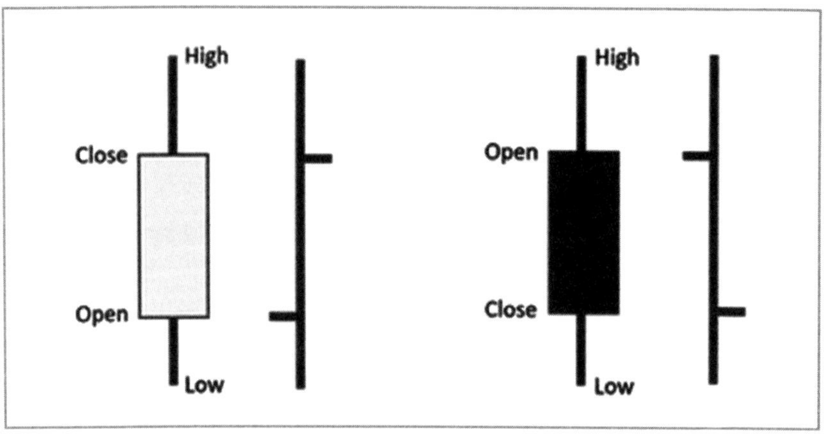


You can see that candlesticks reveal the same information as Western bars, but it's much easier to see if prices were up or down for the day because of the candle body colors. The information in the candlestick depends on your chart's time frame. If you're on a "day" chart, each candle represents the open, high, low, and close for that day. If you're set to a "weekly" chart, each candle represents one week. Monday's opening trade determines the open, while Friday's closing trade represents the close. The high and low trades are the high and lows through the week, regardless on which day they occurred. A "monthly" chart is the same idea, just for the entire month. Charts can also be set to intra-day timeframes. If you're on a five-minute chart, the open, high, low, and close are those prices during that five-minute window. So, from the 9:30am opening bell until 9:35am, you'll get one candle. From 9:35am to 9:40am, you'll get a second candle and so on.

The real power of candlesticks, however, comes from making it easier to see potential *reversal patterns*, which are high and low points where stock prices are likely to reverse direction. And for traders, that's some pretty handy information. There are probably a dozen or so key reversal patterns you should understand, but when you combine candlesticks with other forms of technical analysis, such as moving averages or trendlines, they pack a lot of power to help you see better entry or exit points.

For example, a common reversal pattern is the *bearish engulfing pattern*. Bearish engulfing patterns occur at the top of an extended run, so they signal that prices are about to fall, or turn bearish. This pattern requires two candles. The first is called the *setup* candle, and the second is called the *signal* candle. For candlesticks, it's not just the formations that matter. Instead, you must consider where they occur too. If you see an engulfing pattern in a sideways trend, it's not too meaningful. For reversal patterns, the longer the previous trend, the stronger the signal. So, let's assume the stock has been in a strong uptrend for a while, perhaps months. The next day, we get a white (green) candle, which shows the bullish trend appears to be in full force. The next day, however, we get a black (red) candle whose body completely overshadows, or engulfs, the previous day's candle as shown by the dotted lines:

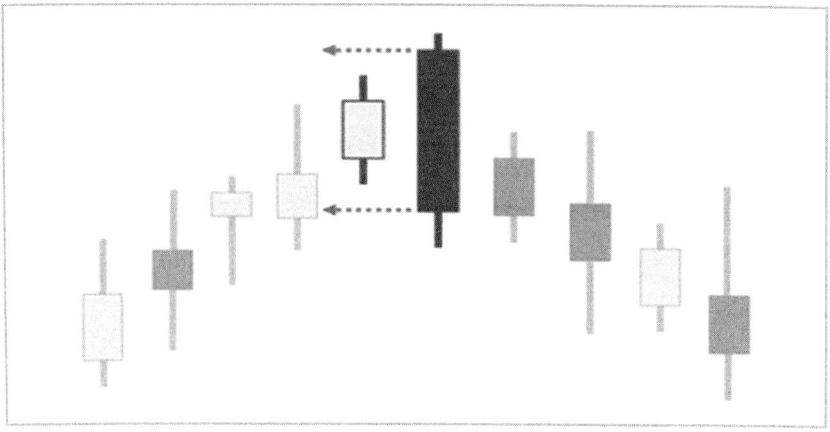

We now see a bearish engulfing pattern occurring at the top of an extended bull run—that's significant. Why?

The only way this two-candle formation can appear is that the second candle (black) must have gapped higher off the opening bell. That's what caused the candle body to sit higher than the previous day's candle. That's significant because, on the opening bell, it looked like prices were going to continue higher—just as they have been for months. We've been in a significant bullish trend, yesterday we closed higher, and today we opened higher. So, it looks like the bull run's going to continue, right?

Well, during the day, something changed. Traders began selling, and the candle closed much lower than the previous day's opening price. That's the only way the second candle body (black) can sit lower than the first candle's body. It's the gap up on the opening bell, and the close below yesterday's opening price, that causes the second candle to "engulf" the first candle. The picture tells an interesting story. The bullish trend appeared to be in full force on the opening bell, but the sentiment radically changed during the day. What happened?

The reason may not be clear, but to traders, it doesn't matter. If you're walking downtown and a crowd of people are screaming and running in the opposite direction, what would you do? You'd probably join in and ask questions later. Even though you don't know why you're running, you'll assume that the crowd knows, so it's better safe than sorry. That's essentially what's happening with a bearish engulfing candle. Something spooked the market and traders began selling. It's a difficult story to explain in words, but so easy to see in the picture. That's the benefit of candlesticks. Again, there are a dozen or so key candlestick patterns you should know. Once you learn them—and combine with other forms of technical analysis—you can greatly improve your chances for great returns. Below is a stock chart of Amgen (AMGN) from May through June 2022, and right there at top of the trend is a massive bearish engulfing pattern signaling the sentiment had likely switched from bullish to bearish:

As a result, traders saw the signal, and began selling. For every bearish candlestick pattern, there's a corresponding bullish pattern. A bullish engulfing pattern is exactly the opposite of the bearish engulfing. It takes place at the bottom of an extended selloff, but the signal candle is white (green) and engulfs the black (red) setup candle on the previous day. These candlestick patterns work in all time frames, so they can be used for any type of trading. Once you learn basic candlestick patterns, they'll help you to see when the crowd is running—whether up or down.

## Moving Averages: It's Good to Be Above Average

Moving averages (MA) are another one of the most basic—but most widely used—forms of technical analysis. Moving averages can be created for any time frame, but some of the most common for identifying long-term trends are 50, 100, 200, 500, and 1000-period MA. For short-term traders, the 9, 12, and 20-period MA are common.

Moving averages are generically referred to as "periods." So, a 50-period moving average selected corresponds to a 50-day moving average on a "day" chart, but a 50-week moving average on a "weekly" chart. If you're set to a five-minute chart, you're looking at the average of the last 50 candles, or 250 minutes.

Regardless of the time frame, the math is identical. To calculate a 50-day MA, you'd take the first 50 days, add up the closing prices, and divide by 50. That gives you the average price over those 50 days. Then you'd take the next group of 50 days, days 2 through 51, add up the closing prices and divide by 50. That gives you the average for the next block of 50 days. When you connect these averages, you'll get a line across your chart that shows how the 50-day average moved through time. Below is a chart of Merck & Company (MRK) with a 50-day MA (black line):

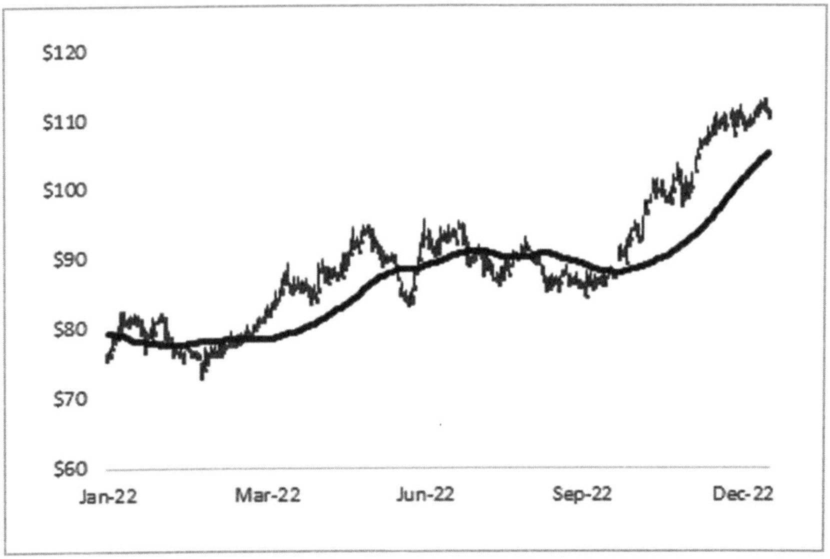


You can gain many insights from moving averages. First, by looking at the moving average, you'll see a smooth version of the stock's trend without all the unnecessary zigs and zags. Moving averages make trends easier to see. Second, in the above chart, you'll see periods where the stock's price is above average and periods where it's below average. Any time the stock's price is *below* the moving average, it's performing *below average*, so it's a sign of recent weakness, and the trend is expected to stay below the average. After all, if it's performing below average and there's no news to make it change course, why should you expect it to suddenly start performing above average?

On the other hand, if the stock's price is *above* the moving average, it's performing *above average*, so it shows a sign of strength. Once the stock's price is above the moving average, it's expected to remain there—unless there's news to push it below. How can moving averages help you make decisions?

One basic way is to use the moving average as a signal. If the stock breaks above the moving average from below, it's a sign of short-term momentum and may be a good time to buy. Conversely, if selling call options as part of a strategy, say covered calls, you may wish to hold off, or sell higher-strike calls. Give yourself some room for the stock to run since it may have some momentum behind it now that it's broken through the average. On the other hand, if the stock price breaks below a moving average from above, it's probably not the best time to go long, but may be an opportunity to go short. Those are basic insights, but moving averages provide so much more.

## Moving Averages as Support and Resistance

If a stock's price is above a major moving average, it's expected to remain above. However, day-to-day fluctuations can make the stock price drift down toward the moving average. If the stock price falls to the moving average, it's expected to "bounce" or in technical terms, find *support* on the moving average. So, if prices are above a major moving average, the moving average acts as a support line. Most of the time, you'll see the stock bouncing along a moving average. It'll fall to the moving average, touch it, and bounce higher. Technical traders sometimes call this the "rubber band" theory. It's as if a rubber band is attached to the moving average and the stock's price. If the stock's price gets "stretched" too far from the moving average, it tends to get snapped back toward the moving average. Once it touches, it tends to bounce off of it.

However, if prices break below a major moving average, it's called a *technical fail* of that average. In other words, the moving average failed to provide support. If that happens, traders expect the stock to find support on the *next* major moving average, whichever one happens to be next in line. Everyone expects the stock to get support, everyone buys, and the stock gets support—just like everyone thought. The chart below is the S&P 500 (SPY) from July 2020 to early January 2022 with the 50-day MA (black line) and 100-day MA (gray line):

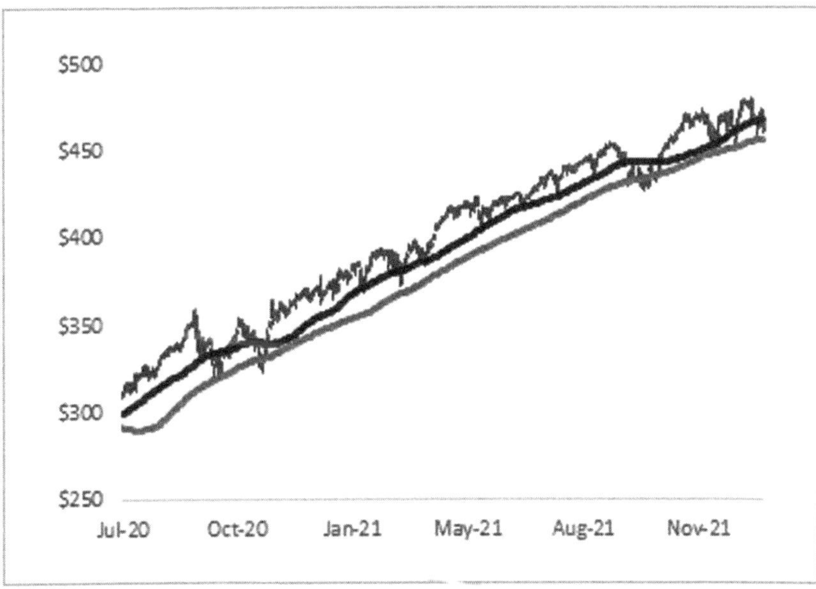


Notice how prices mostly stayed above the 50-day MA. Sure, they can get stretched away, but they'll usually snap back to the 50-day MA. However, once in a while, prices failed the 50-day MA, and then what happened? They found support at the next moving average in line, which is the 100-day MA. Why does this happen?

It's mostly a self-fulfilling prophecy at work with short-term traders. Self-fulfilling prophecies are a powerful force.

Imagine you hear there may be a run on your bank, which means everyone is withdrawing their money, and the bank won't be able to meet reserves and will be forced to close. What would you do? It doesn't matter if you believe the story. What matters is if you think everybody else thinks it's true. If nobody believes it, nobody withdraws their money, and the bank remains in business. However, even if you don't think the story's true, you also realize there's no harm in withdrawing your money—better safe than sorry. You also realize if everyone else thinks the story is true, the sooner you get your money out, the better. You come to the conclusion that no matter what everybody else believes, your best choice is to withdraw your money. Unfortunately, everybody else figures that out too. Everybody rushes to withdraw their money—and the bank fails. Even though the bank may have been perfectly solvent before the rumor, it was the *belief* that it was in financial distress that caused it to fail. That's a self-fulfilling prophecy, and one of the main drivers behind technical analysis. It works because everybody thinks it does. Technical indicators are taught on the belief they work. That's why they get passed on to other traders. Nobody would teach an indicator and say, whatever you do, don't follow this one because nobody else does. So, if everyone learns technical indicators and "knows" they're supposed to get a certain reaction when certain things happen, there's a good chance that's what's going to happen.

Always remember that markets are forward looking. If a stock is $100 today and everyone expects it to be $105 tomorrow, it'll trade for $105 today. The market discounts all available information, which is also a tenet of technical analysis. All available information is reflected in today's prices. So, serious traders and investors are watching for small clues, and that's what technical analysis provides. But when you combine a series of small clues, you can gain valuable insights.

Trading is like solving a 10,000-piece jigsaw puzzle. No single piece provides much information, but when you get half the puzzle solved, you can at least tell what the picture is going to be. If you only use fundamental analysis, you'll have to wait for the next earnings report or economic data release—and hope you can analyze it better than everyone else. Remember, it's not what you think that matters. It's what everybody else thinks that drives stock prices. If everybody thinks that everybody else thinks prices are rising (or falling), prices will move accordingly. Moving averages can provide one more piece of the puzzle that can help you make better decisions. Moving averages are popular because they're versatile, so what else do moving averages reveal?

## The Roles Have Been Reversed!

As previously shown, moving averages act as support when the stock price is above a major moving average. The reverse is also true. If a stock is below a major moving average, that moving average will act as resistance if the stock price climbs up to it. Remember, when prices are below a moving average, the stock is performing below average, so it usually needs a strong piece of news to drive it higher. So, as the price is approaching a moving average from below, traders are thinking it most likely won't rise above it. Speculators begin shorting shares when prices hit the moving average from below, prices fall, and the moving average acted as resistance—just like everyone thought.

Because of this, you can see moving averages flipping from support to resistance, which is called a *role reversal.* Chartists say support becomes resistance, and resistance becomes support at these major moving averages. There are several types of role reversals in technical analysis, and moving averages are one of them. For example, below is a chart of Chipotle Mexican Grill (CMG) from July 2021 to March 2022 with the 50, 100, 200, and 500-day moving averages. Study the chart closely, and you'll see that each time the price approached a moving average from above, it tended to find support on that moving average, even if only for a day or two. At that point, it's expected to bounce. However, if it falls through—a technical fail—it falls to the *next* moving average in line. The reverse is true too. If the stock price rises from below a major moving average, it tended to find resistance at the next moving average in line:

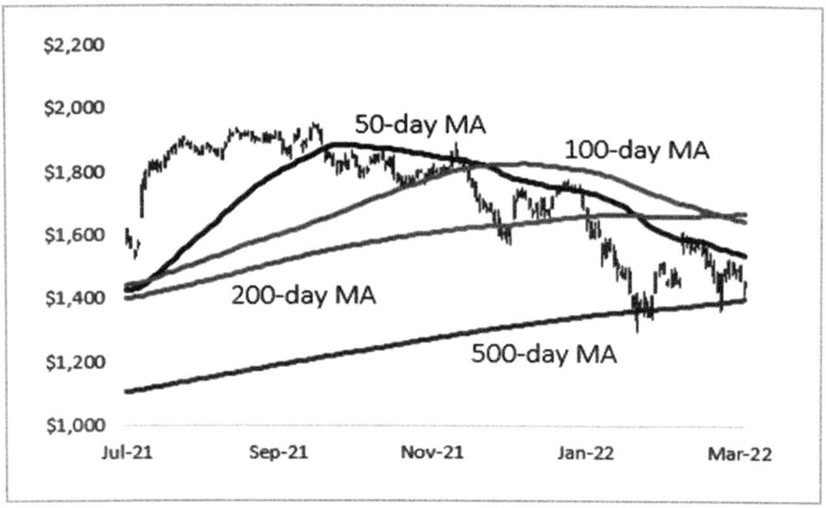


When a stock's price is between two major moving averages, it can just bounce around between them and have a difficult time breaking out—whether up or down. This is why you must be careful when buying shorter-dated options when the stock is between moving averages that are close together, as the price can just get stuck in the mud and bounce between them. This persistent moving-average pattern in the markets works in all time frames and can be used to your advantage for figuring out entry and exit points. So, as a general rule, be careful about entering a bullish position if the stock's price is close to meeting a major moving average from below. Conversely, if you're selling options, perhaps as part of a covered call strategy, you may decide to act a little more aggressively and sell a lower-strike call since there's a smaller chance for the stock to actually break through. Selling a lower-strike call yields more money and will also have a higher theta, or time decay. Or, if you're short the call and the stock breaks out, it may be a good sign it's time to roll the option up and out. Rolling up means rolling to a higher strike while rolling out means rolling to a longer-dated option. So, if you're short the August $100 call, rolling up and out may be rolling to the September $105. Moving averages greatly help you to make better decisions, stay disciplined, and most of all—stick with your plan.

## How Strong is the Trend?

The trend is your friend. That's a trading philosophy you'll hear from all traders. They're continually looking for trends to hop on for a short ride. You don't want to jump in a trade and have the stock whipsaw in the other direction. While there are never any guarantees, finding a strong trend gives you a little more confidence that the trend will remain intact, or at least not come unhinged in the next couple of days. Can moving averages show the strength of a trend?

Yes, any time you have several major moving averages moving roughly parallel to each other, it's a strong trend. The longer the moving average periods, the stronger the trend. In other words, seeing the 50, 100, and 200-day MA moving parallel is a stronger trend than seeing the 10, 12, and 20-day MA. But in all cases, when moving averages are moving parallel, it's a sign of a trend. For example, from November 2020 to August 2021, the S&P 500 (SPY) was in a strong uptrend coming out of the COVID-19 pandemic, which is confirmed by the 50, 100, 200, 500, and 1000-day

MA lined up in order and moving parallel to each other. In other words, the 50-day is on top, the 100-day is second, the 200-day is third, and so on, as shown in the chart below:

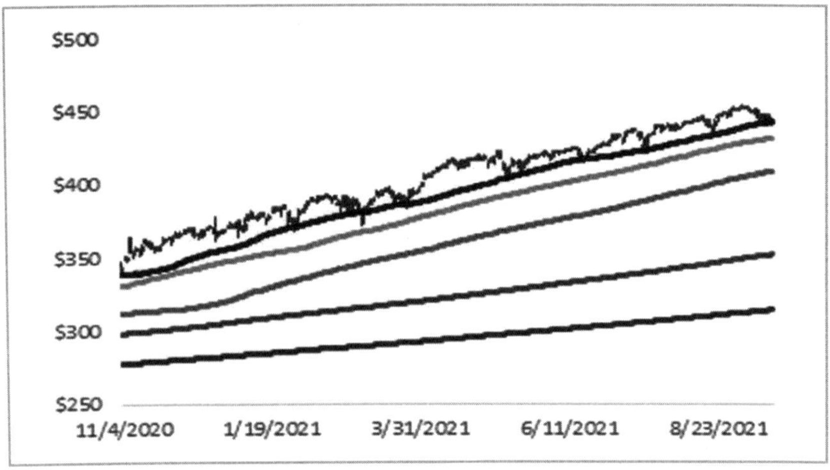


The only way that happens is to have strong earnings from companies in the index and overall positive economic news during that time. As the 50-day MA continues to rise, it pulls the 100-day moving average higher, which pulls the 200-day moving average higher, and so on until all are moving roughly parallel to each other. Looking for strong trends is helpful for many popular option strategies, such as the covered call. For that strategy, you carry a large amount of downside risk since you're holding the shares. While many traders suggest using covered calls in sideways markets, it's actually a risky idea. When stocks are trading sideways, they usually break up or down sharply at some point—neither of which is ideal for covered calls. So, if you're using covered calls, check to see if the stock is in a reasonably strong uptrend. If, instead, the stock was in a strong downtrend, you'd get the opposite picture, which you can image by just flipping the above chart over. The longer-dated moving average would be on top while the shorter-dated would be on the bottom. Rather than doing a lot of difficult fundamental analysis to determine if stocks are performing well through a certain time, a simple glance at moving averages provides the answer.

## Moving to Different Time Frames

Another moving average technique is to switch to different time frames. Short-term traders mostly use daily or intraday charts. However, switching to a weekly or monthly chart can give very different looks at where prices are technically. Every trader can benefit from including longer-term charts, but if you're a longer-term trader, you should definitely watch them. Shorter time frames have more "noise," or false signals, so if you're ever in doubt about a support or resistance level, flip to different time frames. For example, in early March 2020 during COVID-19, the S&P 500 (SPY) dropped off the face of the Earth and plummeted straight through all five major moving averages—including the 1,000-day MA—which is the bottom moving average (black line) in the following chart:

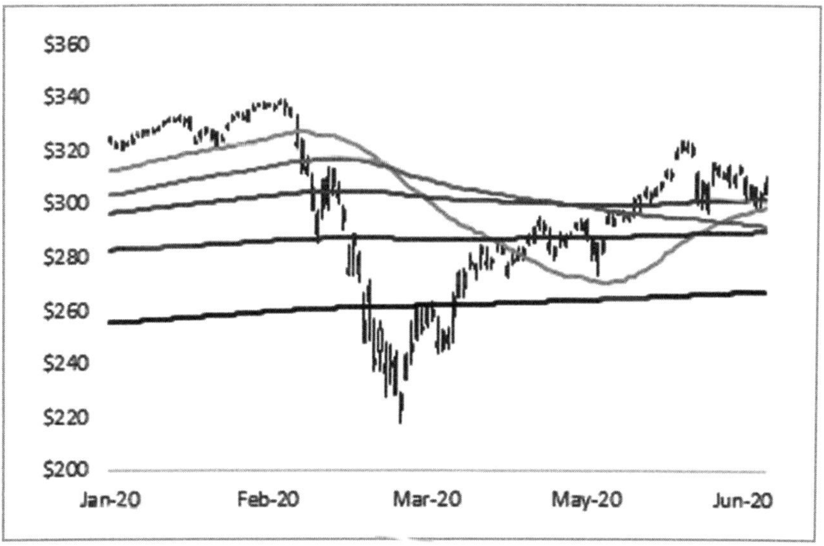

Traders usually look for the next major moving average to get an idea of where support may be. Well, where do you look for support from here? There is no next. It's like being lost at sea at night during a storm—and no lights. You have no idea where you are. All of your points of reference are gone, and that's another thing that adds to the panic and causes traders to abandon plans. Nobody had an inkling of what a share of stock was worth. Instead, it was like screaming "fire" in a crowded theater—everyone made a mad dash for the exits. How do you maintain discipline when everyone's running? This was a great time to flip to a weekly chart. The chart below shows the COVID-19 era in a weekly chart. Now your points of reference are back, and it was easy to see the weekly candles were approaching the 500-*week* MA (black line), and that was where the market turned:

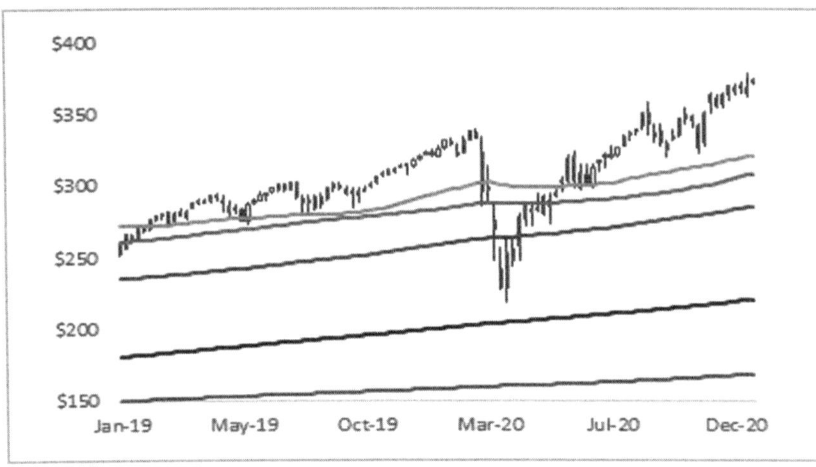


At the bottom of the "V" during this time, there were many technical signals screaming "buy." We had bounces off major moving averages, candlestick kicker patterns, and nearly every oscillator pointing higher. Once you see this, it's the opposite of screaming "fire" in a crowded theater. Now everyone is screaming "huge sale on Wall

Street." Everyone is running for the entrance, and that's what forms the "V" bottoms that we see so many times in the stock market. It's the result of fear and greed.

During this time of panic, you were understandably fearful of buying shares, but now that you understand some of the basics, what if you bought longer-dated OTM calls? What if you could also sell against them when volatility was 80%—and climbing? What if you bought puts to protect the shares, used vertical spreads, sold spreads against shares, used collars, or any number of risk-reducing strategies? Would that be better than having only one choice to buy shares? When you manage risk, you can manage fear, and options were created to manage risk. By default, they also help to manage fear, and that means they create opportunities when everybody else is running.

## The Trend is Your Friend

Didn't we hear that before? Yes, technical traders are always on the hunt for trends, but sometimes trends aren't always easy to find by looking for long-term moving averages to run parallel. What if it's a short-term trend, a trend within a trend, sometimes called a *secondary trend*. To confirm these trends, chartists use trend lines to confirm if a trend is intact—or has been broken. The concept of trend lines is easy.

For uptrends, just connect several prices *below* the candlesticks with a line, and most brokers' platforms allow you to draw directly on your charts. Traders usually agree that it's better if you can connect *closing prices*, but any price at the same general level is okay. It takes two points to create a line, so chartists say it takes a third point to "confirm" the trend. The more points of contact, the better. However, the points should also be roughly equally spaced rather than sitting in one tight cluster. So, if you have a trend line with three points that touch, you'd like to see the points dividing the trend into thirds. For instance, beginning in March 2020, Microsoft (MSFT) went on a massive tear, rising from about $200 to $350 in October 2021, as shown below:

When would the trend break? A trend line has been drawn, and you can see there are about four key points where prices touched the line. You may notice the "touches" aren't necessarily perfect, and they rarely will be. You're just trying to find areas, not specific points. We tell traders to think of drawing the line with a fat magic marker or paint brush, not a finely sharpened pencil. The trend line is a series of higher highs and higher lows, so chartists are trying to determine if this trend is likely to continue. The idea is that if all technical traders identify this trend line, they'll most likely buy when it touches the line. Everybody buys, and the prices bounce off the line. When will the trend break?

Once you see prices drop below the trend line, it's a warning that traders have lost confidence in the trend. In the above chart, it's quite obvious where the candles broke below the trend line. As with all technical analysis, the reason may not be clear. There may not be any news, but again, it doesn't matter. What you do know is that the trend line has been broken, and all traders will see it. Who wants to buy now when prices are more likely to fall?

Once the trend line is broken, it invites speculators to short shares, and that's usually when the trend strongly reverses. Once you see prices drop below the trend line, you can use options to either speculate for profits, or buy puts to guard against the downside if you own shares. If you're selling options, such as with covered calls, you may decide to sell more aggressively since it's less likely for the stock to continue higher with the trend. Regardless of your goals, options give you choices that you simply don't have with shares of stock—and technical analysis helps with decisions.

Downtrends are the same idea in reverse. For downtrends, you'll connect several prices, roughly equally spaced, *above* the candlesticks. You need a minimum of three points of touch to confirm the trend, preferably with closing prices, but the more touches, the stronger the line. Below is Microsoft (MSFT) from December 2021 through July 2023. You can see the strong downtrend, but once prices broke above it, traders recognized the trend was broken, and nobody wanted to short shares off the trend line anymore, and prices continued higher:

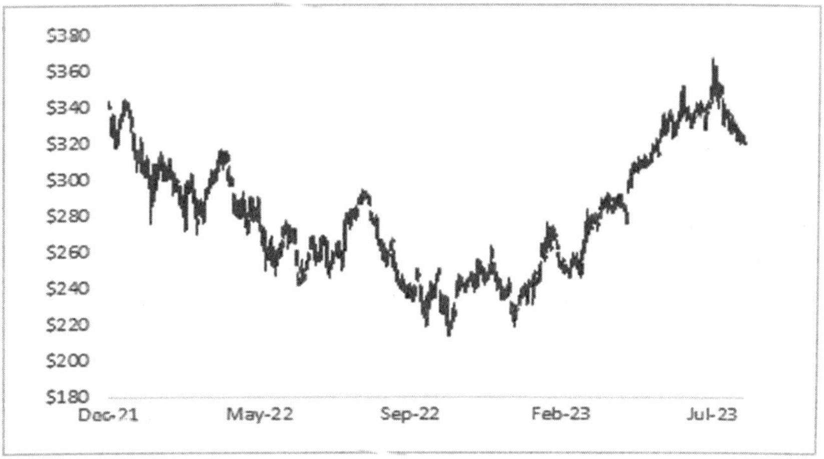

Trend lines are an easy way to determine if a trend exists, the strength of the trend, and when it's most likely been broken. If the trend is your friend, be sure you can identify the times it's friendly—and when it's not.

## Gap Filling

Gap filling is another popular form of technical analysis used by our traders, and it can also help you with entry and exit points. A gap occurs when the opening price is greater than the previous day's closing price. Almost all stocks have some sort of gap each day, as it's rare for a stock price to open at exactly the previous day's closing price. So, when traders talk about gaps, they really mean areas of significant gaps, which are easy to spot. You'll see a lot of space between two candles. For example, below is a chart for Google (GOOGL) showing a large gap up on July 26, 2019, after an earnings release:

The stock closed at $56.80 and opened the next day at $61.40, or 8% higher. The idea of a gap is that when there's good news, everyone rushes to get in. Yes, prices are higher, but traders are expecting them to move even higher. Sometimes, the stocks will continue to run, which is called a "breakaway" gap, but it requires really big news. Most of the time, however, the stock will immediately begin to sell off, which is what happened here. Just seven days later on August 5, the stock fell all the way back to the price where it was before the gap. In trading terms, the stock "filled the gap," which is called *gap filling*. This is another piece of a larger puzzle that can help you make better decisions—and remain disciplined. Retail traders often jump on the gap, expecting prices to continue running away. Sometimes they do. Other times they don't. Unless you're trying to speculate, it's best to give it another day or two to see if it looks like the stock will continue higher—or if it looks like the gap may fill.

Once you learn basic forms of technical analysis, you'll see them appear in multiple places. For example, you can also see a "role reversal" in the chart. Prior to the gap, the candles were "resisting" under the 100-day MA (black line). After the gap filled, however, the stock found strong support on the same 100-day MA, as the candles were now resting on top. The 100-day MA was acting as resistance prior to the gap but flipped to support after the gap. The more forms of technical analysis you know, the more pieces you can connect to see the bigger picture of opportunities. So, if you're trying to trade gaps, what's another risk-management tool to use?

Scaling in and out of trades is a popular form of risk management. Scaling into trades just means you're buying some fraction of the total position you were willing to buy. If you're willing to buy 10 calls, maybe buy five calls, wait to see what prices do, and then buy the second lot of five calls. If it's a volatile stock and you're looking for longer-term investments, you may place five trades, each of two calls. Scaling in allows averages to work for you in volatile situations. What if the stock continues to run higher after the gap?

Scaling will help you here too. You can buy the second lot of five calls at the higher price. Sometimes traders think it's a bad strategy since you're averaging up and increasing your average cost. Well, the options don't know how much you paid. Buying the first lot at $5 and a second lot at $7 is no different than doing the trades in the reverse order. Your average cost is the same, so don't be fearful of averaging up. Plus, you now have a better indication that the trend is continuing higher. By playing the averages, you're reducing the chances for buying at the bottom, but you're also reducing the chances for buying all at the top. It's giving up some potential gains in exchange for reducing risk, so scaling into positions is a form of hedging.

Scaling out is the same idea in reverse. Rather than trying to find the "best" time to sell, consider selling in pieces. Sell five calls now and five calls later. Scaling works in the long run since it's highly unlikely you'll buy at the lows or sell at the highs. If that's true, then by giving yourself multiple chances, at least you'll get some of your contracts purchased or sold at better prices. When it comes to trading in a competitive market, any advantage you can get, no matter how small, counts. Scaling in and out provides a great edge.

## Flat Lines: Trading All-Time Highs and Lows

It's hard to not notice when stock prices are at all-time highs. Is it a good idea to trade at these highs—or too risky? The gut instinct is to be cautious, but that's because there are no prices above the high—but lots below. It just seems that it's more likely for prices to fall.

However, if a stock is at an all-time high today, it was at all-time highs many times before that. Every single high, at one time, was an all-time high. When a stock is at a record high, it's more a sign of strength than weakness. In fact, William O'Neal of Investor's Business Daily created the CAN SLIM method in the 1950s as a way for identifying super growth stocks that were likely to beat the market. Each letter stood for a key characteristic of all great growth stocks, and the "N" stood for something *new*, whether a new product, new management—or a new high. However, because the all-time high puts you on the peak of the mountain, it's usually seen as risky, when it's more likely that traders are missing opportunities. If the rule is to never trade an all-time high, you'll miss the next all-time high.

For instance, if you take all the daily closing prices for Apple (AAPL) from January 2000 to December 2022, the stock made an all-time high 7.4% of the time. In a weekly chart, that number jumps to 14.7%, and in a monthly chart, it increases to 25.4%. So, the longer the holding period, the more likely you are to see all-time highs, but that also means you'll have to ride through the short-term pullbacks. So, if a stock is at an all-time high, it doesn't mean you should avoid the stock, and it doesn't mean you should sell. Instead, manage unwanted risk, and the only way to do that is with options.

The counterpart to trading the all-time highs is trading the all-time lows. The lows are certainly more tempting since you have far more prices above, and as we saw in Chapter 4, the anchoring bias makes traders want to jump on the lows, as it looks like they should trend back toward the highs. However, lows can go lower, so they can also be tricky to trade.

Technical analysis can provide deeper insights for trading all-time extremes by understanding flat line support and resistance levels. A flat line is just what it sounds like. It's a flat line connecting several price highs or lows where the stock had difficulty breaking above or below. Just as with trend lines, you should see at least three points of contact, and closing prices are considered ideal. At flat line at the top is called a flat line resistance while at the bottom it's called a flat line support. Flat lines are important in technical analysis, as they persist through time. On the other hand, as we saw with trend lines, once a trend is over, it's over, never to be seen again. You may certainly start a new trend line, but once one is gone, it's over. That's not true for flat lines, and they can persist for years.

For example, the chart below is for UnitedHealth Group (UNH) from November 2021 through August 2023. You can see a distinct flat line resistance around $550 where prices had a difficult time getting through. You can also see a flat line support around $450 where prices rarely fell below:

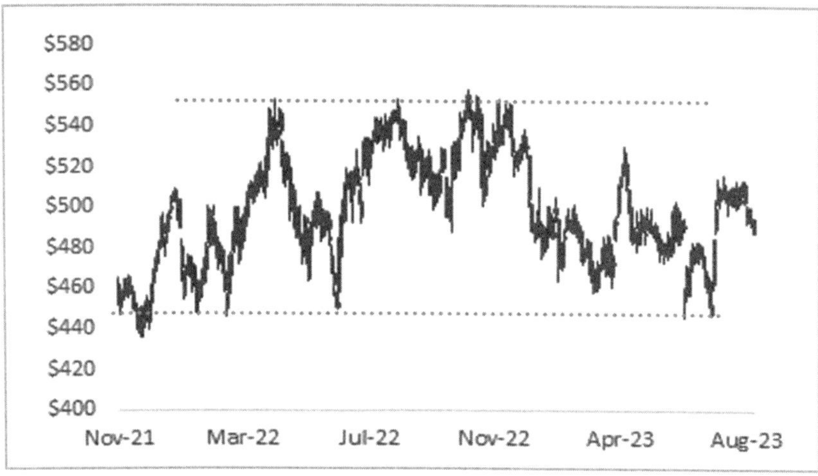


The idea of flat line support and resistance levels is that a stock's "true" price can never be known. Instead, investors are casting their collective votes by buying or selling. However, for many stocks, there's a limit on just how high investors are willing to pay—unless new information warrants it. Once prices hit these levels, investors lean toward selling and speculators join in by shorting shares. The result is that prices fall.

Flat line support levels work for the opposite reason. Price can fall, but there seems to be a bare minimum level where investors agree that it's a bargain. People buy, speculators join in, and the price bounces. Is it a guarantee? Of course not. But if you don't at least entertain the idea that prices may have a tough time getting through the flat line resistance levels, the price can be costly. And if you miss the opportunities at flat line supports, the missed buying opportunities can be just as costly. Use options to trade or invest in the market—but hedge your opinion. All-time highs and lows are other great opportunities for traders who combine flat lines with the hedging power of options.

## Average True Range (ATR)

Average True Range (ATR) is a calculation developed by J. Welles Wilder as an alternate way to measure volatility. Because it's calculating volatility, it's not a directional indicator. A high or low ATR number doesn't mean bullish or bearish. In Chapter 1, we gave a basic definition of volatility, which you can think of as measuring the zigs and zags in a price chart. Volatility calculations are used to determine a potential range of future prices over a given time. For example, if a stock is $100 and trading at 20% volatility, what are the expected highs and lows over the next 30 days? Or over the next year? To answer, you need to know volatility. Traditional volatility calculations use the closing prices of each trading day to come up with a number. Average

True Range is more robust to capture gaps in prices. For example, say a stock closes at $100, but during the next trading day, the price rises to $105, falls to $95, and closes at $100. The close-to-close method would show no variation—no volatility—during those two days, since stock closed at $100 on both days. But there was volatility—a lot—and ATR will capture those intraday gaps. Average True Range uses three calculations: The first takes today's high minus today's low. The second calculation takes today's high minus yesterday's close. The third takes today's low minus yesterday's close. The graphic below shows these calculations:

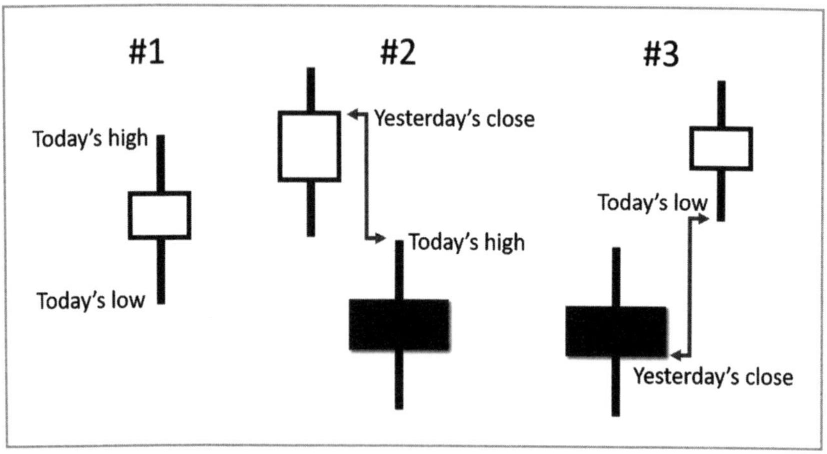


ATR uses the largest of these three values, ignoring any minus signs. It then takes an average of these numbers. There's also a 14-day averaging and "smoothing" process that's done, but that's not necessary to understand the idea. It's essentially a 14-day moving average of these three calculations. Traders use ATR to gauge the strength of stock moves—especially breakouts. If a stock breaks a trendline or moving average and the ATR is large, it reflects a strong move, and shows it's most likely to hold. On the other hand, if a breakout is done with a narrow range of ATR, it's more suspect, and traders may wait a day or two for further confirmation.

ATR is also used to validate potential entry points for short-term trading. If a stock has an ATR of $5, and it's moved $5 so far today, it may be pushing its limits, and you may decide to delay entering the position. However, if it's only moved $1, you may have more confidence in taking the position. It's important to understand that ATR isn't a percentage like traditional volatility calculations, so you can't compare the ATR of different stocks. If one stock has an ATR of $5 and another has $3, you can't say the $5 one is more volatile. Why? If a $200 stock has an ATR of $5 and a $20 stock has an ATR of $3, you can see why comparing total dollars isn't going to work since $3 is a much larger percentage of the $20 stock. Higher-priced stocks will naturally have a greater ATR, but that doesn't necessarily mean they're more volatile. However, traditional volatility calculations can be compared, so if one stock has 20% volatility while another has 30% volatility, the 30% stock is more volatile. Still, ATR is one more way traders can judge the quality of entry or exit points. This chapter was just to introduce you to the ideas of technical analysis and how it can be used to find potential opportunities—and dodge potential risks. Options provide opportunities. Technical analysis provides clues. If you're looking for opportunities, ignoring technicals isn't an option.

# Postface:

## The Archer and the Arrow

They travel at 300 mph. At that speed, it will take one second to hit the target. It's not a lot of time—but a lot can go wrong. Once an arrow leaves the bow, it's out of the archer's control, and in the hands of fate. One gust of wind, an out-of-tune bow, or slight imperfection in one of the arrow's feathers, and the bullseye can be missed—quite possibly the entire target. You can be dedicated, disciplined, and prepared beforehand. You can choose the best equipment, best arrows, and best coach. You can choose the moment to release the arrow. They're all things you can control. But once the arrow leaves the bow, there's not a single thing that can be done during that one-second flight. It's out of your control.

The "Archer and the Arrow" is a parable used in philosophy to show what matters most in life is how you prepare, decide, and control the things you *can* control.

Focus on your decisions, how they'll affect your actions, how they'll guide you toward your target, and that'll give you the best chance to hit it. Whether you hit your life's target or not isn't what matters. The quality of your actions is all you can control, so focus on the process—not the outcome. It's a great philosophy for living but perhaps an even better one for trading.

However, that's not the approach most traders take. Instead, they focus on where the stock is heading, how long it will take to get there, and how big the profits will be if they're right. They focus on outcomes they can't control. To be the best trader you can be, think like an archer. Just as when an arrow leaves the bow, once your finger leaves the "enter" button, the trade is out of your control. Don't think "watching it closely" is managing risk. Scientists have been watching lightning and volcanoes closely for thousands of years.

Focus on things you can control. Manage all unwanted risks before sending the trade. Manage any risks that arise based on new information. Focus on the process and discipline of making the right choices, for the right reasons, at the right times. The rest is out of your control. Just like an archer, you'll still have times when you miss your target, but that's not a reflection of your skills. Sometimes good decisions have bad outcomes, and if you're in the wrong trade—at precisely the right time—there's nothing you can do. It's a perfect shot with a bad arrow, unexpected gust of wind, or just your average collision with a meteorite. They're going to happen.

When you're holding positions in today's global market, like an arrow through the air, they're surrounded with unexpected—and undiscovered—risks that few people can understand or imagine. The one thing you can control is how much of that risk you're willing to take—and how much you want to reject. Throughout the book, we've shown how options give you choices, and now you're now faced with the most important one.

There are three sides to every story: Yours, mine, and the truth. Wall Street has had hundreds of years to tell its story of stocks. We hope the few hours you've spent with us have helped you to understand our story of the untold risks of stocks—and untouchable advantages of options. No matter which side you choose, remember the universal truth: You can only control your actions. So, before you release that arrow, how will you handle the invisible risks, the *unknown* unknowns, the ones that remain after you think you've thought of everything? That's your story.

And that *IS* an option.

## Take the Next Steps in Your Trading Journey

Unleash your full potential! Learn how our team of experts can help you boost your options skills—no matter your experience level.

***Scan the QR Code,***
*Visit:* ***ItsNotAnOption.com/NextSteps***
*Or Call* ***1-800-330-4352***

# Appendix:

## A Starter Guide to Essential Options Strategies

Options strategies begin by understanding the two types of options—calls and puts. If those are the only choices, it sounds like strategies would be quite limited. But remember, you can buy or sell each type, and you can combine them, and that opens the doors to many strategies you never dreamed of. Pete and I have traded every strategy imaginable, but there's a handful we trade most often. You'll also end up with a small stable of go-to strategies, but before you can decide, you must understand all the choices. In this guide, we want to show you some of the most popular option strategies to give you an idea of the flexibility and power they provide. As you study them, see if you can come up with scenarios where each could benefit you. There are no right or wrong answers. Instead, think of them as choices between risk and reward. Can you get the same benefits from only trading shares of stock? Once you discover the ones best suited for you, it still pays to understand them all. Depending on the setup and risks, one may be slightly better than another, and it'll pay to understand the differences. The difference may be win or lose, profits or losses.

# The Classic Covered Call

For many traders, the covered call is the gateway strategy into options. Interestingly, it requires that you sell an option, and you'd think an entry-level strategy would be buying options. However, the reason many investors start with covered calls is that it requires you to own shares of stock. Because most investors come from a stock trading background, they already have shares and are therefore comfortable holding the risk. To enter a covered call, you sell calls in a 1:1 ratio, which means you sell one call against 100 shares of stock. In other words, if you own 100 shares, you can sell one call. If you own 200 shares, you could sell two calls, and so on. You're not required to sell against all your shares, so if you have 400 shares, you could write from one to four calls. However, you do NOT want to write more than four, as that leaves naked call positions.

By selling the call, you have the potential obligation to sell your shares for the strike price. It's a potential obligation, as it's up to the call buyer to decide.

Remember, the call buyer has the right to decide whether to exercise for the shares or not. Let's say you have 100 shares currently at $100 and sell one $105 call for $3. The resulting risk graph looks like this:

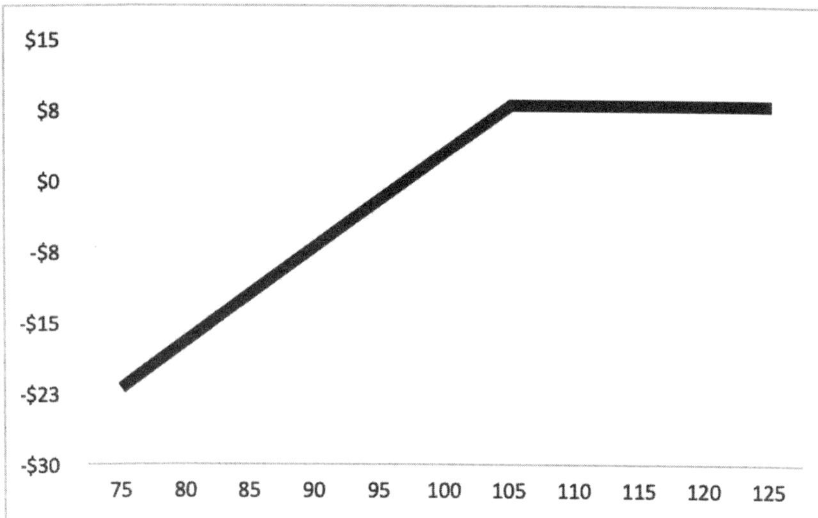


The most obvious feature of this chart is the unlimited downside risk, which highlights why you must be comfortable holding the shares. The reason it's called a "covered" call is that if you sold the call by itself, a naked call, you'd have unlimited *upside* risk. Because you own the shares, however, that upside risk is covered. However, the downside risk remains. Don't let the word "covered" make you think the covered call means all risk is covered. It's only the upside risk if you had sold the option as a naked call. Interestingly, even though the covered call is often advertised as an "entry level" strategy, the risk profile is identical to a naked put—one of the riskiest of all positions. If we drew a risk graph for a short $105 put, it would be identical. How can the covered call be considered relatively safe while the naked put is risky when they share the same risk graph? It comes down to the assumption of risk.

If you own shares of stock, you're already exposed to the downside risk. Selling a call didn't create that downside risk. Instead, it just lowers your cost basis and creates a small downside hedge. On the other hand, if you buy shares for the sole reason of selling calls, then it's more in line with a naked put. That's because your reason for buying the shares was to write the call. You were motivated by selling the call rather than buying the shares, and that makes it a speculative position. Is the covered call right for you?

A good check is to ask yourself if you'd be willing to hold the shares if the stock wasn't optionable. If the answer is yes, selling a call may be a good way to create a small downside hedge. The main reason for using a covered call is to reduce the downside risk.

Each time you sell a call, you're effectively reducing your cost basis. In this example, you owned shares at $100 but sold a $105 call for $3, so your cost basis is reduced to $100 - $3, or $97. So, $97 is also your breakeven price—and the potential maximum loss. If the stock falls to $97 at expiration, you'll just break even on the trade. Had you just held the shares without selling the call, you'd be down 3%, so the covered call offers a small downside hedge. Your potential max loss is also $97, which could only occur if the stock became worthless. The maximum gains are always limited, but the amount of the gains depend on which strike you sell. Below is a chart showing a $100 stock with the $95 (ITM), $100 (ATM), and $105 (OTM) strikes written against it (remember, risk graphs always bend at the strike price):

In-the-money strikes have less extrinsic value—but more intrinsic value. So, they'll offer the bigger downside hedges—but smaller rewards. That's just the risk-reward tradeoff at work. If there's less risk, there'll be smaller rewards. That's why the $95 strike creates the biggest downside hedge but offers the lowest reward. The at-the-money strike always has the most extrinsic value, so it offers the greatest return on your money, as far as the extrinsic value goes, along with a decent downside hedge. However, you're not allowing for any possible capital gains.

Out-of-the-money strikes have relatively low extrinsic value, very much like in-the-money strikes, but they also have no intrinsic value, so they create the smallest of all the downside hedges, but they also create the largest potential gains. If you sell out-of-the-money strikes, you're taking more risk but will also allow for greater rewards. However, most of those capital gains are coming from the stock price rising—not from the short call. It makes no sense to buy a stock at $100 and sell the $120 call for 10 cents but get excited about the 20% potential gain from the "covered call." Nearly 100% of the gains came from the stock rising from $100 to $120—not from the 10 cents you received from selling the call.

Selling OTM options, on the other hand, allows for potential capital gains in addition to the option's premium. If you sell the $105 call for $1, your cost basis is $99, but you have the obligation to sell for $105, which results in a $6 max gain. That gain is the result of $5 of capital gains (the stock rising from $100 to $105) plus one dollar's worth of extrinsic value. Different strikes simply create different risk-reward tradeoffs.

## Which Strike Should You Sell?

With so many expirations and strikes, trying to figure out which expiration and strike to sell can be a challenging decision. For example, in July 2023, Nvidia (NVDA) had 20 expirations, and some had over 150 strikes each. However, there are three simple calculations professional traders use to figure which expiration and strike is right. They are the static return, return if exercised, and the breakeven return. How do they help you make decisions?

## The Static Return

The static return calculates your return assuming the stock price is the same at expiration or remains "static." For example, on July 26, 2023, Nvidia (NVDA) was trading for $450. The stock was trading around 50% volatility, so the options were relatively expensive. The 30-day at-the-money $450 call was trading for $34.

The static return is $34/$450, or 7.5%, which annualizes to 90%. It's a huge reward, but that should give you some pause for concern. The market is willing to pay a big premium for someone else to hold the shares—that's you. However, to collect the entire $34, you must hold the call all the way to expiration so that it expires worthless. Most professional traders won't hold the option that close to expiration, so your return will most likely be something less, but it's still a huge return. Now think about your goals. Are you trying to earn 7.5% per month? If not, perhaps it would be better to sell an in-the-money call to get a larger downside hedge. The $400 call was trading for $63, which has $50 of intrinsic value and $13 of extrinsic value. If you sell this call, your cost basis falls to $450 - $63, or $387. If the call is exercised, you receive $400 per share. Because you've effectively paid $387 and sold for $400, it's a 3.3% return, or 40% annualized. The return isn't as big—but neither are the risks. Professional traders will often look for lower strikes that meet their goals but also create a larger downside hedge.

## Return if Exercised

The return if exercised shows your total return if the option were to be exercised. However, remember it's the long trader's decision to exercise—not yours. The return if exercised calculation only comes into play for out-of-the-money strikes. The 30-day $465 call was trading for $26. If you sell that call, your cost basis is reduced to $450 - $26, or $424. The static return is $26/$450, or 5.7%, which annualizes to 69%. It's still a great return, but it's a smaller static return since you're receiving less extrinsic value. However, you're now allowing for capital gains. If the stock rises to the $465 strike, you've effectively paid $424 but sell for $465, or 9.6%, which annualizes to a 116% return. Remember that the return if exercised can be deceiving. It may look like the option strategy is creating the potential for a 116% gain, but the option itself only provided 70% of those returns. As an extreme example, the $700 call was trading for one dollar. If you sell that call, your cost basis falls to $449, so you've created a $1 downside hedge—nothing at all to speak of. However, if you get assigned, your return is 55%, or 670% annualized. It looks like an amazing return—and it is—but it was nearly all due to the stock price rising to $700. You would have collected nearly that same percentage by just holding the shares. The call only brought in $1, or 0.2%. In other words, don't get fooled by that return because 99.8% of that return was from the stock—not the covered call. Always be sure the premium received from selling the call is adequate to reach your goals. Otherwise, you're just selling off your upside potential—no matter how unlikely—for relatively no money.

## The Breakeven Return

The breakeven return is perhaps the most important of all, as it shows how far the stock can fall and leave you just breaking even. In other words, it's showing the "negative return" you could face and just break even. Because you're focused on hedging risk, that's a good number to watch. With the stock at $450, if you sell the $450 call for $34, your cost basis falls to $450 - $34, or $416. If the stock falls to $416, or 7.5%, you'd just break even. This strike creates a 7.5% downside hedge, so that's the breakeven return. On the other hand, if you sell the $465 call for $26, your cost basis falls to $450 - $26, or $424, which is 5.7% below the current stock price. So, this strike creates a 5.7% downside hedge. What if you liked the $465 strike but wanted a larger premium? Now you'll have to search for a longer-dated option that matches those numbers. For any given expiration, notice that the out-of-the-money strikes create smaller downside hedges—but larger potential returns. Those are always the tradeoffs. So, which strike and expiration is right for you? It depends on your goals, and that's why goals make decisions easier.

## A Classic Cost Basis Mistake

Covered call sellers must always be careful of the difference between the cost basis and the true risk. Traders usually think that by writing covered calls, they can continually reduce the stock's cost basis—possibly into a negative one. For instance, if you paid $450 for Nvidia, and wrote calls with $25 premiums 18 times, you'd receive a total of $450, so your cost basis is zero. If you sold one more call, you'd have a negative cost basis—as if you were paid to own the shares. That's a misperception. If the stock rises to $800 and you're still selling calls, don't be fooled into thinking you have no risk. You could choose to sell the shares for $800, but if you continue to hold, you're putting $80,000 at risk for that next covered call.

## The Versatile Covered Call

One of the regrets that traders have with covered calls is when the stock shoots through the short strike, and they end up getting assigned, or having the shares get "called away." Unfortunately, they see it as a "risk" of the strategy. Remember, though, risk is never defined as missing out on rewards. Instead, getting assigned is an opportunity cost, or a regret. Even though traders know it's a possibility, regret comes when the stock is trading significantly higher. Well, covered calls are more versatile than traders think. Just because the basic definition of the covered call is to sell one call for every 100 shares you own, you're not required to do that. If you have 400 shares, for example, you may choose to sell one, two, or three calls, which will always leave you with unlimited upside potential gains, although more limited. The chart below shows 400 shares of stock (solid black line) compared to selling one, two, or three calls (gray lines). All three choices leave unlimited potential gains. It's only when four calls are sold that gains are completely limited (dotted line):

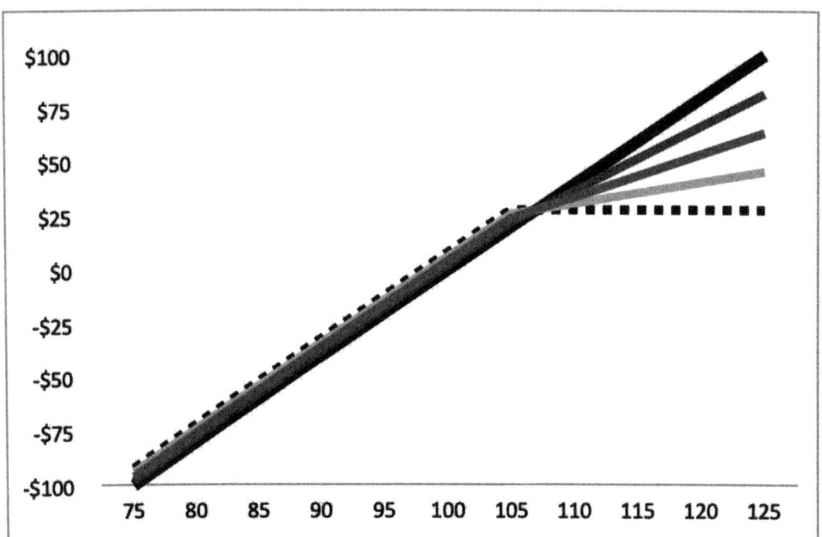

If you're trading shares of stock, the covered call can be a great way to receive option premiums that can bolster returns while creating downside hedges—assuming you're willing to hold the downside risk.

## Why Use Covered Calls?

The main reason for using covered calls is to reduce the downside risk in the underlying. However, because the downside hedge is usually relatively small, be sure you're comfortable holding the long shares before using the strategy. Sometimes this strategy is viewed as one for income generation. Each time you sell a call, you're bringing in more money, which acts like income. However, financially speaking, it's not totally correct because the "income" you're receiving is due to selling off potential future gains—and giving someone the right to buy your shares. Renting out an apartment, on the other hand, is a way to generate income. You receive monthly checks, but you're not giving up any price appreciation in the property—and you're not in danger of losing it. It's important to remember, as many investors see the "income" part of the strategy without fully realizing the potential costs.

## Dividends

If the stock is about to pay a dividend, the long call holder may exercise early to collect the dividend. Exercising an option early to collect a dividend only makes financial sense if the option is trading at parity, or at least very close. Remember, parity means the option is trading for purely intrinsic value with little to no extrinsic value. If a trader decides to exercise early for the dividend, it should always be done as late as possible—the day before the ex-dividend date. A simple rule of thumb is to check the bid of the *corresponding put*, which is the put with the same expiration and strike of your short call. If the put's bid price is greater than the upcoming dividend, it's not a good candidate for early exercise. Why?

If the upcoming dividend is 20 cents, but the put is bidding 50 cents, you'd be better off selling the put to create a synthetic long stock position—long call and short put. Doing so, you have the identical risk as if you exercised for the shares but collected 50 cents rather than 20 cents. Also, you'd hold onto your cash longer to earn interest. If the put's bid is greater than the upcoming dividend, there's a very low chance you'll get assigned. Just remember that very low isn't the same as guaranteed. If you're unsure, roll your short call out to a longer-dated strike. That puts more extrinsic value into the call, which makes it less desirable to exercise early.

## Expiration Actions

If your call is out of the money at expiration, you can let it expire worthless and write a new call on Monday. However, if it's only slightly out of the money, it's not a bad idea to either close it, or close it and simultaneously write a new one. Just because the option may be out of the money at expiration, the long position has the right to exercise until 5:30pm ET, which is one and a half hours *after* the market closes. If news breaks out on the stock in after-hours trading, you may find you've been assigned while holding an option that was out of the money.

# Vertical Bull Spreads

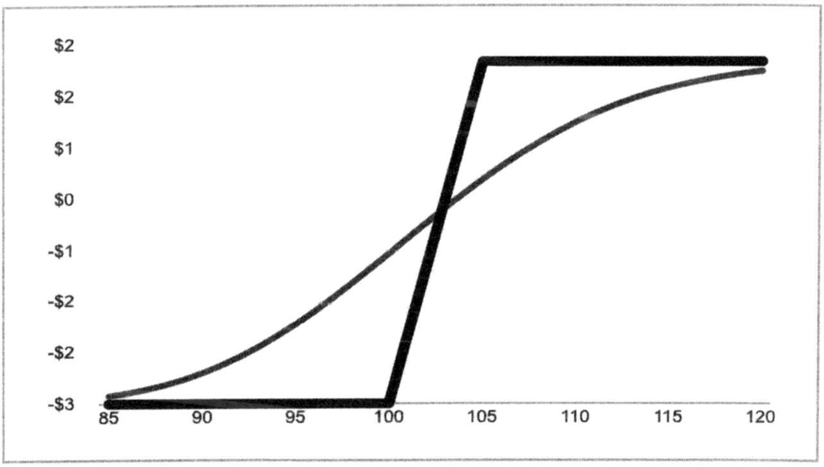


Vertical bull spreads can be created by using calls or puts, and either version results in a limited risk, limited reward profile. Both options must be the same type—both calls or both puts. Whether using calls or puts, a vertical bull spread is created by purchasing one strike and selling another at a *higher strike*. Just remember "buy low, sell high," or BLSH, which looks like "bullish." In other words, if you buy a low strike and sell a high strike, it's a bull spread whether you're using calls or puts.

For instance, if you buy one March $100 call and sell one March $105 call, you'd own the March 100/105 vertical bull spread. Instead, if you bought the $100 put and sold the $105 put, it would still be a March 100/105 vertical bull spread and will have the identical risk graph as the calls. Again, whether using calls or puts, you're buying the low strike and selling a higher strike. What's the difference?

## Vertical Bull Call Spread

If you use calls to construct a vertical bull call spread, it always results in a debit because lower strike calls with the same expiration must cost more money. For debit spreads, the max loss is the debit, and the max gain is the difference in strikes less the debit. The breakeven price is the long strike plus the debit. Rather than memorize formulas, think about why they work.

If you buy the March $100 call and sell the March $105 call, you have the right to buy shares for $100 and the obligation to sell the shares for $105, which is a $5 gain. No matter how high the stock price rises, $5 is the most this spread could ever be worth. If you paid $3 for the spread, the max gain is the $5 difference in strikes less the $3 paid, or $2. To break even, you'd need the long call to make up the cost, so the stock must close at the $100 strike plus the $3 cost, or $103, at expiration. At that price, the $100 long call is worth $3 while the short $105 call expires worthless which means you could close the spread for $3 and just break even.

The delta is mostly positive, as it is a bullish strategy. The maximum delta occurs between the strikes near expiration. However, if the stock price falls well below the long strike or rises well above the short strike, the delta approaches zero.

Because long options have positive gamma and short options have negative gamma, the spread's gamma will be positive near the long strike and negative near the short strike. When gamma is positive, you want the stock price to rise, but when it's negative, you can afford to have the stock remain at the same price but still increase profits. The strategy can be created synthetically by using another popular strategy called a *collar*, which is created by purchasing 100 shares, buying a lower-strike put, and selling a higher-strike call with the same expiration.

## Vertical Bull Put Spread

As mentioned previously, vertical bull spreads can also be created by using puts. Buying the March $100 put and selling the March $105 put is also a vertical bull spread. Notice whether using calls or puts, you're buying one strike but selling a higher strike. Whether using calls or puts, buying the $100 strike and selling the $105 strike creates a bull spread.

However, when using puts, the strategy results in a credit because higher-strike puts must be worth more money, assuming the same expiration.

An interesting pricing relationship exists between vertical call and put spreads. If the 100/105 call spread results in a $3 debit, the 100/105 put spread should sell for a $2 credit. Notice that both prices—the $3 debit and $2 credit—add up to the difference in strikes. Traders are often tempted to only use credit spreads based on the belief that credits are better than debits. However, a debit spread represents an asset—something that can increase in value. If you pay $3 for the 100/105 call spread, it may increase to a $5 value thereby leaving you with a $2 gain. However, if you sell the 100/105 put spread, it represents a liability—it can only lose the $5 difference in strikes. Because you received a $2 credit to enter the trade, the max loss is $3. Because your broker will always require a margin amount equal to the max loss, debit and credit spreads always end up as debit spreads once the trade is placed. Credit spreads aren't better than debit spreads. They're just another way of constructing the same strategy.

While a credit sounds better, both spreads have a max loss of $3, max gain of $2, and $103 breakeven point. They're identical. Buying the call spread for $3 or selling the put spread for $2 are just two different ways of saying the same thing. Because brokerage firms are concerned about max losses, the debit and credit spreads will carry identical margin requirements—both create a $3 debit. So, even though the put spread is called a credit spread, it ultimately results in a debit.

## Should You Use Calls or Puts?

In the previous section, we showed that if the 100/105 call spread costs $3, the corresponding put spread would generate a $2 credit. However, in the real world, this relationship can break down, and when it does, one spread will produce a better risk profile compared to the other. For instance, perhaps there's a bigger demand in the market for the $100 call and its price gets pushed higher, thus driving the spread's cost up to $3.20, which leaves a $1.80 max gain. With the call spread priced at

$3.20, you'd expect to see the 100/105 put spread selling for a $1.80 credit, but perhaps it's trading for $2. Is the call spread expensive, or is the put spread cheap? We don't really know, but we do know the put spread is relatively cheap compared to the call spread. Relative to the call spread, the put spread is the better deal—but not because it's a credit. It's because the max gain is $2 compared to $1.80 for the debit spread. And because the gain is larger, the max loss must be smaller. The put spread's max loss is $3 compared to $3.20 for the debit spread. The put spread's max gain is larger, and the max loss is smaller, so it's the preferred choice, all other considerations equal. Another reason for choosing calls or puts is potential morphs. If you want to release the limited gains or potentially change the directional bias, you may choose the call spread or the put spread.

## Common Morphs

For vertical spreads, whether bullish or bearish, there are two common morphs: First, traders may wish to release the upside cap. Second, they may wish to reverse their directional bias. Whether using bull or bear spreads, there's always one thing in common: *The morph always focuses on the short strike in the vertical spread.* How are these morphs done for bull spreads?

## Releasing the Upside Cap

If you're in a bull spread with calls (debit spread), you can easily release the upside cap by buying back the short call. For instance, if you own the 100/105 call spread, just buy back the short $105 call, and you're left holding the $100 call. You've morphed from a bullish vertical spread with limited upside gains to a long call with unlimited upside gains. However, be careful with your cost basis. Traders often buy vertical spreads to reduce the cost of the long call, but breaking spreads apart can greatly increase your cost basis. Once you buy back the short call, you must add back that cost to the long position, and that changes the overall risk. For instance, say the $100 call is trading for $10, but you don't want to pay that much for the call, so you decide to sell the $105 call trading for $7, which creates a $3 debit. Now assume the stock breaks out, and you decide to close the $105 call, which has now increased to $9. If you buy this call back, you must add the cost back to the original $3 cost of the vertical spread, which means you've effectively paid $12 for the $100 call. Your max loss used to be $3, but now it's now $12. If your motivation for using a vertical spread is that you didn't want to pay $10 for the $100 call, you must question if it makes sense to hold it for $12 now.

If you're using a credit spread with puts, you can also release the upside cap, but you must do it synthetically, as you're trying to create a call option from put options. It's still easy to do—just buy a call with the same strike and expiration as the short put. For instance, if you're short the 100/105 put spread, just buy the $105 call to open, and that leaves you with a synthetic long $100 call. How? The short $105 put combined with the newly purchased $105 call creates a synthetic long stock position. When that's paired with the existing long $100 put, you've got a synthetic long $100 call. Again, you've morphed from a limited gain vertical spread to a synthetic long call with unlimited potential gains. Whether using debit or credit spreads, the morph is easy: Buy the call that's equal to the short strike. If you're in a call spread, it'll be a closing transaction. If in a credit spread, it'll be an opening transaction.

## Switching Directions

To switch from bullish to bearish in a vertical spread is the same idea, just in the other direction. If you're long the 100/105 call spread and wish to turn it into a long put, just buy the $105 put. The existing short $105 call combined with the newly purchased $105 put creates a synthetic short stock position. When that's paired with the long $100 call, you've got a long $100 put. You've morphed from a bull spread to a long put, so your view has changed from a limited bullish view to an unlimited bearish one.

On the other hand, if you have the bull credit spread with puts, the morph is done with the same trade, but this time it'll be a closing transaction. If you're short the 100/105 put spread but now want to own a long put, just buy the short $105 put to close, and you're left holding the long $100 put. Again, you've switched from a vertical bull spread to a synthetic long put, so you've changed your directional bias. Whether your bull spread is built with calls or puts, you're buying a put equal to the strike of the short. For bull call spreads, it's an opening trade. For bull put spreads, it's a closing trade.

## Be Careful with Your Cost Basis—Again

As with debit spreads, it's important to keep track of your cost basis, and just as for debit spreads, just keep track of the net debits or credits. For example, let's say you sold the 100/105 bull put spread for a credit of $2 but later buy back the short $105 put for $9 to turn the bull spread into a long put. If you initially received $2 for entering the vertical spread but spent $9 to close the put, you have a $7 net debit. So, you're left holding the long $100 put with a new cost basis of $7. In the previous example with the debit spread, your new cost basis was $12 by using the same prices. Why is it only $7 here? Remember, credit spreads are liabilities, and by buying back the short $105 put, you no longer have that liability, so your max loss is reduced from $12 to $7.

## Vertical Bear Spreads

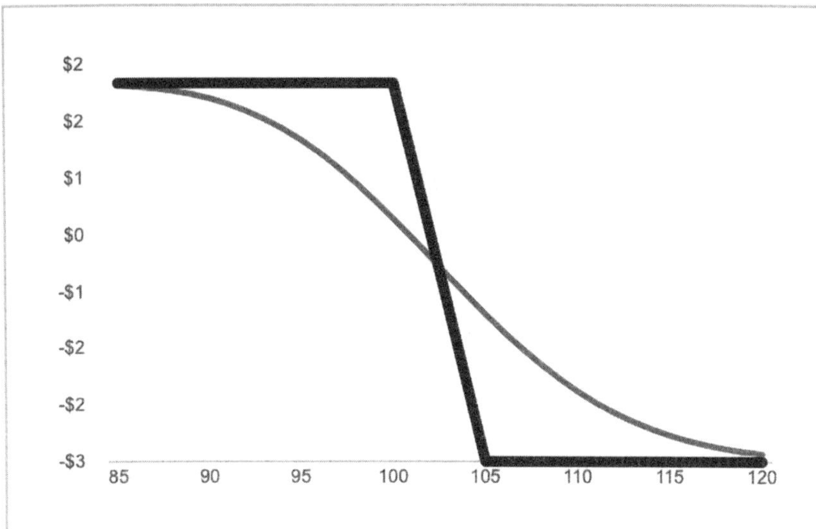


Just as you can create vertical bull spreads with calls or puts, you can do the same with bear spreads. Again, both options must be calls or both must be puts—not one of each—with the same expiration. For vertical bear spreads, you'll buy one strike but sell a *lower strike* of the same option type and expiration. Recall from the bull spreads that buying low and selling high was bullish (BLSH). If you reverse that, buying high and selling low must be bearish. For example, if you buy a June $105 put and sell a June $100 put, it's a vertical bear spread. For any expiration, higher-strike puts are more expensive, so it'll be a debit spread. On the other hand, if you buy a

June $105 call and sell a June $100 call, it'll also produce the identical bear spread. However, lower strike calls are more expensive, so it's a credit spread. In both cases, you're buying a high strike and selling a lower strike, but whether using calls or puts, you're creating a bear spread. Aside from the directional bias, bear spreads work in a similar way as bull spreads.

## Vertical Bear Put Spread

If you buy the 100/105 bear spread, you're buying the $105 put and selling the $100 put. As a result, you have the right to sell shares at $105 and the obligation to buy them at $100, so the maximum value is the $5 difference in strikes. For instance, if you buy the 100/105 put spread for $3, the maximum gain is $2. However, your broker will always have a margin requirement equal to the maximum loss, or $3 in this example. Just as with bull spreads, all vertical spreads end up as debits after accounting for margin requirements. To break even, you'd need the long $105 put to make up the $3 price paid, so the stock needs to fall to $102 at expiration to break even.

## Vertical Bear Call Spread

If you use calls to construct a vertical bear spread, it results in a credit because lower strike calls with the same expiration must cost more money. If the vertical put spread costs $3, the corresponding call spread (same strikes and expiration) should generate a $2 credit. For credit spreads, the most you can make is the amount of the credit. The most you can lose is the difference in strikes less the credit. If you sell the 100/105 call spread for $2, the max gain is $2, and the max loss is $3. Because the broker always guards against the max loss, you'd have a $3 margin requirement. The breakeven point is the $105 strike less the $2 credit, or $103.

Notice that if the 100/105 put spread costs $3 and the 100/105 call spread sells for a $2 credit, both carry the same $3 margin requirement, and both will have the same breakeven points. They are just two different ways of accomplishing the same thing.

The delta is mostly negative, as it is a bearish strategy. The delta gets close to -100 between the strikes near expiration, but if the stock price falls well below the short strike or rises well above the long strike, the net delta approaches zero. The spread's gamma will be positive near the long strike and negative near the short strike.

## Common Morphs

For vertical bear spreads, two common morphs are the same idea as for the vertical bull spreads. You're either releasing the downside cap or switching your directional bias from bearish to bullish. Remember, these morphs are always done by some type of trade at the short strike.

## Releasing the Downside Cap

If you're in a debit spread with puts, you can easily release the downside cap by buying back the short put. For instance, if you own the 100/105 put spread, just buy the short $100 put to close, and you're left holding the $105 put. Remember to add the cost of this newly purchased put to the cost basis of the vertical spread, and that gives you the cost basis of your long $105 put.

On the other hand, if you're using a credit spread with calls, the morph is done by buying a put with the same strike as the short call. If you're short the 100/105 call spread, just buy the $100 put to open, and that leaves you with a long $105 put. As with bull spreads, this is done synthetically. When you buy the $100 put, it creates a synthetic short stock position when combined with the short $100 call. Pairing that synthetic short stock with the existing $105 call creates a long $105 put. In both cases, you're buying the $105 put. It's just a matter of whether the purchase is an opening or closing trade. However, both morphs create a long $105 put.

## Switching Directions

Remember, switching directions is the same morph idea, and you're always focused on buying or selling the short strike. If you're long the 100/105 put spread and wish to turn it into a long call, just buy the $100 call to open. This $100 call combined with the existing short $100 put creates a synthetic long stock position. When that's paired with the long $105 put, you've got a long $105 call. You've changed from a limited bearish view to an unlimited bullish view.

If instead, you had the vertical bear spread with calls (credit spread), the morph is done with the same trade, but this time it's a closing transaction. If you're short the 100/105 call spread but now want to own a long call, just buy the short $100 call to close, and you're left holding the long $105 call. Once again, you switched from a limited bearish view to an unlimited bullish one.

## Don't Forget to Track Your Cost Basis

As covered under vertical bull spreads, be careful with your cost basis whenever you break vertical spreads apart. If the $105 put costs $20, you may not want to spend that much for the option. But perhaps the $100 put is trading for $17. By selling that, the cost basis drops from $20 to $3. However, if you buy back the short $100 put, you must add that price back to the vertical spread's cost basis. Maybe the stock is falling, and the value of the $100 put is rising. If you decide to buy it back for $20, you're now holding the $105 put for $23. You can't make good financial decisions if you don't know the costs of the things you're trying to trade.

## Ready To Dive Deeper Into Options Strategies?

This Appendix detailed only a few essential trading techniques. To access more options strategies, scan the QR Code below to unlock our full digital guide:

***It's NOT an Option:*** *A Guide to Essential Options Strategies*

**NOTE:** The full guide also includes the strategies covered in this Appendix.

# Take the Next Steps in Your Trading Journey

Unleash your full potential! Learn how our team of experts can help you boost your options skills—no matter your experience level.

***Scan the QR Code,***
*Visit:* ***ItsNotAnOption.com/NextSteps***
*Or Call* ***1-800-330-4352***